ON DISARMAMENT

The Role of Conventional Arms Control in National Security Strategy

EDITED BY

Ralph A. Hallenbeck

AND

David E. Shaver

STRATEGIC STUDIES INSTITUTE
U.S. ARMY WAR COLLEGE

Foreword by

WILLIAM F. BURNS

New York
Westport, Connecticut
London

Opinions, conclusions, and recommendations expressed or implied within represent the research and reasoning of the authors. They do not necessarily represent the views of the Strategic Studies Institute, U.S. Army War College, or the Department of the Army. In addition, they in no way indicate acceptance or endorsement of any kind by any other person, party, government, or alliance.

Library of Congress Cataloging-in-Publication Data

On disarmament : the role of conventional arms control in national
   security strategy / edited by Ralph A. Hallenbeck and David E. Shaver.
        p. cm.
   Includes bibliographical references and index.
   ISBN 0-275-93717-8 (hb.). — ISBN 0-275-93726-7 (pb.)
   1. Arms control. 2. United States—Military policy. 3. Soviet
Union—Military policy. 4. Europe—Military policy.   I. Hallenbeck,
Ralph A. II. Shaver, David E.
JX1974.5.O5   1991
327.1'74—dc20   90-44146

British Library Cataloguing in Publication Data is available.

Library of Congress Catalog Card Number: 90-44146
ISBN: 0-275-93717-8 (hb.)
        0-275-93726-7 (pb.)

First published in 1991

Praeger Publishers, One Madison Avenue, New York, NY 10010
An imprint of Greenwood Publishing Group, Inc.

Printed in the United States of America

The paper used in this book complies with the
Permanent Paper Standard issued by the National
Information Standards Organization (Z39.48–1984).

10 9 8 7 6 5 4 3 2 1

Dedicated in memory of John F. Scott (August 13, 1933—February 22, 1990), who retired in 1989 after serving the Strategic Studies Institute as National Security Affairs Analyst for more than 25 years. Thank you, John, for your mentorship, inspiration, sense of humor, and awareness of proportion.

Contents

Figures, Maps, and Tables

FIGURES

MAPS

TABLES

Foreword

Events of the past year in Europe—the "Revolution of 1989"—place regional arms control initiatives into a new context. Conventional arms control negotiations began early in the year, involving NATO and Warsaw Treaty Organization members in more or less traditional roles. The year ended with the virtual paralysis of the Warsaw Pact and serious discussion concerning the reunification of Germany. This timely compendium of contemporary thought attempts to put the crucial issues of European arms-reduction efforts into focus.

To the serious student of foreign policy and international relations, as well as to policymakers and military strategists, conventional arms control has become a puzzle on the paths of both future NATO policies and Soviet-U.S. relations. Where do we begin our research? What are the objectives and how were they derived? What issues are involved? Who are the relevant participants? Where do different nations stand on the issues? What do the current proposals constitute? How close are we to an agreement? Can conventional reductions be verified? What does the post arms-reduction world look like? What is the future of the alliances in Europe? Will we have to change national security strategy? Is arms control still relevant, considering the political changes in Eastern Europe? How can we agree on answers before events change them? The authors of this text provide the answers to those questions plus much more.

To begin to comprehend the conundrum of conventional arms control, the authors start with the earliest events in a process of multilateral arms control negotiations that span more than 17 years. By opening their book with a chronology of conventional arms control events from NATO's Harmel Report in 1967 through the Doctrinal Seminar in 1990, the authors provide a "quick study" for the reader in Chapter 1. This chapter presents a short overview of the activities, conferences, meetings, major speeches, and political initiatives (which have occurred in the past) that continue to influence multilateral negotiations today. The authors briefly describe the architecture of the two sets of multilateral talks ongoing in Vienna: the Negotiations on Conventional Armed Forces in Europe (CFE) and the Negotiations on Confidence- and Security-Building Measures (CSBM). The CFE talks involve the reductions of armaments—tanks, artillery, armored troop carriers, helicopters, and fixed-wing combat airplanes—as well as troop reductions. The objectives of these talks include reductions to a "parity" (nearly equal) level, the elimination of surprise attack capabilities, and the limitation of movement of large military formations to achieve "stability" on the European continent. The objectives of the CSBM talks seek limitations on the activities of military forces through the development of Confidence- and Security-Building Measures, which are designed to make military activities more visible to other nations.

In Chapter 2 the authors provide an academic discussion on how and why we developed the general objectives for the negotiations. Underscoring the basic tenets or propositions in conventional arms control, the authors describe how our current proposals were derived from a strategic framework of do's and don'ts as well as provide a template for the current defensive posture in Europe and how that posture will change as forces are removed from the theater of operations.

Next, political procedures within the U.S. Interagency Group and NATO's High Level Task Force are discussed to paint a picture of how specific objectives are transformed from conception through the complex U.S. and NATO political consensus-building apparatus to formal presentation in Vienna. Chapter 3 supplies the political insight necessary to comprehend current negotiations.

In Chapter 4 conventional arms control issues are presented as mini-historical vignettes to help the reader appreciate the complexity of sophisticated negotiations and the difficulties to overcome in talking across, rather than directly about, various national political positions. Although many issues have been resolved, some have not, nor will they be. Flexibility in our pursuit of a treaty has enabled us to attain a consensus NATO position.

A chapter on definitional disarmament follows, to ensure that readers understand the differences among the various terms described in conventional arms control. Arms limitations, reductions, negotiated and nonnegotiated partial disarmament, and structural disarmament all are explained in terms of their effect on U.S. national security policymaking. The authors note the significant impact of unilateral reductions in their discussion of nonnegotiated disarmament, and they further discuss the exterior (to the arms control process) issues most important to the negotiations—the U.S. budget, allied burdensharing, threat diminishment, and international trading deficits.

At this point in the book the reader should understand conventional arms control history; how objectives for the talks were derived; the political procedures involved; the significant issues that have been addressed; and appropriate definitional and external strategic issues that affect what should be included and excluded from the negotiations.

Next, the authors address in three successive chapters (6, 7, and 8) current proposals and progress in the CFE and CSBM talks, to include the difficulties in attaining consensus on definition and counting rules for Treaty Limited Items (TLI), stationing and sufficiency rules for personnel and equipment, and subregions of the Atlantic-to-the-Urals region. In Chapter 6 the authors describe in detail the current CFE proposals (both NATO and Warsaw Pact) and provide alternatives to areas of potential "gridlock,"—the inclusion or exclusion of Land-Based Naval Air. In Chapter 7 they fully describe and analyze NATO's verification and stability measures. Current CSBM negotiations are presented in Chapter 8, including a summary of the Western proposals and the controversial Warsaw Pact proposals concerning an "Open Seas" measure, designed to open discussions on naval arms control.

Chapter 9 concerns the post-CFE environment. The authors provide a very thought-provoking discussion on a future "nonauthoritarian" world—one that has scrapped the U.S. national security strategy of "containment" in favor of developing a future strategy that looks beyond our current fixation on Europe. This sets the stage for discussion (in Chapter 10) of post–CFE alternative defense strategies and architecture. The authors provide their own versions of post–CFE defensive organization to supplement the existing work of academics and military theorists from both Europe and the United States.

The authors close their discussion of conventional arms control by offering opinions and reflections on what the effects on U.S. and NATO military forces might be after successful conclusions in CFE and CSBM negotiations. Challenges, prospects, and implications for future U.S. and allied nuclear and conventional force requirements are presented for the midterm, with the conclusion that alliance governments need to "come to their senses" concerning the *realpolitik* of peace dividends, increased reductions, divisive burdensharing arguments, and the political instabilities in Eastern Europe.

No study for the serious student would be complete without an analysis of the actual documents involved. The CFE Mandate; NATO's formal proposals in its first, second, and third chapters; and the Western proposal in CSBM are all appended, as well as a necessary glossary of terms.

This book is unique in its field, incorporating the work of practitioners, academics, and actual members of the U.S. negotiating team.

Major General William F. Burns (U.S. Army, Ret.)
Former Director, U.S. Arms Control and Disarmament Agency

ON DISARMAMENT

1

Background

INTRODUCTION

To fully understand conventional arms control we need to view its history. The chronology outlined in Figure 1.1 allows the reader to visualize events over time, and it presents a picture of international events that have had a direct impact on the conventional arms control process and in confidence building among the members of NATO, the Warsaw Pact (WP), and Neutral and Nonaligned Nations (NNA).

Harmel Report

Modern conventional arms control had its genesis in ideas expressed as early as the 1950s, but it was not until the NATO ministers' report (known as the Harmel Report) in December 1967 on the future tasks of the Alliance that the process began to move toward a conference with the East. The report recommended that NATO try to arrange a forum for mutual arms reductions. In 1968, NATO ministers formally proposed force reduction talks with the East.[1] Although the Pact showed no enthusiasm for arms control, the United States and its allies in NATO would not agree to the Conference on Security and Cooperation in Europe (CSCE) unless the East agreed to meet in the Mutual and Balanced Force Reduction (MBFR) forum.

Mansfield Amendments

Various coincident pressures and events moved both sides to MBFR in addition to the quid pro quo for the CSCE. First, Senator Mansfield introduced legislation in 1966 designed to bring about substantial U.S. troop reductions in Europe;

Figure 1.1
Conventional Arms Control Chronology

1967	HARMEL REPORT
1973	MANSFIELD AMENDMENTS MBFR (OCT 73) VIENNA CSCE (JUL 73) HELSINKI
1980	CSCE (NOV 80) MADRID
1984	CDE (JAN 84) STOCKHOLM
1986	GORBACHEV INITIATIVE (APR 86) HLTF FORMED (MAY 86) BUDAPEST APPEAL (JUN 86) BRUSSELS DECLARATION (DEC 86) NATO MTG ON PROCEDURES (DEC 86)
1987	NATO-WP DISCUSS SCOPE (APR 87) MANDATE TALKS START (JUL 87)
1988	GORBACHEV U.N. SPEECH (7 DEC 88) NATO MINISTERIAL MTG (9 DEC 88)
1989	CSCE/CDE VIENNA CONCLUDING MANDATE (15 JAN 89) MBFR TERMINATION (2 FEB 89) CFE MANDATE (9 FEB 89) CFE BEGINS (9 MAR 89) CFE SESSION II (5 MAY 89) CSCE/CDE VIENNA II BEGINS (9 MAY 89) PRESIDENT BUSH'S INITIATIVE (29 MAY 89) CFE SESSION III (7 SEP 89) CFE SESSION IV (10 NOV 89)
1990	CSBM DOCTRINAL TALKS (16 JAN 90)

his efforts continued until 1975, two years into the MBFR talks.[2] The Mansfield Amendments, as they were called, were clear incentives for NATO Europe to negotiate for mutual reductions and, at the same time, to use the potential of MBFR to ward off unilateral cuts by the United States. Senator Mansfield continually called for a U.S. troop reduction in Europe of 50,000 men in 1973.

MBFR—VIENNA (OCTOBER 1973)

When NATO ministers met at Reykjavik in June 1968, they openly expressed interest in a process leading to mutual and balanced force reductions with the East, confirming a conclusion of the 1967 Harmel Report on future tasks of the

Alliance. But in August 1968, the Soviets invaded Czechoslovakia, increasing their occupation force by five more divisions. The NATO ministers renewed their offer to negotiate in 1970, but the Soviets insisted on a European security conference rather than an alliance-to-alliance forum. In July 1973, the Soviets obtained their forum in the CSCE, for which they paid with several concessions and agreements, the most pertinent being agreement to the MBFR forum.

At the signing of the Strategic Arms Limitation Treaty (SALT) I in 1972, Secretary Brezhnev and President Nixon also endorsed the goal of force reductions in Europe. This led at last to the meeting of NATO and Warsaw Pact nations in January 1973 to determine terms of reference for MBFR. Talks were to focus on a zone of reduction sometimes referred to as the NATO Guidelines Area (NGA), which included the Federal Republic of Germany (FRG) and the Benelux countries in the West, and East Germany, Poland, and Czechoslovakia in the East (see Map 1.1). The first MBFR negotiating round began on October 30, 1973.[3]

From the beginning the MBFR, NATO saw the talks as part of a broader effort to reduce the likelihood of war and to strengthen stability. NATO faced a larger ground force (later put at a 170,000-man advantage to the East); geographical asymmetry where the Soviet Union's western border is only 360–420 miles from the eastern border of the FRG, while the Atlantic Ocean lies between the United

Map 1.1
NATO Guidelines Area, Mutual and Balanced Force Reductions

States and the European allies; and limited depth for defense in Europe where one-fourth of FRG industry and 30 percent of its population are less than 60 miles from Pact territory. These differences were true both in 1973 and today. During the 15 years of negotiation, other balances changed: the East matched and then exceeded NATO in short-range and other battlefield nuclear weapons systems; reached parity and perhaps exceeded in capacity the West's strategic nuclear forces; and installed long-range intermediate nuclear forces (LRINF), which NATO countered with its 1979 decision to deploy Pershing II and cruise missiles in Europe. In the interim (1973–89), no force reductions were agreed upon in MBFR.[4]

The MBFR talks that began in Vienna on October 30, 1973 were, with some exceptions, proposals and counterproposals to reduce the numbers of troops on both sides to an equal level. The exceptions were NATO's attempts to break a negotiating impasse in 1975 and in 1976 by proposing reductions in some nuclear forces.[5] The talks foundered on disagreements about providing information on forces and about verification measures. Where initial proposals would have required reducing close to 100,000 troops on each side, the latest proposals in 1985 were for the reduction of 11,500 Pact forces for about half as many NATO troops.

During the course of MBFR, the following events influenced the pace and content of the talks:

- SALT II negotiations began immediately after the signing of SALT I in 1972 and continued until June 1979 with the signing of a treaty.[6]
- The Soviets began to deploy SS–20 intermediate-range missiles and Backfire bombers in 1977. NATO then stopped offering to include nuclear weapons in its MBFR proposals and, in 1979, formulated its dual-track Intermediate-Range Nuclear Forces (INF) decision to deploy cruise missiles and Pershing II missiles in Europe while being willing to negotiate with the Soviets to reduce INF.
- INF negotiations began in October 1980 and resulted in a treaty signed on December 8, 1987 designed to eliminate INF worldwide.

Near the end of active negotiations in 1985–86, when the West proposed reducing 5,000 U.S. troops for 11,500 Soviet troops in Europe, the proposal included verification measures that would include yearly exchanges of detailed information on units down to battalion level, 30 annual on-site inspections, and permanent exit–entry points for the reductions zone. The East reacted with statements that seemed to hold promise for a reasonable verification regime, but the Pact's draft agreements of February 1986 showed no signs of change from the Pact's refusal to open its territory to inspection and monitoring.[7]

The wisdom of retrospect is that the Soviets and their allies did not intend to reach an agreement in MBFR. They were maneuvered into the talks by the West in exchange for the CSCE that the Soviets wanted (but which was shaped substantially by the West), and they may have believed that NATO was acting out a process to avoid U.S. troop withdrawals. The Soviets tried to use the talks to establish the belief that numerical and geographical disparities did not exist between the two alliances. Jonathan Dean, once the U.S. negotiator at the MBFR, said later that the USSR

showed the low priority it assigned to MBFR when it pushed for a follow-on conference [of the CSCE] on European security despite its knowledge that this rival conference, which ultimately took the form of the Stockholm [Conference on Confidence- and Security-Building Measures and Disarmament in Europe] CDE, would undermine the authority of the MBFR forum.[8]

MBFR is a logical source of possible lessons for conventional arms control negotiations. The following observations from the MBFR talks were helpful in preparing for the Negotiations on Conventional Armed Forces in Europe (CFE):

- MBFR's primary focus on troops rather than on units, equipment, and weapons only added to the data and verification issues separating the alliances.
- Late in MBFR, the Pact recognized disparities between U.S.-aligned and Soviet forces in Europe, and its proposals reflected acceptance of the principle of parity. However, this Pact recognition did not extend to the forces of the two alliances as a whole. The Pact never admitted to having overall net advantages in MBFR.
- Both sides recognized the importance of the two superpower members and accorded their forces first priority in force reduction proposals.
- When nuclear and conventional talks were simultaneous, the nuclear talks had priority on both sides.
- Persuasive evidence is not available to support a conclusion that either side was sufficiently motivated to accomplish tangible results in MBFR. NATO lacked consensus on key issues. Reductions in the NGA were not likely to improve NATO's security because the depth of the Eastern NGA allowed nearby stationing of removed Pact troops. And the Pact was intractable on key issues

MBFR talks lacked continuity in negotiators and in top political authorities. The United States had six different delegation heads in the first 12 years; the Soviets had three. Each new administration in the democratic countries brought a wholesale turnover of key people involved with MBFR. About 200–300 NATO officials had to approve each important move in negotiations, and Eastern negotiators were even less flexible than NATO's.[9]

MBFR produced positive results even if it did not produce a treaty:

- It continued and sustained the NATO consensus that arms control negotiations are a necessary component of Alliance defense strategy.
- The talks contributed to a developing East–West dialogue and mutual understanding of some key military issues.
- When the Soviets walked out of INF talks in November 1983, the MBFR forum gave both sides an opportunity to show their continued interest in improving relations through arms control. MBFR also helped offset European pressures on the United States to make concessions in START and INF as a way to get the Soviets back to the bargaining table.

MBFR gave NATO's European members direct participation in arms control, and in that way it played a complementary role in East–West relations in nuclear and space negotiations. As a continuing, active negotiation, MBFR was important to maintaining public support for conventional defense spending.

CSCE—HELSINKI (JULY 1973)

The Conference on Security and Cooperation in Europe (CSCE) convened at Helsinki in July 1973.[10] The talks included all European countries except Albania, the United States, and Canada—35 nations in all. CSCE began primarily as negotiations about unresolved political issues following World War II. Its agenda developed into four areas, called "baskets." Basket I covered interstate behavior, human rights, and the use of force. Basket II addressed cooperation in economics, technology, and commerce. Basket III applied to humanitarian practices and to the flow of information, ideas, and people. Basket IV provided for the continuation of the CSCE at follow-up meetings and conferences that are held in one or another major city in the member states.[11]

On August 1, 1975, the heads of state of virtually all 35 nations met to sign the Final Act. The Final Act was divided into four sections. Section One, involving security, proclaimed the "inviolability of frontiers" and renounced actions "making each other's territory the object of military occupation." Its "confidence-building measures" included 21 days' voluntary prior notification of military maneuvers involving over 25,000 men and taking place within 250 kilometers of national frontiers, and the exchange of observers at such maneuvers. NATO countries observed the provisions on seven occasions in 1975, while the first Soviet notification came later, in January 1976. Section Two concerned economic, technological, and environmental cooperation. Section Three, which engendered most discussion, dealt with humanitarian cooperation; at the end, the talks became largely a defensive action by the Soviet Union against Western and neutral pressure to open up freer contacts of people and ideas. The Final Act embodied limited and voluntary, but not contractual, Soviet concessions on reuniting divided families, marriages between different nationals, the improvement of working conditions for journalists, and the distribution of papers and journals.

Section Four provided for a follow-up conference in Belgrade on June 15, 1977. This was a compromise between the larger powers, who were reluctant to have a continuing organization (the Soviet Union so as to avoid more goading on freer contacts, the West so as to avoid Soviet involvement in Western affairs), and the small ones, who were anxious to make their voices heard more clearly. At the last moment Malta forced the addition of language on the Mediterranean that stressed relations with the Arab states; Turkey fought to exclude ports of embarkation for Cyprus from the notification procedures of the confidence-building measures; a coalition of southern states inserted a paragraph in favor of migrant workers in Western Europe; and Romania conspicuously supported independence on the Warsaw Pact side. In short, the attitudes of the smaller powers suggested that future pan-European diplomacy was likely to produce pressures that could no longer be comfortably contained within the East–West framework. Political diversification became a hallmark of the year.[12]

CSCE—MADRID (NOVEMBER 1980)

On November 12, 1980, the CSCE convened in Madrid to review the results of the Helsinki Final Act. Events in Poland and Afghanistan overshadowed a thorough review, since the Soviets refused to talk about Afghanistan within the CSCE responsibility in Europe.[13] Many Confidence-and Security-Building Measures (CSBM) were proposed, but none were accepted. This conference was important because it established the separate Conference on Confidence- and Security-Building Measures and Disarmament in Europe (CDE) as a subset to the CSCE process on September 9, 1983 (a French proposal).

CDE—STOCKHOLM (JANUARY 1984)

The CDE began at Stockholm on January 17, 1984, to negotiate militarily significant, politically binding, verifiable CSBMs for the whole of Europe, including the European portion of the Soviet Union.[14] Participants were the same 35 nations that took part in CSCE. The CDE forum has not been used to negotiate force reductions; its purpose is to place restrictions on the activities of military forces.[15]

The CDE's first products were insubstantial agreements on notification of major maneuvers of more than 25,000 troops, voluntary notification of smaller movements, and a provision to invite observers.

By the autumn of 1986, the East agreed to most of the measures proposed by the West, marking the first agreement in the CDE process with any substance: control on the activities, rather than the size, of military units in the whole of Europe and the adjoining sea and air space. Briefly, the parties agreed in Stockholm on September 19 to the following points:

- Prior notification of certain military activities. Activities must be reported if they consist of at least 13,000 troops, including support troops, or if they consist of at least 300 tanks.

- Observation of certain military activities. Participating states may send up to two observers to activities that last more than 72 hours and include 17,000 or more troops, except that amphibious landings or parachute assaults must be open to observation when the number of troops meets or exceeds 5,000.

- Annual calendars. Each participating state will exchange with all others an annual calendar of its military activities subject to prior notification.

- Constraining provisions. Activities of 75,000 or more troops should be communicated to other states in a notification that amounts to 15 months' warning; activities of 40,000 or more troops must be communicated by November 15 of the preceding year. "If military activities subject to prior notification are carried out in addition to those contained in the annual calendar, they should be as few as possible.''

- Compliance and verification. Inspection may be requested and carried out by ground or air in any country in the CSBM area; no state need accept on its territory in the zone more than three inspections per calendar year; the inspections may last for 48 hours; inspection teams will have no more than four people, who may divide into two parts.[16]

There were two Western measures not incorporated in the agreement. The first was for an exchange of military information about the structure of ground and land-based air forces, with normal peacetime locations and force composition. The second was development of means of communication to seek additional information on potentially destabilizing events.[17]

Before leaving the discussion of CSBMs, it is noteworthy that the Soviets offered alternative proposals for discussion in the CDE forum: a treaty on the nonuse of force; a pledge of no first use of nuclear weapons; a chemical weapons ban in the zone; and an expansion of confidence-building measures of the Helsinki Final Act.

GORBACHEV INITIATIVE (APRIL 1986)

One certain lesson of arms talks in Europe is that the Soviets place great stock in the forum for negotiations. Diplomatic maneuvering about negotiations seems as important to the East as what goes on in negotiations. Negotiations will differ from the past not only because General Secretary Gorbachev's "reasonableness" is a departure from his predecessors, but also because of the advent of the new Atlantic-to-the-Urals (ATTU) forum.[18]

Gorbachev proposed, in April 1986, "substantial reductions in all components of the land forces and tactical air forces of the European states and the relevant forces of the USA and Canada deployed in Europe."[19] He also proposed that tactical nuclear weapons could be reduced simultaneously and that the preferred area of interest should cover Europe from the Atlantic to the Urals. He stated that both national technical means of verification and, if need be, on-site inspections were possible.[20] This proposal, now known as the Gorbachev Initiative, created the Atlantic-to-the Urals (ATTU) area depicted in Map 1.2.

NATO HIGH LEVEL TASK FORCE FORMED (MAY 1986)

As a direct result of the Gorbachev Initiative, the North Atlantic Council (NAC) formed a High Level Task Force (HLTF) in May 1986 to study the Gorbachev Initiative for its potential impact on NATO and to advise the NAC directly on matters pertaining to conventional arms control and the CDE process.[21] The HLTF still currently operates in that capacity; however, there are those who see that the ad hoc nature of the HLTF may no longer be necessary with the commencement of negotiations in the CFE.

Map 1.2
Atlantic-to-the-Urals (ATTU)

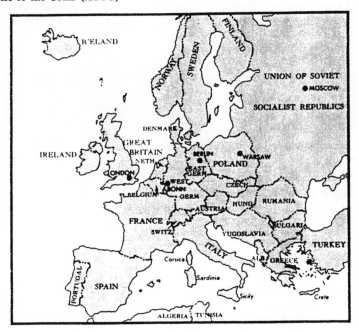

BUDAPEST APPEAL (JUNE 1986)

On June 13, 1986, Gorbachev delivered a speech in response to the latest U.S. proposal in the MBFR talks in Vienna. The substance of that speech became, in effect, an informal proposal. It called for initial troop reductions of 100,000 to 150,000 troops in two years, followed by mutual alliance reductions of 25 percent by the 1990s. The reductions were to be applied to military units, which were to be demobilized and the unit equipment to be returned to country of origin.[22]

BRUSSELS DECLARATION (DECEMBER 1986)

In response to the Gorbachev Initiative, the North Atlantic Council, in its "Brussels Declaration" of December 11, 1986 also concluded that the area for negotiation should be the Atlantic to the Urals with an aim to establish a "verifiable, comprehensive, and stable balance of conventional forces at lower levels." This declaration also called for separate negotiations to build on the results of the CDE.[23]

NATO MEETING ON PROCEDURES (DECEMBER 1986)

As a follow-on to the Brussels Declaration, the High Level Task Force met in December 1986 to develop objectives for the new ATTU talks. This meeting produced the following objectives:

- To establish stable and secure levels of forces, a key to which is the elimination of disparities;
- To negotiate in a step-by-step process so that security is undiminished at each step;
- To eliminate the Pact capability for surprise attack, or to force the Pact to mobilize visibly to initiate any large-scale offensive;
- To expand and improve measures to build confidence, openness, and calculability about military behavior;
- To negotiate measures that apply to the whole of Europe, but in a way that addresses regional imbalances and prevents circumvention; and
- To establish effective verification with detailed exchanges of information and on-site inspections that insure compliance with agreements and guarantee that limitations on forces are not exceeded.[24]

NATO–WP DISCUSSION ON SCOPE (APRIL 1987)

NATO and Warsaw Pact representatives initially met in Vienna in April 1987 to develop the scope offered by the new Atlantic-to-the-Urals talks as a precursor to initiating formal mandate talks scheduled for summer 1987.[25] Discussion involved data exchanges, verification, force modernization and structuring, exclusions, units of account, and stability measures.

MANDATE TALKS START (JULY 1987)

The NATO–WP discussion on scope of conventional arms control negotiations also established a start date for mandate talks. The mandate talks—discussions to set the objectives, rules, organization, and procedures to be used in the formal Negotiations on Conventional Armed Forces in Europe (CFE)—continued to successful conclusion on February 9, 1989 (20 months). Actual mandate provisions are listed in Appendix A.

GORBACHEV'S U.N. SPEECH (DECEMBER 7, 1988)

Perhaps the greatest event since the beginning of the Cold War took place in New York City when Gorbachev announced the unilateral withdrawal of 50,000 soldiers; 10,000 tanks; 8,500 artillery systems; 800 combat aircraft; assault landing troops; and bridging units from Eastern Europe—and an overall military force cut of 500,000. This speech sparked an avalanche of editorials from the political left, center, and right concerning the security implications of such cuts.[26]

Not only did Gorbachev's speech initiate hundreds of articles in the Western press, but also precipitated announcements by other Warsaw Pact members declaring unilateral reductions in troops, armaments, and defense budgets. The reductions amount to some 46,000 men; 2,700 tanks; and 860 artillery pieces.[27]

NATO MINISTERIAL MEETING (DECEMBER 9, 1988)

Immediately subsequent to Gorbachev's speech, NATO ministers announced their planned proposal that would require Soviet bloc nations to make huge cuts in tanks, other armored vehicles, and artillery. Under the plan, equal limits would be established for these units of account, set at limits of 95 percent of the number of current NATO weapon systems.[28] This initial ''going-in'' position was fully supported by the U.S. government, but it proved to be publicly unacceptable as a response to the deep unilateral cuts offered by the Soviets.

CSCE/CDE VIENNA CONCLUDING MANDATE (JANUARY 15, 1989)

On January 15, 1989, the CSCE ended its third session by adopting a concluding document that reaffirms that the resumption of CSBM negotiations will take place in accordance with the Madrid ending mandate. The objectives cited in the Concluding Mandate include building upon and expanding CSBMs established in Stockholm, and adopting new, complementary CSBMs designed to increase transparency and reduce the risk of military confrontation in Europe.[29]

MBFR TERMINATION (FEBUARY 2, 1989)

Rather unceremoniously, the MBFR talks were ended on February 2, 1989.

CFE MANDATE (FEBUARY 9, 1989)

After 20 months of negotiations, the CFE Mandate was finally approved. The text of the mandate is provided in Appendix A. The reader should note the similarities between NATO's objectives and the CFE Mandate objectives as well as the linkage between the CFE and CDE negotiations.[30]

CFE BEGINS (MARCH 9, 1989)

The CFE talks opened on March 9, 1989 and terminated on March 23, 1989. During the two-week period both sides to the negotiations tabled proposals and exchanged force data. The following excerpt from Dr. Lynn E. Davis in ''Arms Control and the Alliance'' discusses the first Warsaw Pact and NATO proposals offered during this period.

The Warsaw Pact proposal calls for the elimination in the first (of three) stage of the most destabilizing kinds and categories of arms, "such as attack combat aircraft of short-range tactical aviation, combat helicopters, tanks, combat armored vehicles and person-nel carriers, and artillery (including launch rocket systems and mortars)." At the same time, each side would reduce its armed forces and conventional arms down to equal col-lective ceilings which would be 10-15% lower than the lowest levels possessed by either alliance. As to the precise ceilings for the different categories of weapons, Foreign Minister Edward Shevardnadze called upon experts to "develop a single method of account" which must be "scientific, fair, and objective." To prevent surprise attack, the Warsaw Pact proposed a zone along the inter-German border in which destabilizing arms would be re-duced, military activities would be limited, and short range nuclear weapons would be withdrawn. In the second stage, lasting 2-3 years, each side would reduce its number of armed forces, including the weapons assigned to those forces, by an additional 25%, or approximately 500,000 men. In the third stage, the armed forces would be restructured so they could only be used for defensive purposes. At the same time, Shevardnadze stated that the Warsaw Pact's negotiating position would be influenced "by the factor of naval arms." The Warsaw Pact also called for rigorous verification measures including land and air inspections "without right of refusal," but it did not define what these might be.

The Warsaw Pact proposal is ambitious in its approach but still vague as to specifics. In contrast, NATO has introduced a quite detailed plan calling for reductions, not in man-power as in MBFR, but rather in a limited number of categories of the most threatening weapons—tanks, artillery, and armored troop carriers. The goal is parity or equal ceil-ings, applied from the Atlantic to the Urals, as well as in geographical sub-zones so as to prevent an undue concentration of forces.

The overall level for each side would be set slightly below the number NATO says it has in Europe, and would be collective: for tanks, 20,000; for artillery, 16,500; for ar-mored troop carriers, 28,000. In addition, the NATO proposal has a "sufficiency rule" whereby no single country may have more than 30% of the total arms held by both sides, in the belief that no single country should dominate. NATO has also defined sublimits for four geographical regions. For example, in the Central Region (Benelux, the two Ger-manies, Poland, and Czechoslovakia), in "active units" there can be no more than 8,000 of the 20,000 tanks, 4,500 artillery, and 11,000 armored troop carriers. Finally, no coun-try may "station inactive units" on the territory of its allies more than 3,200 tanks, 1,700 artillery pieces, and 6,000 armored troop carriers. Reductions in weapons would be taken in units to assist in verification and indirectly to produce reductions in manpower. NATO did not, however, decide whether the weapons to be eliminated in Europe will be destroyed or removed to other theaters. Information will be exchanged on the equipment holdings and personnel in combat and combat support units disaggregated down to battalion level.[31] (See Appendix B for formal NATO proposal.)

Although both East and West seemed to be close on their initial positions, there were challenges to success. These included:

- The categories of weapons systems that should be included;
- Soviet proposals to create zones of low concentrations of offensive armaments;
- An overall ceiling on the number of tanks and artillery in Europe as well as ceilings in each country;

- The place of naval forces and tactical nuclear weapons in the negotiations; and
- The place of the U.S. Follow-on Forces Attack (FOFA) concept in the arms talks.[32]

CFE SESSION II (MAY 5, 1989)

CFE talks resumed on May 5, 1989. In addition to the challenges already mentioned, many other issues were on the agenda, including a revisit to the mandate to clearly define wording about dual capable systems (DCS), zones, and linkage between the CFE and CDE negotiations; stabilizing measures; parity of capabilities; and the disposition of reduced forces. Ambassador James Woolsey headed the U.S. delegation to the talks. The JCS representative was and remains Major General Adrian St. John, II (U.S. Army, Ret).

CSCE/CDE VIENNA II BEGINS (MAY 9, 1989)

The U.S. government fully supports the continuation of the CSCE process, but results must be qualified as "militarily significant, politically binding, verifiable, and cover the whole of Europe from the Atlantic to the Urals. Independent naval and air activities and non-European deployments are not valid subject for (CSBM) negotiation in the CDE."[33] These talks now parallel the time periods of the CFE talks in Vienna. Linkage of the two fora will take place every four weeks. During these linkages CFE participants from the two alliances will exchange views with and have agreed to take into consideration the views of the other CSCE states concerning their own security. Changing the existing CFE Mandate is a potential result of these linkage meetings. These concurrent CSCE/CDE negotiations are now termed Negotiations on Confidence- and Security-Building Measures (CSBM). Ambassador Jack Maresca heads the U.S. delegation to the talks. The JCS representative is Brigadier General Lynn Hooper, U.S. Army.

PRESIDENT BUSH'S INITIATIVE (MAY 29, 1989)

On May 29, 1989, while attending a NATO summit meeting in Brussels, President Bush proposed that the previous NATO CFE proposal be modified to include troops and combat aviation. Specifically, the Bush proposal called for a U.S. reduction and demobilization of 30,000 U.S. combat troops in Europe; a speedup of the CFE negotiating time to 6-12 months; a reduction of both U.S. and Soviet troops stationed outside their respective homelands to 275,000 each; a speedup of actual reductions to take place in the 1992–93 time frame from the currently projected 1997 time frame; and a reduction of combat aircraft and helicopters to 15 percent below current NATO levels for both sides. NATO accepted President Bush's initiative. The Bush proposal now places NATO's position very near the Soviet position and smooths problems within the Alliance concerning the timetable of future Short-Range Nuclear Forces (SNF) talks.[34] (See Appendix C for formal NATO proposal.)

CFE SESSION III (SEPTEMBER 7, 1989)

During CFE Session III (September 7–October 19, 1989), NATO tabled what is known as "Chapter Three" of its proposal. Chapter One (Appendix B) was the original proposal consisting of reductions in Main Battle Tanks (MBT), Artillery, and Armored Troop Carriers (ATC). Chapter Two (Appendix C) was tabled after President Bush's NATO address, which also included personnel and combat aircraft reductions. The Chapter Three proposals (Appendix D) include additional security measures that address exchange of information, stabilizing measures, verification provisions, and measures to prevent circumvention. The proposals contain gaps that will need additional consensus building within NATO but that serve as the framework of supplemental limitations, designed to ensure lasting stability and security in Europe. Many of these measures had their genesis in work accomplished by the Negotiations on Confidence- and Security-Building Measures (CSBM) talks. The reader should note the differences and similarities of Chapter Three in CFE and the CSBMs listed in Appendix E.

In addition to the submission of CFE Chapter Three, another unusual event (witnessed by co-author David Shaver) took place during this session. At a mini-caucus, Major General Adrian St. John, the representative of the Joint Chiefs of Staff, volunteered to develop definition and counting rules for all Treaty Limited Equipment (TLE). The reason for this action was that definitions and counting rules were a major source of argument among members of NATO and between NATO and the Warsaw Pact. The United Kingdom did not want its medium and light tanks to be included as Main Battle Tanks (MBT); Turkey demanded that NATO receive something in return for not counting Soviet T-12 anti-tank weapons, which have a flat trajectory indirect fire artillery capability; and the USSR wanted to exclude its air defense interceptors beyond the Urals and count only strike, frontal/tactical aviation, and naval aircraft, particularly carrier-based aviation; while still other members of the Warsaw Pact wanted to include anti-tank and recoilless rifles. Normally, U.S. negotiators in Vienna are provided positions on issues by the High Level Task Force in Brussels or directly from the Interagency Group in Washington, D.C. (see Chapter 3 in this book).

CFE SESSION IV (NOVEMBER 10, 1989)

NATO presented its draft CFE treaty in CFE Session IV, as a result of the initiative of Major General St. John to develop the NATO version of definitions and counting (accounting) rules in a NATO mini-caucus, which has become the standard for discussion. The WTO also presented its version of a draft treaty. Problems still remain such as the ceiling on troops (the WTO wants a 300,000 national ceiling, not the 250,000 ceiling in NATO's proposal). In addition, this session also produced the scheduled dates for further negotiations in 1990. The dates for these session are:

- January 11 to February 23, 1990 (Round 4)
- March 19 to April 27, 1990 (Round 5)
- May 21 to June 29, 1990 (Round 6).

No further session dates have been scheduled for the negotiations, which leads us to believe that the CFE talks may be concluded in 1990. Upon reaching an agreement in summer 1990, the draft CFE treaty will then have to be approved by the 23 participating countries, in their respective capitals, before the formal conclusion anticipated in November 1990.

CSBM DOCTRINAL TALKS (JANUARY 16, 1990)

During fall 1989 sessions of the CSBM talks, the Untied States introduced the concept of a separate seminar on military doctrines to discuss questions of policies and doctrines in relation to the posture, structure, and activities of conventional forces in Europe. The doctrinal talks will consist of the following subjects:

- Presentations by participating states of their military policy in relation to the military capabilities and structure of their own forces;
- The relationship between military police and military potential and force structures, in particular quantity, equipment, structure, deployment, logistics, and military readiness;
- Military training, including reference to relevant military manuals and educational concepts, and the pattern of military exercises; and
- Military budgets, including questions of comparability in terms of price systems, costs and cost factors, and location of military expenditure in the national budget.

This seminar's purpose is to make the military posture and intent of each nation more open, transparent, and thus, less threatening. The seminar is the "hottest game in town" in Vienna. Doctrinal experts from each nation allowed questions and answers immediately following the formal presentations and an additional hour at the end of each day for follow-up questions. The conference lasted approximately three weeks (from January 16 to February 5, 1990).

NOTES

1. NATO Information Service, *NATO Handbook*, Brussels, Belgium: NATO, 1983, p. 27.

2. Phil Williams, "American Troops in Europe: A New Great Debate?" *The World Today*, December 1987, p. 217.

3. U.S. Department of State. "The Conference on Security and Cooperation in Europe," (hereafter called State, CSCE), *Historical Issues Series*, October 1986; and U.S. Department of State, Bureau of Public Affairs, *Security and Arms Control: The Search for a More Stable Peace*, September 1984, various pages, are the principal sources for this background.

4. U.S. Department of State, *Security and Arms Control*, pp. 47–51.

5. Ibid., pp. 47–48.

6. Ibid., p. 29.

7. Strategic Studies Institute (hereafter called SSI), U.S. Army War College, *Conventional Arms Control in Europe: Army Perspectives*, Carlisle Barracks, Pa: SSI, October 1987, p. 5.

8. Richard Darilek, "The Future of Conventional Arms Control in Europe, A Tale of Two Cities: Stockholm, Vienna," *Survival*, January–February 1987, pp. 5–20.

9. Jonathan Dean, "East-West Arms Negotiations: The Multilateral Dimension," in *A Game for High Stakes: Lessons Learned in Negotiating with The Soviet Union*, ed. by Leon Sloss and M. Scott Davis, Cambridge, Mass.: Ballinger, 1986, pp. 79–106, at p. 96.

10. State, CSCE, p. 1.

11. Ibid., p. 2.

12. The International Institute for Strategic Studies (IISS), *Strategic Survey 1975*, London: IISS, 1976, pp. 57–58.

13. The International Institute for Strategic Studies, *Strategic Survey 1980–1981*, London: IISS, 1981, pp. 83–84.

14. U.S. Department of State, *Security and Arms Control*, p. 55.

15. Darilek, "The Future of Conventional Arms Control," p. 6.

16. "Documentation: Conference on Disarmament in Europe," *Survival*, January–February 1987, pp. 79–84.

17. The complete list of six Western proposals is in U.S. Department of State, "Conference on Disarmament in Europe," *GIST*, January 1986, p. 1.

18. SSI, *Conventional Arms Control in Europe*, p. 8.

19. Darilek, "The Future of Conventional Arms Control," p. 16.

20. Ibid.

21. The International Institute for Strategic Studies, *Strategic Survey 1986–1987*, London: IISS, p. 70.

22. SSI, *Conventional Arms Control in Europe*, p. 44.

23. John Borawski, Stan Weeks, and Charlotte E. Thompson, "The Stockholm Agreement of September 1986," *Orbis*, Winter 1987, pp. 643–62, at pp. 645–46.

24. "Declaration on Conventional Arms Control December 12, 1986," *Department of State Bulletin*, March 1987, p. 43.

25. E. A. Wayne, "Momentum Sought for Talks on Cutting Conventional Weapons," *The Christian Science Monitor*, February 17, 1988, p. 5; and Robert J. McCartney, "NATO Sets Goals for Arms Cuts," *The Washington Post*, March 3, 1988, pp. A27, A30.

26. Mark Helprin, "Hypnotist Gorbachev Conjures an Arms Reduction," *Wall Street Journal*, December 13, 1988, p. A20.

27. Lynn E. Davis, "Arms Control and the Alliance," a discussion paper presented for a symposium, "The Alliance at Forty: Strategic Perspectives for the 1990s and Beyond," co-sponsored by the National Defense University and NATO Defense College, April 24–25, 1989, p. 3.

28. R. Jeffrey Smith, "NATO Arms Cut Proposal Faulted as Too Cautious," *The Washington Post*, April 17, 1989, p. A27.

29. From conversations with staff members of the Conventional Arms Negotiation Division (DAMO-SSC), Office of the Deputy Chief of Staff for Operations and Plans, Headquarters, Department of the Army.

30. Mandate text provided by the Conventional Arms Negotiation Division.

31. Davis, "Arms Control and the Alliance," p. 4.

32. Peter Adams, "Complex Issues Confront Conventional Arms Talks," *Defense News*, February 13, 1989, p. 3.

33. Information obtained from Conventional Negotiations Division.

34. Don Oberdorfer, "Bush Proposes Cutback in U.S. Troops in Europe," *The Washington Post*, May 30, 1989, p. A1.

2

Objectives

The objectives expressed in the CFE Mandate include the establishment of a secure and stable balance of conventional forces at lower levels, the elimination of disparities prejudicial to stability and security, and, as a matter of priority, the elimination of the capability for launching surprise attack and for initiating large-scale offensive action.[1]

The objective of the Conference on Confidence- and Security-Building Measures, simply stated, is improvement of inspection, observation, and notification of military activities in Europe.[2] These objectives (from both negotiations) came from Western viewpoints and were eventually accepted by the East.

NATO's strategy of Flexible Response (MC 14/3) calls for the Alliance to respond flexibly to various levels of Pact aggression while maintaining a forward defense of NATO territories. The intent is to defend the Alliance with conventional means until, at a point at which NATO's defense could no longer guarantee success, NATO would elect to initiate deliberate nuclear escalation. Through such escalation, NATO would attempt to redress the conventional imbalance, seize the initiative in order to regain the lost territory, and halt the war on terms acceptable to NATO. At the heart of Flexible Response is the lack of political and economic will of NATO members to match the WP, tank for tank, and thus resort early to cheaper nuclear forces.

The force imbalance and secrecy of Soviet military activities do not adequately explain in depth U.S. and NATO policies concerning conventional arms control. To provide that depth we will briefly describe the principles involved in conventional arms control, and then we will discuss the strategic, operational, and tactical objectives of the West.

STRATEGIC PRINCIPLES AND PROPOSITIONS FOR CONVENTIONAL ARMS CONTROL

Arms control principles are better stated as propositions because of the ambiguous record of previous efforts to control and reduce arms in this century. Perhaps the only "principle" attracting consensus is that we should use arms control to promote our national security interests when arms negotiations are an effective means to do so. If the following summary of propositions are not principles, they constitute one way to organize our thinking about conventional arms control:

— Arms control is a political process; it deals with the distribution of power and it affects the general welfare. Politics, Aristotle said, is the highest art because it includes everything else; each proposition advanced herein raises political challenges and obligations.

— Arms control can supplement defense in achieving national security. Although they involve dealing with politically hostile nations, arms control treaties do not change ideologies or necessarily reduce hostility. If treaties reduce confrontation and improve predictability, they support diplomatic efforts to reduce tensions.

— Nuclear and conventional arms controls affect each other. They interact not only in how they affect the distribution of military options but also, and often more dramatically, in how their interaction affects the perceptions of national leaders concerned with their countries' security.

— Conventional arms control is more complicated than nuclear arms control. The military resources at issue in conventional talks are complex components of military capability. But the character of conventional negotiations is that they are coalition undertakings, with many nations' political and economic institutions involved in and affected by the results.

— Mutual and Balanced Force Reduction talks provide lessons, not precedents. NATO and the Warsaw Pact disagreed about the fundamental issues of exchanging data on military forces and necessary measures of verification. Still, the MBFR talks are the only example in the nuclear age of many nations in two alliances negotiating with and among each other about the reduction of conventional forces—a process that is, by definition, political.

— NATO strategy is likely to be the NATO perspective for judging conventional arms control. Both the retention of the strategy's main elements and the modification of those elements stemming from arms agreements bear directly on the principle of political control. Nuclear weapons are and will remain a critical component of NATO's deterrent, and their possible use depends on decisions of political authorities.

— Soviet intentions are still unclear but fundamentally political. The possibility that Soviet objectives may be served by reducing Warsaw Pact forces in Europe, thereby possibly improving the stability of the military balance in Europe sought by NATO, is no guarantee that NATO will remain politically cohesive. NATO ministers and parliamentarians must think beyond the immediate effects of arms treaties to the kind and quality of alliance they want in the next century.

— Military criteria and judgment are essential elements of conventional arms control negotiations. Strategy joins political and military considerations. Beyond the details of military hardware and tactics, military advice is always subject to political decisions because it is subject to the availability of national resources. Where strategic goals and security risks depend on calculable warfighting outcomes, unvarnished military advice should be the essential consideration.

— Support from governments and publics is needed to make arms control worthwhile. Military advisors and arms control negotiators can propose; political leaders must dispose in an atmosphere of an aware and alert public—which, in a democracy, is the final arbiter of the value of all political processes. Conventional arms control is a legitimate force for improving national security when it supports, but does not replace, diplomacy and defense.[3]

TRANSITION

In our discussion of objectives, we have completed our consideration of the principles of conventional arms control and now proceed toward understanding the strategic objectives for conventional arms negotiations.

STRATEGIC OBJECTIVES

To propose options for strategic objectives that bear directly on our interests in Europe, we must understand what the strategic objectives are and what they mean. Of special interest are those ideas about objectives that might be stimulated by the coincidence of conventional arms negotiations in Europe and changes in Soviet thinking. It is, therefore, an ideal time to speculate on current NATO objectives and their meaning for our national objectives—before those events might take hold and shape our national objectives and policies for us.

Current U.S. Objectives

National security objectives are published yearly in the President's national security strategy document. In general they consist of:

- Maintenance of the security of our nation and our allies;
- Response of the challenges of the global economy;
- Defense and promotion of the cause of democracy, freedom, and human rights throughout the world;
- Peaceful resolution of disputes that affect U.S. interests in troubled regions of the world; and
- Building of effective and friendly relationships with all nations with whom there is a basis of shared concern.[4]

Most objective are brief descriptions of aspirations that move people and organizations to exert effort cooperatively. Seldom are objectives concrete or precise. They are necessary but not sufficient guides to common effort. Containing the

Soviets, deterring wars, and encouraging democratic tendencies all require at least two or more policies and strategies to achieve them. We should not pretend that identifying and rationalizing strategic objectives constitute any more than the beginning of a process of trying to know what we want of the world.

NATO has a set of objectives for negotiating with the Warsaw Pact to control and reduce conventional and nuclear arms. Theater nuclear forces and weapons will not be considered in the CFE negotiations. NATO has agreed, however, to discuss reductions in the theater nuclear weapons of the United States and USSR during a negotiation to follow immediately upon the conclusion of CFE. In any case, NATO's objectives differ little from the set of objectives the Alliance has posed for itself in earlier nuclear arms talks, with their general thrust being to give each side reason to feel less threatened by the other.

NATO's conventional arms control objectives are instrumental for reaching higher strategic objectives for the Alliance. The same is true of the Warsaw Pact's objectives. Many of us may suspect that what we call the Pact's true objectives for CFE differ from its expressed objectives, as well they should if the Pact has higher objectives. Moreover, we can be sure that each country in each alliance also has its own higher and lower order objectives in relation to CFE talks. Not a few countries probably want to ease their military spending in favor of their economies or reallocate military spending in favor of foreign policy goals. This idea is not alien to the conventional wisdom that arms control is a political process. But what people say this really means is that the objectives of the moment—reducing forces, reducing capabilities for surprise attack, and the details of arms control—are incidental to political objectives for which arms control can only be instrumental. Logically, then, a ''successful'' arms control negotiation or agreement must come that achieves or moves us closer to political objectives. Success or failure are not necessarily inherent to the accomplishments within a treaty.

But to see the objectives of arms control in this fashion requires some vision of a universe larger than the scope of an arms control agreement, larger both in space and time. One theory of the Soviet vision is that Central Europe has been the place where U.S. interests and commitments could be held hostage as a counterweight to U.S. strategic superiority worldwide. Soviet fielding of numerically superior forces, with those of their allies in Eastern Europe, has not been a peculiarity of Soviet strategic culture; the Soviets fully intended to be superior at the one critical place that the United States and its allies could not. Recent Soviet calls for including U.S. naval forces as subject for reduction and control in the CFE probably are neither diversionary nor insincere; they are instead an indication of the Soviet vision of the scope of arms controls and a sense of higher strategic—political—objectives.

Some U.S. pro- and anti-arms controllers forget this predominance of politics at their convenience. Few ''analysts'' of the notorious naval agreements of the 1920s show the slightest acquaintance with the political motivations of the participants. Few of the U.S. strategic intelligentsia who publicly debated the merits of the INF treaty looked beyond its immediate provisions to teach us the right meaning of arms control as a "political process."

Higher objectives—whether we call them global, national, or strategic—are, in turn, important to arms control because they should affect what we want of our opposite number and what we would or would not be willing to do to get it. It could be said, with caution, that in the MBFR talks (1) neither side had any strategic objectives it could further through conventional arms reductions in Europe, or (2) the strategic objectives each side might have had were served better by having talks without a successful outcome in terms of arms reductions. Vague or unstated political objectives cannot be used to rationalize lack of progress or sloppy arms control agreements. Higher political objectives are most important, but the agreements do matter even if they are instrumental.

For convenience, higher objectives related to arms control fall into three categories, each of which overlaps the others in concept and fact so much that it is often difficult to see distinctions. The first is linkage, the usual meaning of which is to make arms controls and reductions contingent on and connected to policies and behavior that are not directly part of the armed forces at issue. Human rights, financial credits, arms exports, interventions, and the like may be linked to arms talks. Linkage seems almost always to be involved in arms control to some extent and is based on the assumption that the other fellow wants an agreement more than you do.

A second category of higher objectives focuses on the area contiguous to the area in which the arms are subject to negotiation. These conterminous objectives can include any and all political aspirations from the reuniting of the Germanies to a more rational burdensharing scheme for NATO's national military forces. Conterminous objectives are, in common speech, the other things one might hope to accomplish because of opportunities opened by arms talks and treaties in the same area covered by the treaty.

Finally, global strategic objectives are national security objectives that transcend arms control objectives but influence arms control objectives and policies and are influenced by those objectives and policies. Although conterminous objectives are a subcategory of global objectives, and although linkage may be a kind of global objective, global strategic objectives are unbound by any definition that might tie them to arms control.

Because strategic objectives are necessarily very broad in how they are stated, they leave ambiguous any sense of means to ends. Policy reduces that ambiguity but may not eliminate it, so it is important to be clear about policies, even more so than about objectives. One of our objectives is to maintain the security of the United States. We can do this by deterring direct attacks by the Soviet Union and by practicing what has come to be called containment of Soviet expansionism. Or we can attack the Soviet Union in an act of preventive war, a policy that was seriously debated in the late 1950s. Clearly, the policy we choose to achieve such an objective affects our lives as people and as a nation more than does an objective stated in a way that admits to numerous courses of action.

Policy in the sense used here is very close to the general meaning of strategy: it is guidance for action contingent on changing circumstances and the actions of others. If Cuba should attempt to interdict U.S. reinforcements to Europe, then policy might be to (1) destroy all Cuban means of intervention and their land-based support with nuclear weapons, (2) destroy enemy forces and facilities with conventional weapons, (3) destroy hostile forces at sea with conventional weapons, and so on. In practice, we tend to see these policy choices as "options," with each having in common the idea of destroying a force that is out to destroy you. But some policy choices make a big difference, as in the first example. An objective for most firms is to make a larger profit this year than last. Associated policies may be that the customer is always right or that one should never give a refund. An unremarkable objective takes on new life when seen in the light of its implementing policies.

Implications for NATO Strategy

NATO should have two strategies, one for before and one for after conventional and nuclear arms reductions and controls. The idea that one strategy is indifferent to circumstances or that substantial arms reductions are not expected. Both reasons are shortsighted.

We should not confuse strategy with labels. Any collection of military forces in Central Europe that includes conventional and nuclear weapons can be called flexible response. Such a collection always will have some element of flexibility as long as one of its purposes is to prevent inadvertent war and crises escalation. A "pure" nuclear defense would be as profoundly stupid as a pure conventional defense against a nuclear-capable enemy who also has conventional forces.

For purposes of deterrence, the move toward conventional emphasis had as its intent to compel the Warsaw Pact to mobilize in large and visible ways before it could attack with any hope of conventional success. It did not follow that war termination must be by conventional denial; clearly implied, and strongly believed by Europeans, was the idea that war must be terminated through nuclear threats. Therefore, large-scale wars—those major enough to threaten the independence of any NATO nation—would be ultimately deterred by nuclear weapons, by the sure knowledge of the enemy that NATO must resort to nuclear means against major attacks not terminated in early conventional stages.

Today, analysts of conventional arms control in Europe perpetuate the assumption that post-reduction agreement strategy should be conventional emphasis as if that were today's status quo. These analysts see CFE as meant to do for NATO what NATO would not do for itself (create a true conventional emphasis posture). It is not at all a bad hope or objective. If a strong conventional force is established at parity, nuclear weapons may become less militarily credible, but may still remain political weapons.

Today's strategy may stay the same pending an arms agreement, but doctrine will be at issue. It defies belief that the collected members of NATO would vote to change the strategy on the eve of or during serious arms talks; however, doctrinal talks are occurring at national and NATO levels. Some future historian is bound to see the current doctrinal issue in CFE as bordering on farce: NATO speaks, at least, about having a warfighting doctrine seen as offensive by the East but existing because NATO sees the East's doctrine as offensive; the Pact has a doctrine promoted as counterattack, which NATO sees as offensive but existing because the Pact sees NATO doctrine as offensive. Logically, if both sides reduce and reposture forces to be defensive, neither would have a threat-based rationale for its doctrine. Therefore, the two sides' attachment to doctrine must be weaned through mutual control and reduction agreements, or those agreements will be meaningless for "stability."

The only policy and objective choices relevant to promoting a revised NATO strategy are encouraging (or not discouraging) Soviet reform, encouraging peaceful evolution in Eastern Europe, and supporting continued movement toward unification in Western Europe—the combination of which promotes substantial conventional arms reductions from a position of political cohesion and strength. Following are some considerations:

- The greater the reductions in U.S. forces deployed in Europe, especially in West Germany, the more likely that strategy must be revised.
- If U.S. forces are cut substantially in Europe, nuclear-capable surface-to-surface systems would be difficult to maintain in Europe unless the allies create their own theater nuclear force.
- Even with conventional stability in Europe, the allies are unlikely to adopt a conventional emphasis strategy and are likely to want to rely on U.S. nuclear power in preference to trying to solve the problem of the FRG's nuclear status.
- Both sides will be vulnerable to short-warning conventional attacks because they would be unable to guard the length of their side of the border after truly substantial force reductions or redeployments. But the price of such attacks is likely to be a meaningless gain, if any, and a return to pre-CFE force levels and accompanying animosity.
- Greater relative reliance on European nuclear deterrents will place unification under constant testing; there is no more, perhaps less, reason to believe that France and Britain would risk Soviet retaliation to save the FRG than would the United States in today's circumstances. Although any new strategy with growing unification need not be of conventional emphasis, it will surely require a strong conventional flavor to be able to handle contingencies imaginable in a post–CFE Europe.

The United States could continue to extend its strategic nuclear deterrent to Western Europe at any stage of unification and European independence from the United States, assuming we still had a strong interest in free Europe. Rather than punish the Soviet Union directly for aggression, fixed and mobile forces and facilities in Eastern Europe could be targeted with precise weapons to deny the Soviets the ability to mass, echelon, and supply an army large enough to be successful in attack. By confining nuclear strikes to areas away from the Soviet border, the threat should be quite credible. The Soviets are unlikely to retaliate on the United States and risk retaliation on the Soviet Union, which, in effect, would be a sanctuary. They are unlikely to retaliate on Western Europe and provoke French and British strategic nuclear strikes at the Soviet Union. The entire idea would be, of course, repugnant to Western Europeans, but if the United States were in the future a minor player in the Atlantic Alliance, Western Europeans could renounce the idea while knowing that they would benefit from it.

OPERATIONAL OBJECTIVES

U.S. operational objectives for the CFE talks were developed nearly two years ago by the Army Staff and subsequently became the forerunners of NATO and CFE Mandate objectives. These objectives are presented below:[5]

- The United States and NATO will not be placed at risk during any stage of the negotiations. This objective means that the negotiations should conclude in a whole product and not in a series of phases. Implementation can be phased, but we cannot afford to negotiate Phase I, implement, and then negotiate Phase II. The latter phase may never happen; therefore, an agreement must include all phases.
- Maintain Alliance unity. Current German objections to SNF modernization and rejection of U.S. burdensharing policy arguments do not support Alliance unity; therefore, this objective was injected to insure that U.S. policymakers understand that certain U.S. policies as described actually support Soviet objectives, not NATO objectives.
- Exclude nuclear weapons. This objective was expressed to keep the focus on the conventional imbalance rather than seek a third zero or nuclear free zone, while keeping the strategy of Flexible Response intact.
- Exclude naval forces. At the time, naval forces were considered by the Army Staff (ARSTAF) and Joint Chiefs of Staff (JCS) as strictly a strategic, not a theater, force and therefore should be kept clear of ground and air negotiations in Europe. In a post-conventional arms-reduction agreement environment, a strong naval force can rapidly respond should the East "break out" of a treaty.
- Preserve existing U.S. Pre-positioning of Material Configured to Unit Sets (POMPCUS) and right to introduce withdrawn equipment. This criterion seeks to insure that the geographical asymmetry is accommodated to establish an ultimate parity of both sides' force regeneration capability.
- Preserve U.S. right to store in Europe all U.S. equipment subject to reductions and limitations. This was expressed not only to reinforce our position on geographical asymmetry, but also to insure that the U.S. commitment under the Long-Term Defence Programme to provide six divisions and more than 1,500 of our first-line aircraft remains intact.*
- No mandatory disbandment of withdrawn U.S. forces. This objective insures that U.S. forces may be preserved for other than European commitments, since even after reductions, Soviet forces will remain the largest military in the world.*
- No permanent limitations on the structure of U.S. forces (e.g., the number of units or mix of forces). The critical paths for and advantages of U.S. force structure are

technology and flexibility. This objective expresses the preservation of these important "drivers" of the U.S. force structuring process.

- Provide for noncircumvention and ability to avoid any agreement in the greater interests of U.S. or NATO security. Two factors initiated this criterion: first, the need to fully describe or define the unit of account of the negotiations so that the East did not develop weapons just under agreement limitations (a non-tank tank), and second, the need for a "trapdoor" to escape a potentially politically driven agreement that makes public sense on the outside but that may actually damage security in the long term. The INF treaty, some believe, has in fact damaged our capability to defend in Europe—even though we attained the elimination of an entire class of nuclear weapons, received asymmetric reductions from the Soviets, and implemented stringent on-site inspections.

- Initially focus on unilateral Warsaw Pact conventional ground manpower and major equipment reductions to achieve parity between NATO and the Warsaw Pact. This was expressed as a priority of conventional arms control to reduce Eastern surprise attack capability, a major concern of NATO. Parity at the time was loosely defined as a close equivalence of military capability and as such, a much more complicated concept than equality of numbers.

- Insure asymmetrical reductions in manpower and major equipment between U.S./USSR and NATO/Warsaw Pact. Obviously, with a military imbalance of forces and firepower in Europe strongly favoring the Warsaw Pact, equal reductions on both sides are not to be considered under any circumstances, even as a symbolic gesture. At the time there was discussion that the MBFR talks should have a concluding mandate and that a symbolic, but small, reduction might be acceptable. This objective sought to eliminate such discussion.

- Priority for initial Warsaw Pact reductions is from the Central European area (i.e., East Germany, Poland, Czechoslovakia, and Hungary). Even though NATO accepted the Gorbachev Initiative to negotiate conventional arms reductions in the Atlantic-to-the Urals (ATTU) region, we never lost sight that the real danger remained in the Central Region, particularly in the Soviet Group of Forces, Germany. An overall ATTU reduction agreement may not diminish the threat in the old NATO Guidelines Area (NGA) unless specific attention were focused on the most important subarea.

- No limitation on U.S. and/or NATO force modernization. As previously mentioned, our strength lies in technology and flexibility. This particular criterion sought specifically to insure that a Lance replacement would not be affected by the negotiations.

- No permanent limitations on right to modernize POMCUS or stored equipment. This criterion was expressed in detail to prevent future allegations concerning modernization.

- No mandatory ceilings on U.S. air forces. Although NATO has reluctantly agreed to address air forces (less naval air) in CFE, the U.S. and NATO air forces actually serve as NATO's immediate reinforcing structure. The ease with which air forces can be reintroduced into the theater prompted early calls for exclusion of air forces. We have since agreed to include them.*

- No U.S. obligation to compensate for reductions allocated against nonparticipants. During 1987 and continuing into early 1988, it was uncertain whether or not France would participate in conventional arms control talks. France wanted the talks under the CSCE umbrella process of all 35 nations in Europe (including the United States and Canada) because she had influence among the 12 Neutral and Nonaligned Nations (NNA) but was not a member of NATO's military structure. France also did not and still does not have a political constituency for arms control. This objective was designed to insure that NATO did not have to "eat" overall reductions without French participation, but with French numbers computed in the military balance. France became the driving force behind today's linkage between the CFE and CDE negotiations and is participating in both fora.

• Maintain the principle of exceptions to ceilings and exclusion of transitory forces. The original framers of the JCS criteria did not want the United States to be trapped by agreement to ceilings that would actually decrease our national security in the end. The exclusion of certain weapons systems, particularly naval forces, and the exclusion of transitory forces might preclude us from using our bases in Europe to support other military operations in the Middle East and North Africa, including support to Israel.

• Establish an effective verification regime which includes on-site inspections as a right. On-site verification may be planned or ad hoc. What was desired was a legally binding inspection for cause; unannounced inspections, as well as announced to preclude cheating or worse, a treaty "break out." (Break out is a term often used by the Navy in describing the level at which a treaty violation becomes less erroneous and more deliberate; this is often presented as a problem in Sea-Launched Cruise Missiles—SLCM— verification.)

• Exchange and acceptance of force data prior to treaty implementation and provisions for notification of information exchange. Because of the data exchange impasses in MBFR, this criterion sought to say, "No agreement on data; no agreement at all." It also supported Senator Sam Nunn's concept of the establishment of risk reduction centers at lower than National Command Authorities' level to exchange information, routinely process ad hoc inspections, and keep misunderstandings on a military level to preclude public misunderstandings and keep propaganda in check.[6]

These 19 criteria and their rationale serve to explain the derivation of NATO's objectives. The next section addresses tactical objectives on the battlefield and at the negotiating table.

(*Editorial Note*: Some of the objectives presented in this framework have been superseded as the actual negotiations progressed.)

TACTICAL OBJECTIVES

Although much of the discussion in this chapter may seem to be overcome by the fast pace of changes in Eastern Europe, the student of conventional negotiations should understand the important tactical principles developed. Tactical objectives presented in this section mean battlefield objectives. They rely on the skill of the players to achieve victory. We will start our discussion with battlefield objectives. Alternate defense concepts will be discussed later in Chapter 10; however, the following section by Captain Daniel M. Gerstein, one of the Army Staff's young "hard chargers," contains the essence of NATO's tactical situation and options, as a result of successful CFE talks, and fully defines NATO's principal concern of establishing an adequate force-to-space ratio.

IN SEARCH OF NATO'S MINIMUM FORCE DENSITY REQUIREMENT

by Daniel M. Gerstein

1. NATO has maintained that there is a minimum force density or force-to-space ratio that must be maintained for defense of the Alliance. Determination of the minimum force-to-space ratio has become critical to Alliance preparation for the CFE talks. This section will examine the force-to-space ratio concept to include the assumptions on which it is based. It will also seek to explain how this ratio can be altered through force modernization and defensive enhancements (such as barriers).

2. NATO Strategy.

a. NATO has chosen a strategy (MC 14/3) that calls for the Alliance to respond flexibly to various levels of Pact aggression while maintaining a forward defense of NATO territories. The intent is to defend the Alliance with conventional means until, at a point at which NATO's defense could not longer guarantee success, NATO would elect to initiate deliberate nuclear escalation. Through such escalation, NATO would attempt to redress the conventional imbalance, seize the initiative in order to regain the lost territory—that is, restore the East–West/Inter-German Border (IGB)—and halt the war on terms acceptable to NATO.

b. NATO's commitment to forward defense requires that NATO maintain a linear, cohesive defense of the Alliance at the IGB, and that, at least initially, there be minimal trading of space for time. It is the maintenance of a linear and cohesive defense that necessitates that NATO man the entire 900-kilometer East–West border. (*Note*: This section will focus on the AFCENT region. There will be no substantial discussion of AFNORTH and AFSOUTH).

c. NATO has divided its forward defense line in the Central Region (AFCENT) into eight forward corps sectors. Several additional French corps could and probably would serve a reserve forces. There is, however, no space between the forward corps sectors and therefore, in theory, there is a linear and brittle defense of the region. Figure 2.1 presents the corps laydown for the Central Region. In general, the northern part of AFCENT contains the least defensible terrain and has the weakest forces. The opposite is true in the southern portion of AFCENT. The "best" terrain and the strongest forces are in the southern portion of AFCENT.

d. Close Air Support (CAS) would be absolutely critical to the defense of NATO in the early stages of a war (before reserves from the United Sates would have arrived). Air forces provide the only rapid capability to respond to any Pact breakthroughs that may occur. CAS is especially important in NORTHAG, where the ground forces tend to be weakest and the terrain is most conducive to large-scale, offensive operations. In this region, air forces are the only readily available "reserves." Recent studies by the U.S. Army Concepts Analysis Agency (CAA) and the RAND Corporation substantiate this assertion.

Figure 2.1
Current NATO Deployment

3. NATO's Strategy (and Implications of Some Alternatives) under a CFE Agreement. The Alliance strategy will need to account for force reductions that could impact on NATO's ability to execute a forward defense of the East–West border. NATO's strategy would need to be altered if forces were cut to levels at which it would become impossible to man the entire border. For this analysis, a generic force laydown, based on the actual laydown depicted in Figure 2.1, will be used. The initial generic laydown is shown in Figure 2.2.

a. Generic Laydown. As noted previously (and depicted in Figure 2.2), there are eight corps that form a continuous defensive line along the East–West border. These forces could be forward stationed in the FRG, home stationed within the Atlantic-to-the-Urals (ATTU), or stationed in CONUS. The only requirement for these forces is that they be rapidly mobilizable and deployable so that they can be positioned at the East–West border by the time the war commences (D-day). Obviously, only a handful of CONUS forces would be able to meet this requirement. The severe lack of strategic lift (i.e., airlift and sealift) available to rapidly deploy U.S. forces precludes greater dependence on CONUS-based units.

b. AFCENT's minimum initial force density requirement (F_{MIN}) can be defined by the following equation:

$$F_{MIN} \leq F_{DEP} + R_{ATTU(t)} + R_{CONUS(t)}$$

Figure 2.2
NATO Generic Force Laydown

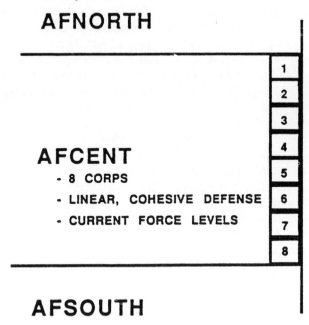

where

F_{DEP} = Forward Deployed Units in FRG

$R_{ATTU(t)}$ = Reinforcing Units from within Western Europe

$R_{CONUS(t)}$ = Reinforcing Units from CONUS

For the minimum force density requirement to be achieved, the sum of F_{DEP}, $R_{ATTU(t)}$, and $R_{CONUS(t)}$ must be greater than or equal to F_{MIN}. Two of the terms, $R_{ATTU(t)}$ and $R_{CONUS(t)}$, have a time factor associated with them; this factor corresponds to the time required to mobilize, train, and deploy a unit from the current peacetime location to the East–West border. If F_{DEP} units are not sufficient for forward defense, then NATO must rely on the timely arrival of reinforcements from within Western Europe or CONUS in order to achieve F_{MIN}. Another implication is that $R_{ATTU(t)}$ and $R_{CONUS(t)}$ might not be initially required if there were forward deployed forces sufficient to achieve F_{MIN}. On the other hand, the F_{MIN} force must be positioned at their defensive positions in enough time to allow for the preparation of the defense. This further complicates attempting to achieve F_{MIN} using forces deploying from CONUS.

c. Small Force Reductions as a Result of CFE. If NATO were to reduce its force structure as a result of CFE, there would be an obvious impact on the laydown of forces. Even small reductions could potentially alter the availability of the F_{MIN} force. (An implicit assumption is that the reductions would come from units rather than theater reserves stocks—TRS—or POMCUS. If TRS or POMCUS equipment were to be reduced, the immediate impact on NATO's ability to man the East–West border would be minimized.) Small reductions (i.e., less than 5 percent) of NATO's current force structure would probably not necessitate a total restructuring or reallocation of forces. It is more likely that reductions of this magnitude would force NATO to "thin its forces," and to either accept greater risk that NATO's forward defense would be decisively penetrated or require NATO to accept, as an alternative, a more flexible defensive strategy (i.e., trading space for time). In any of these alternatives, NATO would retain the same number of corps, albeit with a reduced structure. The smaller corps would still be able to defend initially roughly the same frontage as before. Thus, at a macrolevel the laydown presented in Figure 2.2 would still be valid. However, as the size of the reduction approached 12.5 percent of NATO's current levels (i.e., one-eighth of the AFCENT force or approximately one corps), analysis indicates that it would be necessary to reorganize into a seven-corps defensive front or implement other alternatives that would allow NATO to compensate for the lost corps.

i. Seven-Corps Defense of AFCENT. This alternative would require NATO to distribute its forces such that gaps would have to be accepted between or within the corps sectors. As the Pact attacked, the NATO corps would have to move laterally to cover any areas that had been left open. This situation is depicted in Figure 2.3. By the nature of this sort of defense, it would be militarily less stable than when NATO was able to completely cover the border, and it would place an increased importance on C^3I systems. The timeliness of detection and capacity to respond to enemy attacks/penetrations would make or break the forward defense of the Alliance.

ii. Seven-Corps Defense of AFCENT with Barriers. Implementation of this alternative could be done in a couple of ways. Barriers could be constructed at many points along the IGB (i.e., the gaps between the seven corps depicted in Figure 2.3. could be filled with barriers to restrict forward movement of Pact forces). Another alternative for implementing a barrier system would be to create a large barrier that would essentially "replace" the withdrawn corps. However, a barrier system of any sort has to be covered by fire. Thus, while the combination of fewer forces and barriers may be relatively cheap (as compared to manning, equipping, and sustaining a corps), some force level must nevertheless be maintained. There are still some drawbacks to a barrier system. As with the Maginot Line in World War II, barriers should not be considered to be impenetrable. With any barrier system, there are always countermeasures that could be implemented; the real question is whether barriers would be cost effective. Another significant drawback is the political ramifications of barrier systems, especially along the IGB. While some barriers are already planned in the event of a conflict, it remains problematic whether the FRG would permit the installation of a massive barrier system (which is what would be required to make this alternative meaningful in peacetime).

Figure 2.3
A Seven-Corps Laydown

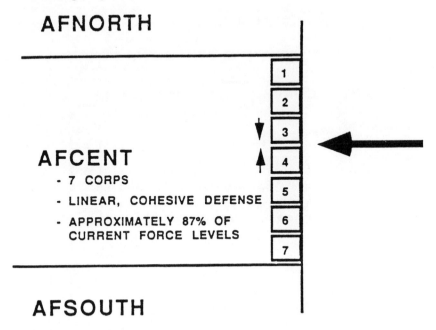

iii. Seven-Corps Defense of AFCENT with Augmentation from Early Arriving U.S. Forces. This alternative would require an increased commitment to dedicated, fast sealift for the transportation of the M + 10 Essential Force Unit—that is, III Corps (U.S.)—that would take the place of the withdrawn forces. This alternative is considerably more risky than having the F_{MIN} forces in the ATTU. This situation is portrayed graphically in Figure 2.4. However, in combination with a barrier option, this might nevertheless prove to be the best of several "risky" options.

d. Large Force Reductions as a Result of CFE. The previous analysis has focused on small reductions that could be compensated for through various programs, and that would still allow NATO to maintain its current forward defense strategy. This section will examine the impact of large withdrawals on NATO's ability to defend in accordance with MC 14/3.

i. Barriers. The barrier systems discussed previously could be implemented. The discussion concerning the advantages and disadvantages of barriers still applies; however, the reduction of three corps would magnify the problem. In simple terms, in the case where barriers replaced one corps they might account for approximately 12.5 percent of the IGB, whereas in the case where three corps are removed, they would have to account for as much as 37.5 percent (i.e., three-eighths) of the IGB. Reductions of this size (even if complemented by a massive barrier system) would be very risky to the Alliance and would do little

Figure 2.4
The Reinforcing Corps

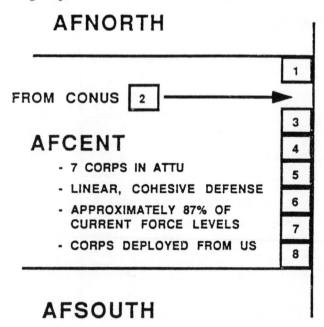

to promote stability and security in the ATTU (which is one of the objectives of the CFE negotiations). Under this defense, NATO could still possibly be able to mount a forward defense, but the operational art and tactics used in the defense would have to be modified substantially.

ii. Force-on-Force Defense. If NATO were to take large force reductions without compensating for these reductions with barriers, increasing fast sealift, and so forth, then the current forward defense strategy of the Alliance would have to be abandoned. To wit: forward defense would have to be replaced by some form of a force-on-force defense in which defender would be required to give ground while seeking favorable opportunities for counteroffensive maneuver. Since NATO could not cover the entire East–West border, enhanced C^3I would be required to detect and deploy delaying forces to the points where the Pact would be attempting to conduct a breakthrough. Unless NATO could be confident of its ability to regain the initiative, such a defensive strategy could become militarily unstable and might greatly decrease public confidence in the Alliance. As an example of this force-on-force defense, consider the hypothetical case depicted in Figure 2.5. In such a case, NATO takes a 50 percent reduction in corps so that only four corps remain in the ATTU. Assuming that no barrier systems have been erected (and CONUS units have been unable to deploy prior to D-day), NATO would find itself in a position where it would be attempting to determine where Pact forces were being massed. NATO would be required to deploy to

Figure 2.5
Force-on-Force Defense

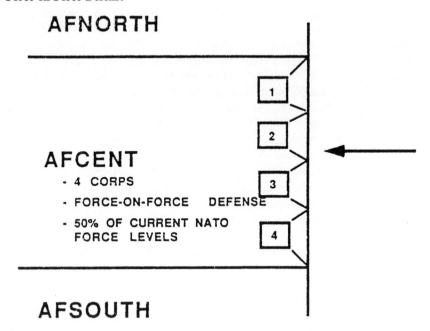

the anticipated point of attack and set up a hasty defense (vice a prepared defense when the entire border was manned) and wait for the enemy to strike. If NATO miscalculated, the Pact would almost certainly be able to achieve a penetration. In the example, a NATO corps would be expected to move laterally and completely realign itself in order to stem even a small penetration. Success or failure would hinge on (1) NATO's agility until reinforcements arrived, and (2) NATO's ability to continuously reconstitute a reserve until sufficient reserve forces became available to permit an Alliance counteroffensive.

e. Impact of Modernization on Force-to-Space Density. Modernization is a term that refers to several types of enhancements that could be implemented to increase the efficiency and/or cost effectiveness of a force. Modernization includes force structure changes (i.e., TOE changes), integration/substitution of new equipment (i.e., substituting Mls for M60s), and changes in strategy and doctrine. In most cases, one associates modernization with an improvement in total force capability. Therefore, it stands to reason that modernization has the potential to alter force-to-space density requirements. There are, however, other variables that also would need to be considered. The relative modernization of the Pact would, for example, play an important role in this equation, as would the magnitude of the total force improvement. As new systems were developed that might radically alter the effectiveness of NATO (e.g., Line of Sight

Anti-Tank—LOSAT), the minimum force density requirements might also decrease (e.g., to a level reduced from eight to six corps to defend AFCENT).

4. Previous Analysis. Several analytical organizations have examined the minimum force density required to defend AFCENT. The British Ministry of Defense, the FRG Ministry of Defense, the Joint Staff (J-8), and the SHAPE Technical Center (STC) have done some work in this area. The initial FRG analysis concluded that NATO could tolerate reductions to only 95 percent of current NATO levels, although recent studies indicate that NATO could go as low as 90 percent. The British analysis concluded that the point at which NATO could no longer defend under its current strategy was at approximately 80 percent of its current levels, and the J-8 analysis concluded that this "breakpoint" was somewhere between 80 and 95 percent of NATO's current levels. The most recent study conducted by STC concludes that NATO can drop to 90 percent of its current levels and still defend forward in accordance with MC 14/3; this analysis has become the basis for the virtually unanimous belief that an initial NATO proposal should call for the reduction of NATO and the Pact to approximately 90 percent of NATO's current levels.

5. Proposed Evaluation Methodology. The previous analyses have been conducted using static techniques without regard to terrain or computer simulations, which do not accurately reflect NATO's strategy to arrive at the aforementioned conclusions. While this is adequate for an initial examination of the issue, it is prudent to examine how this density requirement is affected by the terrain. The methodology outlined below considers terrain and makes use of computer simulations to validate the terrain analysis. The methodology is recommended for the determination of the minimum force density.

STEP:

1. Conduct an Intelligence Preparation of the Battlefield (IPB) to determine the minimum force density requirement (F_{MIN}). The IPB consists of a terrain analysis to determine what size threat force can fit through each of the corridors. Terrain, built-up areas, and obstacles are considered in this analysis. For each corridor, the NATO force required to defend is determined. These NATO force requirements represent F_{MIN}.

2. Validate F_{MIN} using a computer simulation model. F_{MIN} should be able to stop the first operational echelon forces. If the initial F_{MIN} cannot stop the first operational echelon, then the IPB should be repeated to determine a new F_{MIN}.

3. The follow-on forces/reserves should be added to the force list in the combat simulation in 10-day increments (according to their mobilization and deployment time-lines) to determine NATO's overall ability to defend the Alliance.

6. Conclusions. At least initially, the force density requirement for NATO should be based on the overall Alliance strategy (MC 14/3) that calls for forward defense and Flexible Response. It is neither militarily nor politically prudent for NATO to alter its overall strategy simply to reach a CFE agreement. Analysis should be

conducted to determine the force levels that, while lower than current NATO force levels, still allow for NATO to execute its strategy with an equal or enhanced prospect of success.

NOTES

1. Strategic Studies Institute (SSI), U.S. Army War College, *How to Think about Conventional Arms Control: A Framework*, Carlisle Barracks, Pa: SSI, June 24, 1988, p. 13.

2. Ibid., p. 23.

3. Ibid., p. 17.

4. U.S. President Ronald W. Reagan, *National Security Strategy of the United States*, Washington, D.C.: The White House. January 1988, pp. 3–4.

5. Strategy, Plans, and Policy Division, Office of the Deputy Chief of Staff for Operations and Plans, Headquarters, Department of the Army, "A Framework for Conventional Arms Control Negotiations," unpublished, Washington, D.C.: January 15, 1988.

6. Sam Nunn, U.S. Senator, "The American/Soviet Disarmament Negotiations and Their Consequences for NATO," Speech to the Wehrkunde Conference, Munich, West Germany, February 8, 1988, p. 6.

3

Procedures

This chapter consists of two sections written specifically for this book. The first, written by Lieutenant Colonel David R. Tanks, is entitled "Intragovernmental Policy Development" and addresses the interagency system of U.S. policy formulation. The second, "From Issues to Policies: The NATO High Level Task Force," was written by Colonel Arthur W. Bailey and addresses the HLTF internal process and its relationship with arms negotiations. The reader should note the extraordinary Alliance policymaking architecture that was necessary prior to formal presentations in Vienna. Understanding these two processes and their interrelationship with the actual arms negotiations delegations will assist the reader in comprehending the complexity of multilateral arms control.

INTRAGOVERNMENTAL POLICY DEVELOPMENT

by David R. Tanks

Introduction

The U.S. government develops the details of security-related policy positions in interagency groups. While each administration usually stamps the interagency process with its own terminology and organizational structure, the end result is constant: some type of a committee-based hierarchy that develops and shapes U.S. government security policy. The U.S. arms control policy is developed and coordinated within this interagency system. This section will discuss the interagency system as it has been organized in the Bush administration, the strengths and weaknesses of the interagency process, and then it will narrow the focus to examine how CFE positions have developed and what influences sway decisions made in interagency forums.

Organization of the Interagency System

On January 30, 1989, President Bush signed National Security Directive 1 (NSD-1), which specified the organizational structure for the National Security Council (NSC) and its subordinate committees that form the U.S. interagency system. Based on an unclassified government summary of NSD-1,[1] the U.S. interagency system is arrayed in a hierarchy that flows from the NSC. This hierarchy is depicted in highest to lowest order in Table 3.1.

Table 3.1
Hierarchy of U.S. Interagency Committees

National Security Council (NSC)
   Principals Committee (NSC/PC)
   Deputies Committee (NSC/DC)
   Policy Coordination Committees (NSC/PCC)

The composition of these groups is accurately reflected by their titles. The National Security Council is made up of its statutory members plus the President's Chief of Staff and the Assistant to the President for National Security Affairs. In addition, the Secretary of the Treasury and the Attorney General are generally included in most sessions.[2] The Principals Committee (PC) is essentially the NSC less the President and Vice President. In reality, the NSC/PC seldom meets since most actions move from the NSC Deputies Committee (DC) directly to the full NSC. The DC is composed of the deputies to the members of the PC (e.g., Under Secretary of State, the Vice Chairman of the JCS, etc.). The Policy Coordination Committees (PCC) are composed of assistant secretaries responsible for the areas governed by each PCC. It should also be noted that each of these committees may include representation from other agencies with specialized areas of interest. For example, the U.S. Arms Control and Disarmament Agency (ACDA) and the Department of Energy participate in PCC and DC meetings that deal with arms control issues.

There are ten Policy Coordinating Committees (PCC) identified by the Bush administration. These include six regional committees and four functional committees. These committees and the responsibility for chairing each are shown in Table 3.2.[3]

Table 3.2
Regional and Functional Policy Coordinating Committees (PCC) of the National Security Council

Policy Coordinating Committees	Chair Responsibility
Regional:	
Europe	
The Soviet Union	

Policy Coordinating Committees	**Chair Responsibility**
Latin America	Secretary of State
East Asia	
Africa	
Near East/South Asia	
Functional:	
Defense	Secretary of Defense
International Economies	Secretary of Treasury
Intelligence	Director of the CIA
Arms Control	Assistant to the President to the President for National Security Affairs

Each PCC has an Executive Secretary appointed to it from the NSC Staff to assist the chairman with administrative matters.

There are two points worth noting in the composition and makeup of these bodies. First, with a few exceptions (e.g., representatives from the Joint Chiefs of Staff and the Intelligence Community), most members of the interagency bodies discussed so far are political appointees. They are generally well qualified to examine proposed policy positions from a broad, overall policy perspective, but their knowledge of technical issues is often uncertain. Second, the areas that they must be prepared to deal with are extremely broad. For example, the Arms Control PCC deals with all arms control issues: conventional, nuclear, chemical, etc. For the Deputies Committee, the issues are broader yet, since it must deal with the issues that are handled by all ten PCCs. As a result, it is desirable to resolve most technical issues below the PCC level.

The PCCs usually establish subcommittees, mostly composed of career personnel, to work the technical issues within a more narrowly defined context. For example, the Arms Control PCC has a number of subcommittees that work the technical issues associated with a particular negotiation (such as CFE). The CFE Subcommittee is constituted at the Deputy Assistant Secretary level but is often represented by office heads, division chiefs, and special assistants that are responsible for day-to-day CFE issues. It is at this level that most of the technical details and interagency-blessed instruction cables to U.S. delegations are generally worked out and coordinated.

How the Interagency Process Works

The interagency system is not well suited for generating new policy proposals. The nature of the beast is such that it tends to maintain the status quo. Therefore, most new policy proposals tend to originate with the President, his close advisors, or the NSC. Once a general policy thrust is determined, the interagency process deals with the details. To illustrate how the details are developed in the process, this section will use CFE to examine how security issues are generally managed.

Earlier in this book, the history of CFE was outlined starting with the Gorbachev Initiative of April 1986. Under the Reagan administration, CFE issues were handled almost exclusively at the technical level of the interagency process.[4] The CFE negotiations achieved their current high level emphasis in U.S. policy after President Bush declared it to be the United States' highest priority arms control objective. However, since the President does not have the time to work out all of the details for each of his objectives, his overall policy declarations become the marching orders for the interagency process.

The shape of the U.S. proposals for the CFE negotiations was hammered out in the PCC Subcommittee (SC) and the SC Working Groups composed of staff experts from the agencies represented on the Arms Control PCC. While these meetings tend to be unexciting, they do provide a forum for coordinating the labor required to develop policy details.

Typically, these meetings work as follows. A two-to-three hour meeting is held to work agenda issues. Proposed position papers that have been prepared by various agencies are usually on the agenda, along with selected draft cables containing instructions to the U.S. delegations to the CFE High Level Task Force (HLTF) in Brussels and/or the U.S. CFE Delegation in Vienna. The group meets and picks the papers apart, sentence by sentence, has a brief discussion on what new issues need to be dealt with in the near future, and then agency representatives volunteer for or are tasked by the chair to develop a proposed position paper on those subjects—with due dates of usually one day to two weeks into the future.

The papers required at this working level are designed to answer the who, what, when, where, how, and why questions that must be considered in policy development. While it is not a complete listing, the example shown in Table 3.3 is designed to illustrate the types of issues that are dealt with in the interagency process.

Table 3.3
Illustrative CFE Verification Issues for Resolution

Limits on equipment input/output into the ATTU zone:

— Establishment of a baseline (start point) for equipment accountability?

— Monitoring reductions from current levels to treaty levels?

— Equipment production monitoring?

— Entry and exit control into or out of the zone?

CFE Inspection Regime:

— Degree of accountability accuracy required?

— Cheating possibilities?

— On-site inspections?

— Aerial overflights?

— Permanently stationed roving inspectors?

— Sensitive site exclusions?

— Inspections at privately owned facilities?

— Threshold for notification of status change?

— Counting rules for look-alike equipment?

— Paramilitary equipment?

— Civilian industry owned equipment (helicopters)?

— Equipment tagging regime?

— Data exchange required on equipment?

Other CFE-Related Considerations:

Accountability of

— Foreign military sales production?

— Transiting equipment accountability?

— Training restrictions on allied forces?

— Vulnerability to espionage?

— Verification costs?

Obviously, there are some issues on which the group cannot agree, or issues that have important political ramifications for the United States. The objective is to resolve as many of these issues as possible at the lowest level feasible. If consensus develops among most agencies, but one or two agencies favor a different course of action, those in the minority position can (1) try to soften the effect of the proposal in contention (water it down), (2) allow the majority to rule, or (3) force the issue to the next higher level for resolution. The action followed is often determined by how important the issue is to the agency involved, and the degree of tenacity that a particular agency's representative shows in holding out for a review by a higher committee. Since remaining silent in these meetings signifies consent to the proposal under review, the majority usually try to isolate the holdouts and pressure them into silence.

Those issues that cannot be resolved in the PCC/SC become agenda items for the PCC. If the PCC cannot agree, then they are sent to the DC. It also happens that issues that have significant political or security implications sometimes bypass lower committees and are immediately addressed at whatever level is considered appropriate based on the overall importance of the issue. As an issue is raised within the interagency hierarchy, the prospects become greater for resolving the issue based on its broader political ramifications rather than on its narrower technical merits. This fact often acts to pressure agencies to resolve technical issues at the working level and settle for the best deal possible, rather than pushing the issue up the committee ladder and risking an unfavorable ruling or high level criticism for making primary policymakers deal with relatively trivial matters.

Key issues that are referred to higher levels usually deal with extremely contentious issues. Verification has been the CFE issue that has absorbed the lion's share of PCC and DC attention. The PCC has also been heavily engaged in resolving some of the contentious aspects of the CFE equipment definitional issues. The PCC also reviews many of the proposals raised by the U.S. CFE Ambassador, particularly if they involve a suggestion to modify an existing U.S. position. This review process provides a mechanism for adjusting U.S. policy proposals.

The Strengths and Weaknesses of the U.S. Interagency System

On the positive side, the interagency system provides a number of benefits to U.S. policy development. As can be inferred from the foregoing discussion, many of the positions taken by agency representatives are personality dependent. As the personnel assigned to these positions change, so might the positions taken by that agency in interagency fora change. However, as other players are often still in place, the policy momentum usually continues in the same general direction as it had been going. One of the strengths of the interagency process is that it limits the degree of swings in U.S. policy and provides for greater consistency and stability in U.S. security policy.

A second benefit from this system is that it allows for a greater amount of U.S. government resources to be brought to bear on issues. Data and assistance can be easily obtained as necessary from all involved government agencies in compiling the facts required to formulate the problem and develop proposed solutions. This allows policy proposals to be formulated based on a more in-depth review of the available information.

The third benefit is that the interagency process tends to screen out many of the "half-baked" or parochial proposals that are focused too narrowly on the perspective of just one or two agencies. This screening process often helps ensure that U.S. policy positions are more balanced in protecting U.S. interests in their broadest terms.

There is also a significant downside to this committee system of government. Most agencies represented in interagency fora only develop a primary position on current issues—they normally do not have any fallback positions. Many of the players in the interagency process consider fallback planning to be dangerous, since information leaks regarding the existence of the secondary position tend to undermine the primary position on controversial issues. The backup plan becomes a self-fulfilling prophecy. In addition, the work load is often such that agencies do not have the time to develop a fallback position. All of the effort is expended trying to keep up with the ongoing action. However, the lack of a fallback position means that representatives to interagency meetings are often not prepared to move away from their only position even when it becomes obvious that they are the only agency that supports that position. This means that additional meetings must be scheduled to reconsider the issue, or the issue is needlessly raised to the next higher level.

A second weakness of the interagency process is that it seldom operates from any grand design that provides a picture (or target) for where U.S. policy is going—particularly if the end objective might represent a change from the status quo. If the end result might require a new policy direction, few want to be in front of the president in formulating a potential policy that differs from the current approved policy. This means that in fluid situations, the interagency system will seldom be a driving force in turning the direction of U.S. policy.

The third weakness, which is probably a symptom of the foregoing weakness, is that the intragovernmental system does not usually focus on strategy; most of the focus is on the tactics of winning the interagency dispute under active consideration. When papers are examined, the focus of the effort is usually to ensure that the wording of the issue is acceptable to all agencies (does not harm the agency's self-interest). This often means finding the lowest common denominator. In working these issues, citing existing policy or past agreements is a common ploy used to prevent any new direction from emerging. Since the focus is on protecting agency or pet interests, little attention is usually given to determining where the process is headed in terms of long-term national strategy.

The fourth weakness is that the President is the first and last point at which firmly held interagency disagreements can be ruled upon. Naturally enough, there are many issues in dispute that do not warrant presidential attention. Yet, without a lower single authority with the power to make a binding decision, many issues require an inordinate amount of time and effort to hammer out a compromise solution, In a fast-paced negotiation, this type of committee system can be a drag on rapid progress.

Interagency Management of CFE

Elsewhere in this book, the CFE proposals are described in some detail, thereby making it unnecessary to rehash that material here. However, the process by which those positions were developed and modified as required by developments in the negotiation process is worthy of some attention. In examining CFE policy development it is critical that one fact be kept firmly in mind: CFE is a multilateral negotiation—the United States is but one country among 23 participants. This makes the process much more difficult to manage in comparison to a bilateral negotiation involving only two parties.

In reality, the CFE negotiation has four separate and distinct negotiating fora. First, there are the negotiations among the Washington agencies to determine what the U.S. position should be on each specific proposal, such as what the definition of an Armored-Vehicle-Launched Bridge (AVLB) should be. Second, there are negotiations in Brussels at the NATO High Level Task Force (HLTF) meetings to decide the Western negotiating policy on each primary issue. Third, there are negotiations within the Western Caucus, which meets in the Canadian embassy in Vienna, regarding position details and what negotiating strategy should be followed in presenting Western proposals to the East. And last, there are the actual CFE negotiations between the 16 Western countries and the seven Eastern countries. Many who are familiar with all facets of the CFE Negotiation claim that the East–West facet is the simplest piece of the process.

The coordination between these four focal points is clumsy; essentially, it works as follows: the Washington interagency process produces a U.S. policy position or a negotiating proposal. This position is described in a cable (telegram) that is sent to the U.S. interagency representative who is attending the HLTF meeting at NATO. This cable specifies exactly what the U.S. representative should propose and what can be accepted by the United States. The cable also specifies how much flexibility exists for the U.S. representative to use his or her own judgment in gaining a Western consensus on the issues under consideration. Once the HLTF, which usually meets every two or three weeks, concludes its meeting, the staff at the U.S. Mission to NATO prepares a cable to Washington reporting on the meeting, describing the discussions and decisions made.

Based on the HLTF reporting cable, and any additional reports made by agency representatives in attendance, the State Department prepares a proposed cable of instructions for the U.S. CFE Delegation in Vienna. This cable is interagency staffed (usually at the PCC/SC level), modified as required, and agreed upon prior to dispatch. In cases where there is minor disagreement on wording, the NSC Staff usually determines the outcome. Unresolved issues arising from the HLTF meeting become agenda items for the interagency work program.

In Vienna each Western CFE delegation receives instructions from its own capital based on the general agreements made at HLTF meetings. Some of these agreements may require the Western Caucus in Vienna to fill in the details of a skeletal concept outlined in Brussels. The interagency instruction cable to the U.S. CFE Delegation usually limits the range of options that may be pursued by the delegation. At times, an impasse develops in the Western Caucus that must be referred back to the various governments for resolution. For the United States, this again requires interagency deliberations regarding the U.S. position on the issue in contention.

In the CFE negotiation, positions often must be modified to gain agreement. The negotiations that take place gradually define areas of agreement and disagreement. Where positions are sharply at odds, it usually requires some position modification by several parties to move toward a common position. For the United States, significant position changes require interagency approval and may also require reconsideration of the issue by the HLTF.

Within the interagency, significant disagreement often arises based on the legitimate concerns and needs of each agency. For example, in determining the requirements of a verification regime, conflicts can occur based on the responsibility of each agency concerned. For those agencies that represent the defense establishment, a verification regime that can detect militarily significant levels of treaty violations, but does not unduly interfere with normal military operations and training, is an acceptable regime. For other agencies, such as ACDA, which is required by its charter to certify to the Senate that a treaty is verifiable, the verification proposals and requirements may be viewed more legalistically:

can violations of whatever treaty provisions the United States agrees to be detected? For the Intelligence Community, the issue of concern may be more focused on ensuring that the treaty provisions are crafted in such a way that insures that it will be easy to distinguish between treaty-limited equipment and equipment that is outside of the scope of the treaty when the equipment is viewed from a distance. Obviously, resolving the differences between these conflicting goals requires time and effort to accomplish. Even so, once consensus is reached, it often proves to be unacceptable to the allies or to be nonnegotiable with the East, and the process starts over again.

Ideology also becomes a player in the interagency process. Some officials may have a dim view of the whole arms control process; others may be extremely distrustful of the East and want to ensure that the CFE treaty is airtight in its basic formulation. Others may have a different outlook altogether. As is sometimes seen in CFE interagency fora, the personal ideology held by those in a position to influence the details of the action (usually at the Assistant Secretary level) will often direct their personnel to take hard-line positions on topics of key concern, which deadlocks the progress for significant periods of time.

With the huge numbers of issues that the interagency must deal with in keeping up with the CFE negotiation, and given the cumbersome system in which decisions are made, it should not be surprising that there are times at which the CFE progress seems to be dragging. However, if the interagency process solves most of the conflicts, and if it is successful in clearly defining for the NSC and the President the political decisions that must be made on those few major issues where consensus cannot be reached, then it has accomplished its intended purpose.

In essence, the interagency process, and the Western Alliance's structure for managing CFE, is a direct reflection of the democratic process. While it is difficult to move very swiftly, it does ensure that all the parties concerned receive a hearing.

FROM ISSUES TO POLICIES: THE NATO HIGH LEVEL TASK FORCE

by Arthur W. Bailey

The principles of national sovereignty and political consultation are inherent in the basic North Atlantic Treaty of 1949. In addition to being a defense alliance, NATO provides a forum for consultation and political-military decision making. This consultative background was underscored by the 1956 Report on Non-Military Cooperation, which broadened the consultation process to include all matters of Alliance interest during the formative stages of government decision making.[5] Although the principal forum for consultation is the North Atlantic Council (NAC), consultation now occurs in other NATO bodies, such as the Senior Political Committee, the Political Committee, and the Economic Committee.

The principal extant group dedicated to addressing matters pertaining to arms control (including the CFE and CSBM negotiations) is the NATO High Level Task Force (HLTF). This body forms the policy link between members' capitals and the two conventional arms control negotiations now taking place in Vienna. The results of the political consultations in the HLTF on issues confronting the Negotiation on Conventional Armed Forces in Europe (CFE) and the Negotiation on Confidence- and Security-Building Measures (CSBM) form the basis for the operational guidance for the group of NATO negotiators in Vienna. The HLTF has its origin in the NATO Halifax meeting on conventional arms control of May 1986. A major item on the Halifax agenda was consideration of the Gorbachev Initiative of April 1986 in which he proposed "substantial reductions in all components of the land forces and tactical air forces of the European states and the relevant forces of the USA and Canada deployed in Europe."[6]

In its final communiqué, the Halifax group spoke of the need for bold new steps in the field of conventional arms control. It is in the communiqué that the basic charter of the HLTF is most clearly stated. These points are quoted from the communiqué:

Our objective is the strengthening of stability and security in the whole of Europe, through increased openness and the establishment of a verifiable, comprehensive and stable balance of conventional forces at lower levels.

- To work urgently towards the achievement of this objective, we have decided to set up a High Level Task Force on Conventional Arms Control.
- It will build on the Western proposals at the CDE Conference in Stockholm and at the MBFR negotiations in Vienna, in both of which participating allied countries are determined to achieve early agreement.
- It will take account of Mr. Gorbachev's statement of 18th April expressing, in particular, Soviet readiness to pursue conventional force reductions from the Atlantic to the Urals.[7]

In addition to serving this immediate need, the creation of the HLTF served to assuage French concerns about the formal NATO defense planning process, while at the same time allowing French participation among "the 16" in NATO arms control negotiations that necessarily involve defense planning.

From its inception in 1986, the HLTF has had its share of conventional arms control issues to address. In November of that year, within the framework of the Conference on Security and Cooperation in Europe (CSCE–Helsinki, 1975), 35 countries of Europe and North America met in Vienna for the convening of a European arms control conference. This conference was the follow-up of a previous conference held in Madrid that closed in 1983. Drawing on both the success of the CSCE process and the lessons of the difficult Mutual and Balanced Force Reductions talks, the Vienna conference worked from 1986 to 1989 to explore new avenues for cooperation and strengthening European security. Two major products were agreements to convene the CFE and the CSBM negotiations, although it must be noted that the CFE Mandate was developed within the CSCE framework by a separate caucus of the 23 states that together constitute NATO and the Warsaw Treaty Organization (WTO). The HLTF developed as a functioning body during this period, providing a forum for Alliance partners' consultation and taking a management role.

Notwithstanding its four-year history, the HLTF remains an ad hoc body. It is a gathering of national representatives, sent as a rule from capitals, who meet to discuss common issues on conventional arms control in consideration of both their national policies and instructions, as well as the objectives of the Alliance, general and specific. These national representatives are aided by the NATO International Staff, which provides a chairman, analytical and administrative support, translation services, and facilities. The chairman is the Deputy Secretary General, with a large measure of support from the Political Affairs Directorate of the Political Division. Decisions and recommendations are reached by consensus through a meeting process that is structured but also dynamic, engendering earnest and productive debate. Discussions are managed by the chairman with representatives addressing themselves primarily to the chair rather than to each other. This procedure permits useful expression of positions without the potential conflict inherent in having a personal focal point or debating opponent.

By sending its representatives to Brussels to meet in the HLTF, member countries take advantage of the centralized consultative mechanism provided by NATO, and in turn simplify the passing of NATO positions on to negotiators. In the case of the United States, the HLTF representative carries instructions developed through the interagency policy development and coordination process in Washington. In this way the U.S. representative is able to express a position developed and approved by the major agencies of the executive branch of our government. The recommendations or decisions of the HLTF are reported back to capitals, which in turn pass them to negotiators, in the case of CFE and CSBM, in Vienna. In addition, the International Staff will record the HLTF actions in official documents and distribute those to capitals through the permanent national representatives at NATO.

To deal with the complexity of specific conventional arms control issues, the HLTF has created several subgroups. The most significant of these are as follows: the White Team to specifically cover CSBM matters; the Green Team for verification issues; the Red-Blue Team to record force structure data; the Stabilizing Measures Team for those proposals that create or lead to stability in the security area; and the deputies-level subgroup at which national representatives may be up to the level of (in U.S. terms) an agency assistant secretary.

As conventional arms control issues have grown in international and historical significance, particularly in light of the recent rapid and sweeping political changes in Eastern Europe, the existence and operation of the HLTF has proven its merit. Although it remains an ad hoc group, it offers a continually available forum for Alliance partners (including France) to meet and discuss consensually derived guidance. In this way NATO is better prepared to preserve its influential role in what has proved to be a very dynamic period in European history.

(*Comments*: The HLTF only meets for a few days at a time. Thus, representatives shuttle between their respective capitals and Brussels armed with national positions on salient issues. However, they frequently lack the flexibility to bargain or compromise, and tough issues tend to get pushed off to the next meeting.)

Because the negotiators in Vienna remain in Vienna, and because they have more or less continuous opportunities to meet, discuss, bargain, and seek potential compromises, they are frequently impatient with the HLTF process. More to the point, the CFE ambassadors have occasionally sought to bypass the HLTF by working proposals on their own. This has worked with mixed success, but the suggestion that the HLTF has outlived its usefulness as the forum in which to arrive at Alliance negotiating positions appears to be gaining steam. In part, this is due to the aforementioned modalities. In part, it is due to a desire on the part of the negotiators to retain greater bargaining flexibility; and, in part, it is due to the mounting workload of unfinished business before the HLTF.

In fairness to the HLTF, however, the Brussels meetings have produced many successes. Furthermore, the international military staff of NATO is in Brussels, not Vienna, and has been an important contributor of papers, proposals, and data for HLTF consideration. Finally, unlike the ambassadors, the HLTF representatives are acutely aware of the thinking in their capitals.

This is not to say that the HLTF should remain the forum of first resort either for CFE or the CSBM negotiations. A strong case can be made that the current division of labor is not optimal. More important, there is a pressing need for some Alliance body—ostensibly the HLTF—to get on with the task of deciding issues dealing with implementation. For example, the apportionment of reductions among NATO's members, the disposition (destruction or transfer) of the reduced TLE, the modalities of data submissions, information exchange, and verification inspections have yet to be addressed by the HLTF owing to the magnitude of its tasks in support of CFE and CSBM proposal production. Also, because NATO's force reductions may require rather significant modifications to the roles and missions of Alliance members in a post–CFE environment, this issue may also be grist for HLTF consideration.

Unless and until the HLTF is divested of its control over proposal formulation, however, these implementation issues are unlikely to get the attention they deserve. Thus, the editors are inclined to recommend as of this writing the responsibility for formulating Alliance positions in CFE and CSBM be transferred to the negotiators in Vienna.

NOTES

The counsel of Mr. Keith Eddins, United States Foreign Service, Political Adviser to the United States Mission to NATO, in the preparation of this chapter is appreciated.

1. U.S. National Security Council (NSC), "Description of the National Security Council Organization," Washington, D.C.: NSC, April 18, 1989.

2. Ibid., p. 1.

3. Ibid., p. 3.

4. One high ranking political appointee was heard to say on December 8, 1988, that he had just participated in his first White House discussion of conventional force issues. He also noted that it was the only high level discussion that had been held on the subject of which he was aware.

5. NATO Information Service, NATO Headquarters, *NATO Handbook*, Brussels, Belgium: NATO, 1985, p. 22.

6. Richard Darilek, "The Future of Conventional Arms Control in Europe, A Tale of Two Cities: Stockholm, Vienna," *Survival*, January–February 1987, p. 16.

7. NATO, "Halifax Communique," Brussels, Belgium: NATO, 1986.

4

Issues

INTRODUCTION

At this point the reader has been provided the background, objectives, and procedures of conventional multilateral negotiations in the CFE and CDE. The principle of complexity should stand out among others. This chapter addresses issues involved in the negotiations that have been the most difficult to resolve, and the positions taken by relevant actors. It serves as a primer for advanced discussions in Chapters 6 and 7 concerning the most significant and influential positions on the issues that may well determine CFE and CSBM ultimate outcomes or minimally affix the role of conventional arms control in national security strategy.

In attempting to understand conventional arms control, a number of issues emerge for discussion and debate. These issues comprise two types: "strategic" and "operational." Strategic issues are ones that may impact on U.S. military force structure and may determine the role that conventional arms control can and should play. These issues are important to assess because of their synergistic relationship with each other. The strategic issues presented in this chapter include Allied burdensharing, diminishing threat, international trade, and the U.S. defense budget decline.

Operational issues generally deal with the mechanics of arms control. They concern what should be controlled, how it will be controlled, and the regime to monitor the agreement and prevent its circumvention. It is clear, of course, that these two types of issues overlap because one's position on strategic issues will often play a controlling role in deciding one's position on the final form an agreement will take. Nonetheless, the distinction holds up well enough for analytical purposes.[1]

This discussion will serve the purpose of introducing some of the problems that the United States and NATO face in the coming decade, the role that conventional arms control can play in ameliorating those problems, and the manner in which conventional parity may be attained in the ATTU region. The discussion of operational issues will serve to illustrate the complexities inherent in attempting to obtain effective arms control through choices of inclusion and exclusion.

STRATEGIC ISSUES

Issue A: Allied Burdensharing

Burdensharing is the most problematic and emotional issue facing the NATO Alliance. It can be defined simply as sharing the risks, roles, and responsibilities among NATO partners on a "fair" basis, commensurate with each nation's ability to contribute. The issue is cyclic in nature; it takes on added importance during periods of U.S. defense budget decline. At the heart of the issue is NATO's failure to define what constitutes a "fair share" of the Alliance defense burden. Since neither the United States no: our NATO allies have been willing to systematically negotiate burdensharing standards that could be acceptable for all parties, we are deluged with a number of reports, commentaries, and articles on the subject from both sides of the Atlantic. Some highlights are:

- *Report of the Defense Burdensharing Panel.* This so-called Schroeder Report concludes that, based on military expenditure percentage of Gross Domestic Product (GDP) figures, neither our NATO allies nor the Japanese are spending enough on defense and are instead still dependent upon the United States. It further suggests that since Europe and Japan are world economic powers, they must break away from their regional perspectives and take a worldwide defense role.

- *Fair Shares: Bearing the Burden of the NATO Alliance.* A U.S. Defense Budget Office project, this report finds that the burdens of the Alliance are so complex, they cannot be measured by a single simplistic formula such as GDP figures.

- *Pooling Allied and American Resources to Produce a Credible Collective Conventional Deterrent.* Ambassador David M. Abshire calls for a rethinking of the NATO Alliance by developing a new two-pillar treaty based upon U.S. nuclear deterrence.

- *Report on Allied Contributions to the Common Defense.* This annual Department of Defense report concludes that U.S. allies contribute far more to defense than is normally recognized. The report also concludes that the Alliance must do more to ensure Western security.[2]

There is an entire "cottage industry" of writers contributing to the burdensharing debate. Whether this debate will be settled in time to influence force structuring decisions in the near future is doubtful, but if the issue were resolved, the results might have a dramatic impact upon NATO force structure and the Negotiations on Conventional Armed Forces in Europe (CFE). If the burdensharing issue is not resolved, this too may impact on CFE by increasing national pressure for reducing national contributions to NATO defense on a unilateral basis, and by sustainment or improvement of European defense contributions based upon specific NATO assignments of roles and responsibilities at strategic, operational, or tactical levels at which each nation does best.

Issue B: Soviet Threat Perception

Soviet threat perception is an important issue that has potential for causing a dramatic impact on the CFE talks. Mr. Gorbachev is dedicated to taking the threat away from the West by intention, if not in capabilities. By restricting naval operations to near Soviet coastal waters; hinting at pulling out of Cam Ranh Bay; announcing unilateral force cuts at the United Nations; withdrawing from Afghanistan; encouraging Communist allies to disengage in Eastern Europe and throughout the Third World; and allowing openness through his policies of "glasnost and perestroika," Mr. Gorbachev has seized much of the "high ground" in the diplomatic arena. His political actions appear to many to raise the threshold of war.[3]

Since the United States and its major NATO Alliance partners have relied heavily on a threat-driven strategy to construct military budgets, the diminishing threat (perception) logically leads to diminishing military budgets, which in turn lead to diminishing force structure, and the ever smaller budget spiral continues unabated as the threat continues to diminish.[4]

This issue may severely impact on U.S. and European force structures of the next decade and, thus, directly upon the CFE talks. The U.S. government will continue to caution others against irrational force structure reductions based upon Soviet intentions rather than capabilities; but how long can we sustain that position if the Soviets do everything they have stated they will, including substantial reductions in their defense capabilities? This issue appears to have no satisfactory resolution, nor has a competitive strategy been developed to counter it.

Issue C: International Trade

Trade is critical to the very existence of nations today. Trade imbalances, protectionism, and interdependence among nations have the attention of governments and publics. This overall issue encompasses 282 agreements among European nations and may have a greater impact on the CFE than any other. In 1992, the European Economic Community (EEC) will drop its national trade barriers to form an integrated European trade structure. With the wealth of Western Europe taken as an entity having a GDP greater than the United States, and with the rise of Japan as a leader in world trade, the United States may become outflanked. Interdependence is deemed essential in today's world; however, trading partner deficits, debtor nation status, the "buy out" of the United States, heightened competition from emerging nations, and continuing Soviet internal economic pressure can all lead to economic conflict. Military alliances could fracture because of economic conflict.[5]

Issue D: Negative U.S. Defense Budget Growth

Zero-to-negative defense budget growth is simply a reality for the next several administrations, until the federal deficit is finally resolved. The same future awaits many of our allies in Europe. This reality means we have to "do more with less" (which doesn't work very well over time) or we must "do less with less" (which doesn't work very well either). The choices are tough. Budget "enhancers" such as base closures, burdensharing, and arms control may not be national security enhancers. In such an environment, strategic risk must be balanced by sound planning, creative ideas, and leadership judgment; but, in the end, results rest in the hands of external determinants such as national policies, the environment, resources, and capabilities. We have moved from threat-driven strategies to resource-driven strategies. We need to meld a joint effort for the President's budget and Six-Year Defense Program (SYDP). We need to shrink commitments we make to ourselves, like protecting the world's sea lines of communication. If we pare down our commitments, the void will either be filled with allied "out of area" forces or it will not be filled at all.

Zero-to-negative defense budget growth will precipitate headquarters consolidations, unit inactivations or conversions, and procurement stretchouts, cancellations, and postponements. On the positive side, NATO host nation support, cooperative research and development, standardization, and interoperability may flourish. Real defense budget decline may force us to return to successful U.S. business practices like lease versus buy, sale and lease back, leveraging assets, and subcontracting. When ethical business procedures are overlaid upon the military, we may be purchasing more defense with less money. In any event, the budget issue looms as a strategic issue that may independently affect CFE outcomes because of the strain budget reductions place on forward-deployed forces.[6]

OPERATIONAL ISSUES

The Strategic Studies Institute developed 21 issues that might impact on conventional arms control negotiations in its study *How to Think about Conventional Arms Control: A Framework*, published in June 1988.[7] Although a number of those potential issues never surfaced as preliminary meetings between the East and West progressed, the majority of the issues have never been resolved and new issues have developed. In this section we will present 13 issues, their derivation, and positions of the relevant actors. The positions will be discussed in terms of higher and lower case. If the position is an Alliance consensus, we will describe the position as NATO or WTO, which means that national members also take the position. If the issue remains contentious, we will identify national government positions. If the issue is known to have significant diverse positions within governments, we will identify the internal relevant actor positions, particularly in the U.S. government.

Issue 1: CEO Mandate

Early in 1987, the issue concerning the East-West conventional arms control mandate was: Should the United States and NATO agree to negotiate conventional arms control in the CSCE/CDE forum, an expanded MBFR, or a new forum? At one extreme the CSCE includes the Neutral and Nonaligned Nations (NNA), and at the other is a direct Alliance negotiation without the NNA.

The Conference on Security and Cooperation in Europe (CSCE) and its arms control creation, the CDE, have been discussed in Chapter 1. CSCE's primary purpose is to address nonmilitary issues such as human rights, information flow, technology, and trade. CDE's purpose has been Confidence- and Security-Building Measures (CSBMs). CSCE/CDE consist of the 16 NATO members, the 7 Warsaw Pact members, and 12 NNA members (in sum, the United States, Canada, and all European countries except Albania).

The NNA are:

Austria	Lichtenstein	Sweden
Cyprus	Malta	Switzerland
Finland	Monaco	The Vatican
Ireland	San Marino	Yugoslavia

With the exception of Yugoslavia, the NNA obviously are not formidable military powers. But they have a deep security interest in NATO–WTO confrontation and competition in Europe. The principal argument for including negotiations in the CSCE/CDE was that outcomes of conventional arms control negotiations could have significant impact on the NNA.

- Arguments for a forum that included the NNA in the CSCE/CDE were:
  - Most NNA are pro-West (culture, tourism, etc.).
  - Few are directly influenced by the WP.
  - Many have had bad experiences with the USSR since World War II.
  - Yugoslavia is seeking closer ties to the West.
  - Most perceive the USSR as a threat.
- Arguments against negotiating in CSCE/CDE were:
  - NNA are not militarily relevant to the threat facing the West.
  - NNA input is not germane to military issues.
  - NATO might lose control.
  - An Alliance/NNA forum is too large; too much delay for all to be heard.
  - NNA do not have nuclear weapons; they may desire denuclearization.

An expanded MBFR was another choice open to East and West. The expansion referred to geographical scope and to membership. The scope was determined as the ATTU and membership would hopefully include France.

- Arguments for this MBFR–plus forum included:
  - MBFR was already established.
  - MBFR excluded the NNA which could still be consulted.
  - MBFR was a Western creation.
- Arguments against the MBFR–plus were:
  - The East would lose face if it changed positions it took to block progress in the past in MBFR.

— It would have to build on a history of failure.

— It would confuse and complicate negotiating mandate issues.
A third choice, a new forum that included only the two alliances, could have possible links to the NNA through the continuing CDE discussions of CSBMs.

• Arguments in favor were:

— A fresh start allowed both sides to save face on positions taken in the past that they would rather forget or change.

— It allowed concentration on force reductions and associated measures.

— It provided the Soviets and the French a forum they seem to favor over MBFR.

• Arguments against were:

— The Soviets would claim credit for the idea.

— It might alienate NNA sympathetic to NATO.

— In the context of MBFR, CDE, and CSCE, it might confuse Western publics, especially if the West seemed intransigent on some issues because the issues belonged in another forum.

France wanted the arms control negotiations in the CSCE for two reasons. First, since France is not a member of NATO's military command structure, more autonomy from NATO would be provided in CSCE. Second, France would have substantial influence with the NNA. The United States and Britain favored a new, 23-nation forum for the reasons outlined in the previous discussion, but both nations recognized the need for consultative links with the NNA. The Soviets apparently wanted a CSCE forum because they proposed the ATTU area specifically to allow participation of all Europeans in what the Soviets consider a European-only issue. The NNA wanted, obviously, to participate.

Both East and West finally achieved a compromise solution and the CFE Mandate (presented in its entirety in Appendix A) was agreed upon on February 9, 1989. Although this issue appears to be resolved, the mandate contains ambiguous wording, which facilitated the compromises and procedures on how to change the mandate during the course of the negotiations.

On the eve of the CFE Mandate Agreement, Turkey wanted the ATTU to exclude a portion of its territory that borders on Syria, Iran, and Iraq, because this part of Turkey is not a part of Europe geographically and contains units of the Turkish military that are not committed to NATO. The United States and other NATO members agreed to this change and so did the Soviets, who did not ask for similar relief in the Transcaucasus. In the eleventh hour of preparing the details for the mandate, Turkey tried to exclude its air base at Incirlik and a major port city that supports Turkish operations on Cyprus. Naturally, the Greeks objected to these details, so the mandate wording was made ambiguous so that NATO could resolve this argument at a later date.

Although both sides agreed on a new forum in accordance with NATO's position, the linkage between the CSCE/CDE process was formalized and could become onerous. Not only do the CFE participants have to report formally to the 35 member signatories in CDE (to include the NNA), and informally have decided to report to the CDE four weeks after conclusion of each of the four planned CFE sessions, but the mandate requires the participants to report their progress to the next full CSCE session in Helsinki in 1992. The CFE Mandate includes a provision that empowers the full CSCE to change it. To enforce the CSCE position, the CFE mandate is included as an annex to its CSCE/CDE Vienna Concluding Mandate of January 15, 1989. To achieve agreement on the CFE Mandate, NATO felt compelled to compromise on this linkage between the different fora, and the U.S. government is concerned that the CFE "rules of engagement" may be subject to change in 1992.

Issue 2: Dual-Capable Systems (DCS)

Initially, the issue concerned how to deal with dual-capable systems including Dual-Capable Aircraft (DCA) and short-range Surface-to-Surface Missiles (SSM) in the negotiations, since the West did not want to discuss nuclear weapons in conventional talks and these particular weapons systems have both nuclear and conventional capabilities.

At one extreme, an early position on this issue dealt with such systems in a totally separate forum. At the other extreme was the position of including such forces in the conventional talks. A middle course was also taken to deal with these forces in a separate forum, which would be linked such that progress on DCS would be connected to progress in the conventional negotiations.

There were fairly clear reasons why relevant actors might hold each of the major positions noted between the issue extremes. First, totally separating the fora would allow NATO to avoid making any concessions to the Soviets on DCS in exchange for Soviet concessions in conventional talks. Indeed, this position would allow NATO to avoid talking about DCS at all, if it so chose.

Discussing DCS in a forum linked to conventional talks would require NATO to discuss DCS but would link agreements reducing such weapons to Soviet agreement to parity in conventional forces. This position would be adopted by those who hoped to increase the likelihood of achieving conventional parity in Europe by offering the Soviets something they wanted in return.

The third position, that DCS should be "thrown into the same pot" with conventional forces, would be taken by those who feel that the main capability of DCS is conventional and that all conventional weapons should be available for trades. Those who argued for this position considered that the treatment of DCS in a separate forum linked to conventional progress would place too many limitations on the possible trades that might be made.

The Soviets, who have the advantage in Surface-to-Surface Missiles (SSM) and Dual-Capable Aircraft (DCA), wanted all such systems included in the conventional talks. NATO agreed to discuss DCS in the conventional talks but did not want such systems included in the initial mandate. Within NATO, the FRG wanted to initiate a separate Short-Range-Nuclear Force (SNF) forum, to run concurrently with conventional talks. France wanted to keep DCS totally separate from the conventional talks. Indeed, the French appeared to prefer that no negotiations take place on such systems at all, at least until conventional parity was attained. The British position was similar to that of the French.

In the United States, the position of the Reagan administration also was similar to that of the French. Administration officials regarded a mix of nuclear and conventional forces as essential even if conventional arms control was successful. Within Congress, the statements of Senators Levin and Nunn placed them in opposition to the inclusion of DCS in the conventional talks, but not as vehemently as the administration.

Then, in early 1988, the Chairman of the Joint Chiefs of Staff met one-on-one with Marshall Akhromeyev, the Soviet's top military officer. During the informal discussions, Admiral Crowe and Marshall Akhromeyev agreed to include DCS launchers in the conventional negotiations, but not nuclear warheads, thus clearing the way for the final U.S. government position for specified inclusion of artillery (tube and missile) and DCA. Given the current state of conventional imbalance, this position focused on the conventional capabilities of DCS. One can only speculate as to why the Chairman agreed to this position. We believe that what was envisioned at the time was an agreement that placed a ceiling on artillery (tube and missile) at a level slightly below NATO current totals, which would dramatically improve NATO's position in a conventional war while also improving NATO's relative capacity to launch Artillery-Fired Atomic Projectiles (AFAP) when and where desired. The only apparent problem seemed to be that a limit of the Multiple Launch Rocket Systems (MLRS) might also limit future fielding of the Army Tactical Missile System (ATACMS). This problem could be resolved if each side was allowed to "mix and match" artillery and MLRS subject only to an overall ceiling.

The CFE Mandate now includes agreement on how to resolve the DCS issues in its "Scope and Area of Application":

No conventional armaments or equipment will be excluded from the subject of the negotiation because they may have other capabilities in addition to conventional ones. Such armaments or equipment will not be singled out in a separate category; nuclear weapons will not be a subject of this negotiation.[8]

The issue seemed to be resolved; however, in the final Soviet version of the mandate, they used their Russian word for "weapon," which translates as warhead and its delivery system. This ambiguity in the mandate started an additional debate on SNF as to whether to include launchers or launchers and warheads in CFE, or whether to initiate a separate SNF forum that would operate concurrently with CFE or start functioning after CFE negotiations are successfully completed.

NATO wants to exclude nuclear warheads from the CFE. The FRG wants separate SNF talks but wants those talks to be immediately initiated and to operate concurrently with the CFE. The Soviets want their translation of "weapon" to be accepted, which in effect violates the agreed-upon mandate scope, which states that "nuclear weapons will not be a subject of this negotiation" and, in fact, reneges on its compromise. Finally, the U.S. government wants no SNF talks initiated until after conventional parity is implemented as a result of an agreement in CFE; and the government supports NATO's position that "weapons" in CFE must be translated to mean launchers, not nuclear warheads and launchers. In effect, the issue has come full circle from two years ago and was again placed on the agenda for the second session of CFE.

Issue 3: Force Modernization

The issue here is whether a conventional arms control agreement should regulate the extent and/or pace of modernization of each side's equipment. There are two main views on this issue: at one extreme, the modernization of forces in the ATTU region should be highly regulated, perhaps even banned; at the other, that modernization should be left totally unregulated.

The case for detailed regulation of modernization is simple. There is no sense in taking the time and effort to obtain a successful agreement only to have the purpose of that agreement circumvented by arranging for a new and expensive qualitative arms race (similar to the one begun by the Washington Naval Agreements of 1922), which would have unforeseeable consequences.

The argument for leaving modernization unregulated is just as simple. Since technology is the main strength of the West, a qualitative arms race would tend to favor NATO. As a result, over the long run, leaving modernization unregulated would tend to place NATO in a superior military position relative to Pact forces. The U.S. government has not formally committed to one side of the argument or the other; however, we think that the relevant actors in the U.S. Interagency Group are moving to accept a moderate Army concept that permits modernization of weapons systems under predetermined conditions set forth as "stability" measures, which normally refer to constraints or transparency agreements applied to other than Treaty Limited Items (TLI), the final inclusive treaty units of account.

A great deal of attention should be paid now to the problems of maintaining a rough parity of capabilities during the transition to greater sophistication, and beyond. Three factors would appear central to this process. First, decision-makers must understand what it is that they can (and cannot) reasonably expect to achieve through a CFE arms reduction agreement. Second, they must eschew all notions that they can prevent modernization, and instead seek to achieve agreement on a process for the management of modernization. Such a process could entail measures to promote mutual adjustment and self-restraint, properly verified. Finally, decision-makers should understand that this cannot be done, and should not even be attempted, through legalistic "definitions" and contrived "counting rules," for various equipment types; e.g., tanks, artillery, and ATCs. Strict definitions and counting rules would be very unlikely to constrain circumvention opportunities, such as those that would derive from new engineering designs.[9]

The concept of using CFE information exchange to manage the force modernization issue is described in detail in Chapter 7, but in general, a system of limiting the fielding on a self-limited basis, commensurate with the fielding activities of the other side, would seem to resolve this issue. Without such a concept, CFE could bog down as the East and West polarize their positions on this issue.

Issue 4: The Unit of Account

Defining the unit of account for conventional arms control was and still is not an easy matter. To decide on units of account requires not only analysis of the inclusions, but the potential, tactical results of the exclusions. As previously indicated, units of account in CFE are now called Treaty Limited Items (TLI).

Initial thought in 1987 was that there were basically two main choices when dealing with equipment. One can attempt to limit one or two major types of equipment (say, tanks or tanks and artillery), or one can attempt to limit many types of equipment including, perhaps, even equipment that is not itself weaponry, such as trucks or communications equipment.

The case to be made for limiting only one or two types of equipment was clear. The fewer items limited, the easier it should be to agree on data. In addition, the fewer items limited, the easier it should be to verify compliance, since monitoring resources could be concentrated on those few items.

The case for limiting a large number of equipment types rested on the belief that unless the Soviets are tightly regulated, they will attempt to circumvent the treaty. This could be done in two ways. First, armies could be reorganized and doctrine rethought to emphasize systems that have not been controlled. Thus, limitations on tanks and artillery alone might well lead to a Pact army just as large as before CFE, but now heavy in Infantry Fighting Vehicles (IFVs) and attack helicopters. Second, the way weapons and other equipment are defined could also leave loopholes to be exploited. For example, a tank could be defined as a tracked vehicle weighing at least 50 tons and carrying a main gun of at least 90 millimeters. If so, we might find the Soviets building large numbers of tracked vehicles weighing 49 tons and carrying a main gun of 89 millimeters. Ingenious modifications might even be made to supply trucks. As a result, this argument goes, virtually all types of equipment must be defined and regulated.

NATO's initial proposal in CFE cites tanks, artillery, and Armored Troop Carriers (ATC) that include various models on both sides (e.g., Armored Personnel Carriers [APC] and Infantry Fighting Vehicles [IFV] on the U.S. side). The WTO's initial proposal cites tanks, artillery, and armored personnel carriers as well, but also includes combat aircraft and helicopters. The inclusion of combat air by the Soviets had earlier been discarded by NATO as too difficult to verify. NATO has accepted requirements for significant reductions in allied air forces, and for fixed ceilings that could easily be detected over WTO territory. The Soviets initially exempted medium bombers and fighter-interceptors from their proposal because NATO has no medium bombers and the WTO has a 4:1 advantage in fighter-interceptors. NATO did not allow such exclusions.

Since the tabling of the initial proposals from both sides on March 9, 1989, the discussion shifted to whether or not Land-Based Naval Air (LBNA) and other independent aircraft operations conducted on a national, rather than alliance, basis should be included in CFE and/or included in CDE Confidence- and Security-Building Measures (CSBMs). Prior to President Bush's proposal, NATO said no, while the WTO said definitely yes to inclusion.

To achieve the CFE objectives of increased security and stability and to eliminate large-scale offensive operations and the ability to mount a surprise attack, the TLI will eventually be agreed upon; however, other than currently debated TLI may be equally important for inclusion and/or exclusion. This means that Combat Support (CS), Combat Service Support (CSS), and general support infrastructure to include facilities should be included in any CFE agreement, to constrain or eliminate this capability of force regeneration. Whether or not this force regenerating capability will be spelled out and detailed as TLI, or dealt with through stability measures aimed at achieving transparency is not as important as selection as agreement to accomplish at least one or the other. There remains considerable work for the negotiators and military planners to accomplish before a CFE agreement on units of account is established.

Issue 5: Disposition/Destruction of Reduced Forces

Assuming that conventional arms control is successful, what is to be done with the forces that the agreement mandates eliminating? Initially, there were two primary positions on this issue. At one extreme was the position that the equipment reductions should be destroyed, with associated manpower demobilized. At the other extreme was the view that all equipment reduced should be removed from the theater with manpower disposed of as each side saw fit.

The reasons why either major position might have been adopted are as follows: the first extreme position—equipment destroyed and personnel demobilized—ensures that no TLI will ever again enter the controlled region. In addition, the demobilization of associated personnel ensures that personnel liberated by TLI reductions cannot be used to circumvent the agreement in any of the ways alluded to in the section on Unit of Account.

The second extreme position—removal of equipment from the theater but making the disposition of that equipment and any personnel liberated by equipment cuts a matter of national discretion—could have been adopted on the basis of flexibility. This position allows each side the greatest flexibility to adapt to the reductions most effectively from its perspective. The Soviets have been very clear but fickle in their position. Initially, they publicly stated that forces and equipment subject to reduction agreement should be demobilized and destroyed, respectively. Since this initial position was expressed, the Soviets have modified their position to one that includes monitored storage. NATO has taken the position that

NATO equipment disposition should be a NATO decision based upon the outcome of final agreement and its positional stance on geographical disparity. The USG position currently recognizes that destruction, demobilization, and monitored storage must all be part of the disposition resolution. The government recognizes that we must destroy some of our TLI to get the other side to make asymmetrical destructions; however, it wants to insure that NATO is the political level that should determine how Alliance reductions will be apportioned among NATO's members. Thus, NATO has insisted the CFE agreement between NATO and the WTO prescribe only that each side will reduce to the agreed levels, and that TLI currently in the ATTU and in excess of those levels will be destroyed.

Issue 6: Subzones

Should CFE mandate subzones within the ATTU area? There are two major positions that bound this issue. One extreme is that any reductions mandated by a CFE treaty should be allowed to be taken from anywhere within the ATTU area. The other extreme is that the location of reductions should be regulated by one or more subzones.

Those in favor of the first position desire flexibility and simplicity. This position would allow each side the greatest flexibility in dealing with the impact of reductions. The simplicity of this position would also present the least difficulty to negotiators attempting to reach agreement. The possible requirement for an elaborate set of subzones will raise problems in defining them, obtaining data for each subzone, etc., which may make negotiating a final agreement difficult.

Those in favor of subzones maintain that they are required to address the threat in the Central Region. This position, however, allows each side to attempt to direct the other's reductions to its greatest advantage and insure that monitoring resources are employed most efficiently by being concentrated on the subzones of greatest concern. In addition, the existence of one or more subzones implies that movement between them would have to be monitored. This would help deter any concentration of offensive forces and provide unambiguous warning of activities inimical to the security of all participants.

NATO has taken the position in its current proposal that ceilings be placed on TLI in active units located anywhere in Central Europe, which it has defined as in an area extending across the middle of Europe from Spain to the Urals and including the Benelux, FRG, Denmark, France, Britain, Italy, Spain, and Portugal in the West, and the German Democratic Republic (GDR), Czechoslovakia, Poland, Hungary, and the Baltic, Byelorussian, Carpathian, Moscow, Volga, and Urals Soviet Military Districts. Any successful CFE agreement will include a "Central European Subzone." Without such a subzone, the Soviets might be able to take most or all of their reductions from their reserve military districts. NATO, on the other hand, due simply to the distribution of its troops, will have to take the bulk of any mandated reductions from the FRG or the Benelux nations. Thus, without a Central European subzone the balance of forces at and near the inter-bloc border could be worse after arms control than before. With a Central European subzone, however, the Soviets could be required to reduce in such a manner that the balance in the Central Region is rectified. This would reduce the Pact's capacity for surprise attack by improving NATO's conventional position where it needs improvement most.

More stringent subzones have also been introduced in CFE by Alliance members. However, a judgment must be made as to the trade-off between the additional safety derived from further zoning and the complexity that further zoning would inject into the negotiations. With regard to the exact nature of the Central European subzone, our judgment is that it should include the old NGA plus the Soviet Union's western military districts to avoid flank nation objections that they do not seem to be part of NATO's current subzone. More will be said about subzones in Chapter 6. Subzoning in arms control seems to be like gerrymandering in politics.

Issue 7: Verification

This issue involves the extent and intrusiveness of any verification regime adopted in support of a CFE agreement. There are two main positions on this issue. At one extreme is the view that an extremely elaborate and intrusive regime is required. At the other is the view that such a regime is not required and that National Technical Means (NTM) of verification, transparency (information exchange), and self-restraint on the part of the participants can do the whole job.

The argument in favor of an extremely extensive and intrusive verification regime rests on requirements to deter cheating, to include cheating of small proportion. Only such a regime, it is argued, can insure sufficiently against Soviet cheating. Secondarily, an argument can also be made that extensive onsite verification is essential to transparency, and that greater transparency with respect to Soviet force levels and activities should be one of NATO's primary objectives.

The argument for the position taken against such a regime is twofold. First is the problem that any such regime would have to be reciprocal. Thus, it is argued that such a regime would enable the Soviets to do too much "snooping" around our installations and those of our allies. In addition, it is argued that a very extensive and intrusive verification regime is not really necessary, since as long as cuts concern only TLI, National Technical Means (NTM) may provide sufficient insurance against militarily significant cheating scenarios.

The Soviets objected to highly intrusive verification measures in MBFR, but accepted them in INF and have said they will accept them in CFE. They will also accept nonintrusive measures. There are those in the United States who think that if the cuts are substantial, intrusive measures will be required, but not many. Congress must be fully satisfied that verification measures are intrusive enough to detect significant patterns of cheating. The concept of using moderate stability measures expressed earlier in our discussion of force modernization may satisfy

Congress when fully meshed with on-site inspections, manned and unmanned surveillance, and NTM as a package concept.

Issue 8: Counting POMCUS and War Reserve Materiel (WRM)

To determine military balances for data exchange, both alliances made up their own rules as to what to count. Should we count Pre-positioning of Materiel Configured to Unit Sets (POMCUS) and War Reserve Materiel (WRM)?

Initially, military service planners opted to exclude POMCUS and WRM from the balance figures presented to the WTO; however, there was insufficient justification to adequately support this position. The JCS then proposed to NATO that the United States be allowed to exclude POMCUS from NATO "stationed forces" totals. Once again, NATO did not deem the position defensible, but later reversed its position to embrace the U.S. initiative. The USG now accepts a British compromise that includes POMCUS and WRM in the equipment totals in ATTU, but places them in a "stored equipment" category. More details concerning the military balance will be presented in discussion of Issue 12, Data Exchange, in this chapter.

Issue 9: Inclusion of Air Forces

The U.S. Army's initial position on this issue was that air forces should be included in conventional arms control talks. The U.S. Air Force was not convinced and posed verification, transitory, and independent national operations issues as its rationale.

The USG defeated military positions that opposed the inclusion of air forces, and NATO ultimately accepted the inclusion as agreed in the scope of the CFE Mandate by addressing inclusion of "all conventional armaments and equipment." The mandate also excluded naval forces. The government position was that naval forces are excluded from CFE by mandate, but that does not include Land-Based Naval Air (LBNA). It is not readily apparent from open source literature as to why NATO agreed to the inclusion of LBNA, while it stands firmly on the mandate's exclusion of naval forces. Reportedly the deciding factor was verification, and U.S. insistence on a "look alike count alike" rule. It is as yet unclear whether NATO will sustain its position, however, especially inasmuch as the USG refuses to count its carrier-based aircraft.

This issue will be discussed more in Chapter 6, "Current CFE Negotiations."

Issue 10: Inclusion of Naval Forces

Not only is the issue of inclusion of LBNA somewhat in doubt, but the explicit exclusion of naval forces, as expressly stated in the CFE Mandate, is under Soviet attack. Recently, Mr. Shevardnadze stated that the WTO's negotiating position would be influenced "by the factor of naval arms."

Perhaps what Mr. Shevardnadze is saying is in effect a hint as to what kind of "bargaining chip" the East will require to make the large asymmetrical reductions in land and air forces proposed by the West. That said, sea-based forces will not be opened to negotiation in CFE, although they may be grist for arms controls in the CSBM negotiation, or in some other, as yet unspecified forum.

Issue 11: Stablizing Measures

CSBMs are the products and responsibility of the Conference on Confidence- and Security-Building and Disarmament in Europe (CDE). In early 1988 it was still not certain whether or not stabilizing measures would be a subject for negotiation in CFE or left exclusively a subject for CDE.

In MBFR, measures that enhanced security through inspections, constraints, calendar and information exchanges, designed to make WTO military activities more transparent as to mobilization for surprise attack, were called Associated Measures. In CFE, these subagreement designed to reinforce and supplement security are called "stability" measures. CSBMs were relegated to negotiations in the CDE.

The following discussions and examples of each kind of measure are presented to clarify their differences:

- In the MBFR talks, Associated Measures included information exchanges, noninterference with National Technical Means of gathering intelligence, scheduled but limited number of on-site inspections, advance notification of division-size out-of-garrison activities, mandatory invitations for training activities, advance notification of movements into the NATO Guidelines Area (NGA), and establishment of permanent troop entry and exit points to observe unit movements into and out of the NGA.

- In the CFE, Stability Measures are judged by how well they constrain and/or make transparent any transition from peace to war (mobilization) and how they affect the other side's reaction to such a transition to war. Stability Measures are classified by national governments prior to tabling them to the other side. Tough stability measures could generically restrict or limit stored TLE; the size, frequency, and duration of training activities; callup of reservists; and equipment other than TLE. They are generally designed to make both sides less "ready" and less able to initiate surprise offensive actions.

- In the CDE, Confidence- and Security-Building Measures (CSBMs) are not part of or necessarily complementary to TLI, the units of account in the conventional arms control negotiations. The newly established linkage between the CFE and CDE/CSBM fora, however, will ensure that only complementary proposals are adopted. CSBMs are, in fact, a return to the Associated Measures of MBFR and seek to advance transparency beyond the Stockholm Document summary presented in Chapter 1.

There are two principal differences between the Stability Measures in CFE and CSBMs in CDE: first, CSBMs in the CDE forum are politically binding, but not legally binding as the CFE measures are by treaty; and second, the focus on CSBMs is on transparency, while the focus of Stability Measures is constraint.

Invariably, a nation on one side or the other tries to introduce constraining measures in CDE and promptly receives admonition from its colleagues.

Issue 12: Data Exchange

At present, the exchange of force data bases for the CFE conflict in many technical areas of selective accounting techniques used by both East and West. These same data problems plagued the MBFR talks and may inhibit CFE progress unless resolved. Four examples of the conflicting data base for NATO and WTO conventional forces are presented:

- Ground Forces. Soviet figures claim rough parity with 3.5 million Warsaw Pact soldiers facing 3.6 million NATO troops. Soviet data includes naval forces but excludes most support or construction units. NATO excludes naval forces, but it counts most Soviet construction troops and claims a Warsaw Pact advantage of 3.1 million to 2.2 million troops.

- Tanks. Soviet data concedes a Warsaw Pact advantage of 2:1 in total numbers of tanks (59,470 to 30,699). NATO claims a 3:1 Soviet advantage (51,500 to 16,424). The Soviets count all tanks—heavy, light, light-amphibious. NATO figures include only heavy, main battle tanks (MBT).

- Artillery. NATO figures include only heavy artillery (100mm and over). Soviet forces have these weapons in great abundance to support ground forces. By contrast, NATO has far fewer of these weapons, but large numbers of smaller (below 100mm) weapons that are organic to its ground forces. Soviet data initially included all artillery regardless of caliber (down to 75mm artillery and 50mm mortars), but the Soviet position is now comparable to NATO's position.

- Combat Aircraft. The Soviets insist that NATO has a 1.5:1 advantage in front-line combat aircraft. This contrasts with NATO estimates of a 2:1 Warsaw Pact advantage. The large discrepancy is explained by Soviet exclusion of combat-capable training aircraft, and aircraft in strategic aviation.[10]

The data exchange issue must be resolved soon so that the delta between agreed-upon ceilings and current levels can be determined and the reduction monitored and verified.

Issue 13: Size of Reductions

As a conclusion to our discussion on strategic and operational issues, we need to determine the outcome that compromise and resolution of issues will bring, which leads us directly to the size of the reductions agreed upon. NATO has tabled its proposal with reductions to 90-95 percent of NATO current levels of tanks, armored troop carriers, and artillery. The WTO proposal sets the level of reductions at 35-40 percent below the level of the lowest side in each of the weapons categories. These levels of reductions were selected as a result of prenegotiation analyses, but the real issue is how low can we afford to go?

Senator Nunn and former Ambassador Jonathan Dean have both proposed reductions to 50 percent of NATO's current strength. Many other analysts also seek what is becoming a very popular 50 percent figure, since it seems to rhyme with START reductions. Most recently, General Andrew Goodpaster, former Supreme Allied Commander Europe (SACEUR) and current chairman of the Atlantic Council, has published the paper "Gorbachev and the Future of East–West Security: A Response for the Mid-Term," in which he recommends strengthening the Western European Union (WEU) and then seeking parity in CFE to no more than 50 percent of present NATO strength.

This "50 Percent Club" of distinguished relevant actors is going to impact on U.S. and European publics as the CFE talks continue. Colonel Hallenbeck, in a quick analysis of General Goodpaster's paper, sets the tone for the military response to 50 percent reductions:

Such deep reductions would require the abandonment of forward defense and a shift to a "force-on-force" defense which could entail an initial deep Pact penetration of FRG territory in wartime. This shift in strategy would seriously undercut the utility to the FRG of its association with NATO. Indeed, a force-on-force strategy could actually be destabilizing because it would place a high premium on preemptive attack and it would encourage NATO and the Warsaw Pact to field defensive forces with a very high counter-offensive potential.[11]

The key to determining the answer to "how low can we go" does not lie in the selection of a post–CFE strategy and alternative defense plan, but in ultimate political solutions to German reunification.

NOTES

1. The selection of issues to be discussed was originally determined by contributing authors Michael F. Altfeld, John F. Scott, Regina Gaillard, and David E. Shaver while preparing *How to Think about Conventional Arms Control: A Framework*, published by the Strategic Studies Institute (SSI), June 24, 1988. The study team framed the issues from numerous newspaper articles, periodicals, political speeches, and from unclassified discussion in Department of Defense classified literature. The updated version of the issues stems from this initial research in October 1987 to the present.

2. David E. Shaver, *Force Structures: The United States and Europe in the Coming Decade*, Carlisle Barracks, Pa: Strategic Studies Institute, U.S. Army War College, June 12, 1989, pp. 7–8.

3. Ibid., pp. 8–9.

4. SSI, *How to Think about Conventional Arms Control*, p. 80.

5. Shaver, *Force Structure*, p. 13.

6. Ibid., p. 14.

7. SSI, *How to Think about Conventional Arms Control*, pp. 35–63.

8. See Appendix A for a full presentation of the CFE Mandate.

9. See Chapter 6 for an all-inclusive look at current negotiations.

10. Conversation with Ralph A. Hallenbeck, Colonel (U.S. Army), Director, Conventional Arms Negotiation Division, Office of the Deputy Chief of Staff for Operations and Plans, Headquarters, Department of the Army, April 1989.

11. Gary L. Guertner, "Conventional Deterrence after Arms Control," *Parameters*, U.S. Army War College Quarterly, Carlisle Barracks, Pa: Vol. 19, No. 4, December 1989, p. 70.

5

Definitional Disarmament

The reader should now be familiar with the background, objectives, procedures, and issues in multilateral, conventional negotiations. In this chapter we will discuss the various types of disarmament by definition. The focus is on negotiated, non-negotiated, and structural disarmament. An understanding of these kinds of disarmament will help to view the details of conventional arms control in a strategic context.

ON DISARMAMENT

Arms control and disarmament are distinct and often value-laden terms. Disarmament is the most stringent and utopian term, which carries a common assumption that it means a "zero" outcome. Clearly, we are not writing about disarmament as purely defined. We are addressing arms reductions of weapon systems and associated force structure. The term "disarmament" here is used to subsume arms reductions and/or controls and simplifies an explanation that may encompass limitations (as in SALT I or II), reductions (as in CFE, START), and disengagements (as in armistice or war termination).

When discussing disarmament it is necessary to qualify the discussion as meaning "partial disarmament," since the word formally means "the laying aside or depriving of arms." Disarmament can be unnegotiated; negotiated in bilateral and multilateral fora; or can be brought about almost accidentally, as in "structural disarmament." In this section we will discuss all three forms of disarmament.

NEGOTIATED DISARMAMENT

The Negotiations on Conventional Armed Forces in Europe (CFE) and the Conference on Confidence- and Security-Building and Disarmament in Europe (CDE) are examples of multilateral, negotiated disarmament. The development of NATO strategies and positions to take in negotiations to advance these strategies is dependent on the resolution of the issues discussed in Chapter 4. Professor Edward N. Luttwak states the difficulty of the negotiating process:

Given the inherent complexities of arms control negotiations, and the great scope for sharp disagreements on hard technical questions, it is evident that issue-by-issue bargaining may sometimes make agreement quite impossible. . . . But in trying to negotiate significant arms control measures, one must almost invariably trade across the issues, since the variety of weapons characteristics and all the other asymmetries make issue-by-issue bargaining very difficult [indeed].[1]

Before we can begin to predict the outcome of successful conventional arms control in Europe, which means attainment of our objectives, we must first determine the roles that the strategic issues of allied burdensharing, diminishing Soviet threat, international trade, and the U.S. defense budget decline will have on the environment that will shape future strategy development.

The impact of successful allied burdensharing agreements may lead to a reduced U.S. active force structure in Europe. If CFE operational issues and burdensharing are not addressed in consort, separate resolutions may further result in reductions well beyond those proposed in CFE. Coordinating the issues by attempting to resolve the burdensharing issue prior to negotiating a CFE agreement would enable the United States and NATO members to restructure NATO's risks, roles, and responsibilities, and it would assist NATO to resolve how the reductions in CFE will be allocated within the Alliance.

We should also simultaneously coordinate cuts in the U.S. defense budget with burdensharing and conventional arms control activities, since budget issues have the potential to unilaterally reduce U.S. forces in Europe.

We cannot afford to exclude the negative impact that a diminishing Soviet threat will have on NATO member defense budgets and resulting force structures—and the rise of economic power in relation to military power promised as a result of the EEC action to drop its national trade barriers to form an integrated economic trade structure in 1992.

In general, then, while we seriously negotiate issue by issue and across issues in CFE, the strategic issues provide clues to new strategy formulation. Each in one manner or another has the potential to reduce NATO force structures unilaterally beyond required treaty reductions, in what might be considered non-negotiated disarmament.

The operational issues identified in Chapter 4 may support negotiated disarmament, even if such negotiatons are as difficult as Professor Luttwak predicts. Clearly, all of the operational issues have been difficult to negotiate, but the issues that impact on determining a future strategy include selection of units of account (or TLI), determination of subzones, and resolution of the size of reductions.

- Units of account. By limiting CFE talks to the current NATO and WTO proposals, which include Main Battle Tanks (MBT), artillery, Armored Troop Carriers (ATC), attack helicopters, and combat aircraft, we are limiting how we can restructure the remaining forces and may be creating a potential arms race in other than TLI, which may naturally develop as offensive weapons of choice in future restructuring. Units of account thus become increasingly important when attempting to devise alternative strategies and defense plans, regardless of the final, negotiated ceilings on TLI.

- Subzones. Determination of subzones is also important to the development of alternative strategies and defensive concepts. We must understand the "where" of the reductions as well as the "what" (TLI) and the "how much" (size of reductions). As previously discussed, subzones have a tendency to ignore subregions that are not included in any description of a Central Zone. The old NATO Guidelines Area (NGA) in MBFR excluded most of the NATO membership.

- Size of reductions. The answer to the question of "how low can we go" is the toughest and most uncertain issue to resolve NATO's opening position was for reductions as high as 10 percent of current structure, later revised to 15 percent. The WTO has also proposed that reductions below the level of the lowest side would be 15 percent initially, with a further reduction of 25 percent later on. That would have amounted to a 40 percent reduction by weapons system; however, the WTO proposals were based on highly inflated estimates of NATO holdings.

The original notion of deep reductions was nevertheless intriguing and would be considered favorable by the 50 Percent Club mentioned earlier.[2] The key to appreciating this position is not a matter of determining true military sufficiency for either side to mount a defensive defense, but it becomes a true matter of political negotiation alone. Based upon the presentation by Captain Gerstein, "In Search of NATO's Minimum Force Density Requirement," in Chapter 2, if the size of negotiated reduction in CFE is 10 percent or less for NATO, a replacement strategy for Flexible Response would not be required. Since NATO's initial proposal was for about a 10 percent reduction, this indicates that an alternative strategy and alternative defense plans should be developed. President Bush's 225,000/195,000 U.S./USSR troop ceiling proposal definitely establishes the need to develop new alternatives.

In summary, our discussion on "negotiated disarmament" prophesizes reductions caused by the concurrent nonnegotiated issues of allied burdensharing, diminishing Soviet threat, international trade, and/or the U.S. defense budget decline. The key operational issues to be resolved in alternative strategy development are those that will determine the "what," the "where," and the "how much."

NONNEGOTIATED DISARMAMENT

We have seen how the strategic issues of allied burdensharing, diminishing Soviet threat, international trade, and U.S. defense budget decline may create synergistic pressures for unilateral force reductions without a negotiated agreement. A series of alliance unilateral reductions may also impact on partial disarmament.

Conferences are being conducted in Western Europe, in the United States, and in the USSR that seek to resolve arms control through a series of unilateral actions by both alliances, without the formality of the CFE. Mr. Gorbachev's December 7, 1988 announcement at the United Nations was strictly a unilateral act of disarmament, which precipitated similar unilateral actions from other WTO members. Additional announced reductions in Soviet SNF to be included as part of the unilateral withdrawals are also nonnegotiated disarmament actions designed to encourage corresponding acts of disarmament in the West. The FRG through its 1990 military restructuring; budget constraints impacting on Canada, Belgium, and the Netherlands; new calls for Soviet expulsion from Eastern Europe; and U.S. reductions associated with the INF treaty are all actions resulting in partial disarmament, external to the CFE talks. Should members of NATO (other than the United States) and East European nations continue to announce and carry out further reductions, pressure will return to the West to announce even more reductions, and thus nonnegotiated disarmament progresses to some unknown stop point in the future. Recent legislative action by the U.S. Senate to link U.S. unilateral reductions with corresponding NATO member unilateral reductions attempts to freeze the current status of allied burdensharing contributions. This legislation purports to put pressure on the West to resist unilateral action until CFE agreement is attained, and thus halt this kind of nonnegotiated disarmament. We will have to wait and see if this works.

In spring 1989, President Bush emphatically announced that the U.S. strategy of containment had ended. What are the implications in terms of disarmament? It seems that resources dedicated to achieving the objectives of such a concept would now become unnecessary. The strategic concept of deterrence will remain, of course, but how about the strategic concept of forward stationing? With the death of containment as a national security strategy, it becomes more difficult to justify the implementing strategic concept of forward stationing and, thus, to politically rationalize our position in Europe. The President's announcement may become a landmark in East–West relationships, but it may become a lodestone for both those who must explain implementing military strategy to Congress and for those in Congress who challenge those explanations. The death of containment may also strengthen calls for a stronger European "pillar," which will only proceed, however, if the Europeans are allowed a greater leadership role within NATO, something the United States has not yet adequately addressed.

In summary, nonnegotiated disarmament can occur with or without formal arms control talks. Strategic issues can initiate nonnegotiated disarmament, as can planned and unplanned unilateral actions. With the death of containment as a national security strategy and the new political realities taking shape in Eastern Europe, the implementing concept of forward stationing and its dedicated resources may also see political extinction.

STRUCTURAL DISARMAMENT

More subtle than negotiated or nonnegotiated disarmament is the concept of structural disarmament.[3] In the author's view, there are two types of structural disarmament: technological and logistical.

Technological structural disarmament stems from the "bill payer" philosophy used informally within the U.S. Department of Defense. This so-called bill payer philosophy amounts to paying for new or anticipated military hardware from within organizational budget structures, rather than seeking additional funding external to the organization. The bill payer philosophy seeks to avoid competition among the services for scarce defense funding by selecting reductions from within a military service budget to fund the new equipment. Within each service there are those constituencies who favor high cost, high technology equipment, and those who favor low cost, low technology solutions.[4]

Advocates of high cost, high tech equipment make a strong case that science and technology can replace costly force structure with costly but more effective and more lethal weapon systems. Those who support this argument propose that limited dollars should be spent on such things as aircraft carriers, submarines, and strategic lift, and modern, survivable strategic missiles and bombers, because they perceive that time is the critical path to mobilization, and there will not be enough of it to build these high ticket items in the next war.

Those who favor low cost, low tech solutions see a different war tomorrow, one that will be fought in the deserts, jungles, and plains of Third World countries—low intensity conflicts, special operations, military assistance and training—concepts that require soldiers and marines, lightly but lethally equipped. These advocates are against force structure cuts as acceptable bill payers for the high cost, high tech equipment.

One of these advocate groups is right and one group will lose the argument. The Army and DOD leadership must determine which of these arguments is the right one for the next decade or consider that this kind of advocacy game is not a zero sum game, but one in which both constituencies may be served.

The results of the bill payer philosophy are evident in force reductions to pay for the new technologies, and in the high cost of new technologies and fewer quantities purchased. These reductions are defined here as technological structural disarmament, a unilateral nonnegotiated disarmament nonetheless, and unconnected with negotiated disarmament arising from the modernization issue in CFE.

Logistical/structural disarmament occurs when a NATO member, in accordance with its national security priorities, elects to purchase or lease needed weapons systems but fails to purchase the associated logistical supplies that would be needed to support them in case of war. The lack of adequate repair parts and ammunition stockage by NATO members, including the United States, is an example of logistical, structural disarmament. Logistical disarmament is important because of its impact on NATO's warfighting capability.

The current and previous SACEURs have said that NATO can only fight a conventional war "for days, not weeks," with current firepower and ammunition.[5] Their rationale considers the overwhelming superiority of WTO numbers of offensive weapon systems and the 60–90 days of WTO ammunition that is stockpiled well forward on the potential battlefield, as well as the lack of modernization and fair share defense budget commitments of NATO partners to produce the numbers of systems and ammunition stockpiles necessary to counter a WTO offensive. Senator Nunn wanted to switch around days and weeks to be able to fight for "weeks, not days," and proposed a simple program to reverse the conventional weakness (logistical disarmament) in NATO:

— Eliminate automatic escalators
  • increase NATO member ammunition stockpiles
  • build aircraft shelters and refuel/reloading capabilities
  • continue the Balanced Technology Initiative
— Expand cooperative research and development.[6]

Such a program would have certainly improved our conventional deterrent, but the Soviet massive numbers and closing technology gap still raise concerns as to whether the NATO Alliance, with its very independent member-state convictions, can fight outnumbered and win, even with solid improvements in capabilities. In any case, logistical structural disarmament is an important factor in determining an alternative strategy, should reductions be kept at current CFE ceilings.

In summary, our discussion of structural disarmament takes on two different perspectives: technological and logistical. Both have dramatic impact on a future battlefield, and both are important to round out the total realm of disarmament and its role in national security strategy.

NOTES

1. Edward N. Luttwak, "Why Arms Control Has Failed," in *Military Strategy: Theory and Application*, ed. by Colonel Arthur F. Lykke, Jr., U.S. Army-Ret., Carlisle Barracks, Pa.: U.S. Army War College, 1989, pp. 383–91, at p. 387.

2. It should be noted that the arbitrary 50 percent figure may not actually represent the true size of the reductions that 50 Percent Club members have suggested. In a personal conversation with Ambassador Dean, Colonel Shaver asked what Ambassador Dean was looking for in his 50 percent proposal. The ambassador replied, "Something on the order of 25 percent. . . . The 50 percent figure was designed to encourage NATO to fall off its unrealistic 5-10 percent reduction figure." Ironically, President Bush's initial position in the now famous Kennebunkport meeting was also 25 percent reduction.

3. Sam Nunn, U.S. Senator, Speech to the DMS Symposium on Industrial Cooperation within NATO, "NATO Challenges and Opportunities: A Three-Track Approach," *Congressional Record*, Washington, D.C.: April 28, 1987, Vol, 133, No. 66, pp. 4–5.

4. David E. Shaver, *Force Structures: The United States and Europe in the Coming Decade*, Carlisle Barracks, Pa.: Strategic Studies Institute, U.S. Army War College, June 12, 1989, pp. 10–11.

5. Henry van Loon, "An Exclusive AFJ Interview with: General John R. Galvin, USA, *Armed Forces Journal*, March 1988, p. 50.

6. Sam Nunn, U.S. Senator, "The American/Soviet Disarmament Negotiations and Their Consequences for NATO," Speech to the Wehrkunde Conference, Munich, West Germany, February 8, 1988, p. 5.

6

Current CFE Negotiations

In the Negotiation on Conventional Armed Forces in Europe (CFE), NATO has two interrelated tasks, each of which must be addressed effectively if the CFE objectives of greater security and stability are to be achieved and sustained. First, relative to any Alliance reductions, NATO must insist on very large, asymmetrical reductions in the quantities of Soviet and other Warsaw Pact forces and their associated weapons systems. Large, asymmetrical reductions, in combination with appropriate stabilizing, transparency, and verification measures, should leave both alliances with comparable military capabilities, equally sufficient for defense, but equally unlikely to be sufficient for aggression.

Second, beyond achieving even these ambitious military objectives, NATO's leaders need to come to grips with appropriate political, economic, social, and other objectives. While the latter are not (and cannot be) the technical subject matter of the CFE negotiation, they are very much a part of the calculus of CFE. The success of Soviet perestroika, for example, depends on the creation of far more cooperative Eastern political and economic relationships with the West. Thus, whereas NATO's immediate CFE interest may be in redressing the military imbalance in Europe, the driving force behind WTO participation in the negotiation appears to be the potential that might be created for much more cooperative political and economic interactions with the West. NATO's interest can be achieved at the negotiating table in Vienna, but the interests of the WTO will need to be addressed as well (albeit between capitals, not in Vienna) if the basis for a mutually beneficial and lasting East–West relationship is to be created.

The purposes of this chapter are to describe the state of play in the negotiations to reduce conventional forces in Europe, and to underscore the relevance of NATO's reduction proposals to achieving the objectives of greater stability and security. The chapter concludes with an examination of possible ways to resolve differences that still separate the two sides.

THE FIRST STEP: MOVING TOWARD A ROUGH PARITY
OF NATO AND WARSAW PACT MILITARY CAPABILITIES

While reducing the quantities of weapons on both sides may provide the most obvious and workable topic for negotiation, the stable and secure balance of military "capabilities" that both sides purport to seek cannot be achieved directly just by reducing and constraining armaments. Armament reductions might, however, serve as a stalking horse for reductions in military force structure, and force structure reductions and operational constraints, effectively verified, might lead to conditions favoring much greater military stability and mutual security.

If one categorizes those capabilities most essential to an effective defense, five broad groups emerge. They are (1) early warning of preattack activities (force generation and concentration); (2) ready and rapidly mobilizable forward defenses sufficient to repel a "limited warning" attack along high speed axes and against critical nodes in the rear and forward areas; (3) reinforcement/mobilization capabilities sufficient for responding effectively to a more "fully generated" attack against the full width and depth of the battlefield; (4) capabilities to sustain a successful conventional defense; and (5) a mix of conventional and nuclear capabilities sufficient for escalation control. Collectively, these same capabilities provide the basis for credible and effective deterrence, the sine qua non of both stability and security.

Greater security for all parties will also depend on reducing offensive capabilities. As agreed in the CFE Mandate, the common NATO and WTO objective is to eliminate capabilities for surprise attack and for large-scale offensive action. This aspect should include (1) large, asymmetrical reductions to Warsaw Pact and NATO forces, resulting in roughly equal residual force levels; (2) the wholesale elimination of large numbers of the major weapon systems found in the active and reserve forces on both sides, resulting in equal ceilings on these Treaty-Limited Equipment (TLE) items; and (3) the imposition of subceilings and stabilizing measures to constrain the geographic disposition, composition, and operational activities of the residual forces (and TLE). Any concentration or mobilization for an attack should be made highly unambiguous, complicated (politically as well as militarily), and unlikely to be decisive in the face of the defender's ability to react.

Adequate verification of compliance will obviously be essential to the effectiveness of all force reduction, TLE elimination, and stabilizing measures. Transparency with respect to the permitted size, armament, composition, geographic disposition, and activities of the residual forces on both sides will also be essential to the longer-term maintenance of security, not to mention the future stability of the military balance.

Enhancing defensive capabilities relative to offensive capabilities must proceed along both axes: reducing offensive capabilities while sustaining defensive capabilities. In broad terms, it would not seem all that difficult to describe what this might mean. For example, NATO's March 9, 1989 CFE proposal called for a quantum reduction in the number of tanks, artillery pieces, and ATCs in the combined holdings of the two alliances. In accordance with NATO's proposals, the number of WTO and NATO tanks, artillery pieces, and ATCs permitted to remain in the ATTU region following reductions would be no more than 40,000, 33,000, and 56,000, respectively, with each alliance retaining an equal share of the residual treaty limited weapons systems.[1] See Map 6.1 for a breakdown of current NATO and WTO holdings in the ATTU.

In March 1989, NATO called for reductions by both sides to equal numbers of the three most important weapon systems for seizing the holding terrain. Following reductions, the WTO and NATO would each retain only 20,000 tanks, 16,500 artillery pieces, and 28,000 ATCs. Furthermore, only 12,000 of the 28,000 ATCs would be permitted to be turretted Armored Infantry Fighting Vehicles (AIFVs).[3]

Such a substantial reduction in the total quantities of tanks, artillery, and ATCs/AIFVs on both sides would be very significant. Were the WTO to accept such an outcome in CFE, there could be no doubt that NATO's security and the stability of the military balance in Europe would improve dramatically. For most of the 40 or so years since the end of World War II, NATO has faced Warsaw Pact ground forces armed to the teeth with the weapons most associated with offensive warfare. This is not to say that tanks, artillery, and ATCs are not also required for defense. Rather, it simply says that when one side (in this case the WTO) insists on amassing and retaining an overwhelming quantitative advantage in these major weapon systems, the other side (NATO) has had an obvious reason to feel threatened. NATO's proposals to eliminate the current asymmetries were, therefore, an appropriate beginning to the CFE negotiation.

During the week of May 15, 1989, the WTO responded positively to NATO's tank, artillery, and ATC reduction proposals. Significantly, the Pact counterproposal also included helicopters, aircraft, and military manpower as categories for reduction.

The WTO agreed to ceilings of 20,000 for tanks and 28,000 for Armored Fighting Vehicles (AFVs), but it proposed that the ceiling for artillery be 24,000 instead of 16,500. The WTO also proposed that neither side retain in the ATTU area more than 1,700 helicopters, 1,500 "strike" aircraft, or 1,350,000 personnel.*[4]

---

*AFVs appear to be roughly equivalent to ATCs. "Strike aircraft" are roughly equivalent to "fighter-bombers." WTO manpower levels appear to apply only to selected ground and air forces.

Map 6.1
The Atlantic-to-the-Urals Region

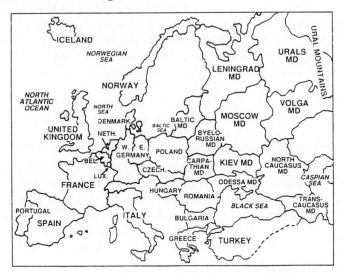

CURRENT NATO AND WTO HOLDINGS*

	TANKS	ARTY	ATCS
NATO	22,600	17,700	28,800
WTO	51,500	46,200	53,500

NATO and the WTO have both published data bases. The NATO data is similar to the data shown. The WTO data differs substantially from NATO numbers. Differences are due, at least in part, to the definitions and counting rules that were applied.

*The data shown throughout this chapter were derived from the BDM and NATO High Level Task Force (HLTF) unclassified data bases.[2]

CURRENT LEVELS OF HELICOPTERS, AIRCRAFT, AND MANPOWER IN THE ATTU (NATO'S DEFINITIONS AND COUNTING RULES)

	HELICOPTERS	COMBAT AIRCRAFT	MANPOWER
NATO	2,200	6,700	3 Million
WTO	3,500	13,500	4 Million

The tank and AFV ceilings specified in the initial Warsaw Pact proposals were obviously identical to those in NATO's proposals; the difference between NATO's proposed ceiling on artillery (16,500) and the Pact proposal (24,000) was also potentially negotiable (the primary difference reflected a different counting rule, which has since been resolved).[5] The proposed helicopter ceiling also appeared negotiable, especially inasmuch as NATO subsequently offered, and the WTO accepted, a ceiling of 1,900 on these weapon systems. It remains to be seen, however, whether the two alliances can reach agreement with respect to the definitions and counting rules applicable to tanks, ATCs, aircraft, and helicopters; and, just as important, whether they can also agree to equal ceilings on air and manpower.

In September 1989, NATO responded to the WTO with a proposal for reductions to parity at levels 15 percent below NATO's current levels of combat helicopters and aircraft. Based on Alliance definitions and counting rules, the ceilings would be 1,900 for combat helicopters and 5,700 for combat aircraft.[6]

At the same time, NATO also proposed that the United States and the Soviet Union reduce the forces each stations on foreign territory to equal manpower levels of no more than 275,000 for either superpower.

NATO had agreed in principle to the addition of aircraft, helicopters, and manpower as TLI. However, the definitions and counting rules on which the Pact proposals had been based—especially the manpower and air proposals—had been rejected out of hand by all Alliance members. First, NATO was not prepared to focus only on fighter-bomber and other ground-attack (strike) aircraft. From NATO's perspective, all types of aircraft (e.g., bombers, fighter-bombers, interceptors, and combat-capable trainers) would have to be included if a basis for serious negotiation were to be achieved.

Recognizing this reality, the Warsaw Pact subsequently modified its position by raising the proposed ceiling on aircraft to 4,700, applicable to all combat aircraft in "frontal aviation" units.[7]

Obviously, this WTO concession went partway toward closing the very large gap that had initially separated the air proposals of the two sides. On the other hand, major differences remained. These differences focused primarily on how combat-capable trainers, land-based naval aircraft, intermediate-range bombers, fighter-interceptors in Soviet strategic air force, and various other combat air-craft not in frontal aviation would be dealt with. NATO had not been prepared to accept the exclusion of any aircraft on the basis of its mission or unit of assignment. Furthermore, Alliance members had stressed repeatedly that the capabilities of both sides' aircraft had to be the determining factor, and that aircraft that "looked alike" would need to be "counted alike."

Second, manpower also remained a major issue. Although manpower reductions, such as those that might occur as the natural consequence of reductions in equipment holdings, had been viewed by NATO as necessary, alliance-to-alliance manpower ceilings had been resisted. Such ceilings would be virtually unverifiable, especially given the potential for circumvention through fuzzy definitional distinctions between active military personnel, reserves, paramilitary personnel, and supporting civilians. By limiting the manpower reductions to only U.S. and Soviet forces stationed on foreign territory, however, NATO sought to eliminate such difficulties. That is, the forces stationed abroad by the United States and USSR tend to be active military, and organized in more or less standard and, therefore, relatively more verifiable configurations.

For the United States, the proposed 275,000 manpower ceiling would require the withdrawal of 30,000 U.S. military personnel from Western Europe; for the USSR it would require the withdrawal of more than 300,000 men from Eastern Europe. NATO's proposal was not, however, at all congruent with the Pact's proposal for a manpower ceiling on all forces, nor did it include a ceiling on all stationed forces. NATO justified its omission of the relatively modest numbers (170,000) of stationed British, French, Belgian, Canadian, and Dutch manpower in terms of keeping the focus on the dominant members of the two alliances, in terms of minimizing the verification problems, and in terms of maintaining defensive sufficiency.

NATO's strategy of forward defense was dependent on the contributions of both U.S. and Western European forces deployed along the Inter-German Border (IGB), and, in particular, on the ability of Germany's European allies to reinforce the IGB rapidly if Germany were threatened by Pact aggression or intimidation. A low ceiling on all stationed forces would probably require NATO to reduce not only U.S. forces, but also French, British, and other allied forces critical to the forward defense of the FRG. A relatively high alliance-to-alliance stationed manpower ceiling would, on the other hand, provide the Soviet Union a large entitlement, which was precisely what NATO's members (along with several of the non-Soviet members of the WTO) were eager to avoid.[8]

In an effort to force the withdrawal of most of the Soviet forces stationed in Eastern Europe, NATO also tabled proposals to reduce and constrain equipment in "stationed forces." That said, there was (and still is) an obvious anomaly in NATO's proposals governing stationed forces. NATO's manpower proposal would provide the Soviets an entitlement to stationed personnel equal only to the U.S. stationed manpower level. NATO's TLE proposal, on the other hand, would provide the Soviet Union an entitlement to stationed tanks, artillery, and ATCs equal to the entitlement of the entire North Atlantic Alliance.

NATO proposed that no more than 3,200 tanks, 1,700 artillery pieces, and 6,000 ATCs be permitted in the active, stationed forces of either side.[9]

While this anomaly may prove difficult to sustain at the negotiating table, it is not entirely without practical justification. Because NATO's defenses depend on the contributions of so many members, and because each of those members provides its stationed combat forces independent administrative and logistical support, NATO has always had a much higher "tooth-to-tail" ratio than stationed Soviet forces (which are the only stationed forces in the WTO). Thus, a case might be made that NATO's stationed manpower levels need to be higher than those afforded by the USSR, even if the two sides were entitled to the same quantities of stationed TLE. Only time will tell whether the USSR will be willing to accept either the principle or the consequence of NATO's proposals for ceilings on stationed manpower and TLE. There have been several indications that the anomaly is of less importance to the Soviet Union than other aspects of NATO's stationed force proposals.

For example, NATO's proposal to cap stationed TLE does not address stationed aircraft or helicopters; nor would it constrain the quantities of any treaty limited equipment that a member of either alliance might retain in storage outside its territory. From NATO's perspective, limits on stationed aircraft and helicopters would be militarily meaningless inasmuch as these weapons types could be returned on very short notice. Furthermore, ceilings on stationed aircraft and helicopters would be unverifiable but could impose on NATO very substantial costs associated with restationing forces in peacetime. For reasons that will be discussed in greater detail, NATO also distinguishes TLE in active stationed forces from the TLE that the United States and Britain maintain in unmanned storage.

CURRENT LEVELS OF "STATIONED," ACTIVE WTO AND NATO FORCES

	TANKS	ARTY	ATCS	HELOS	AIRCRAFT	MANPOWER
NATO	3,400	1,800	5,400	950	700	470,000
WTO	10,800	6,600	10,800	1,200	600	600,000

The WTO responded to NATO's stationed forces proposals with proposals of its own. Each side would be required to reduce the quantities of TLE it had stationed on foreign territory without any distinction between active and stored equipment. This would add more than 4,000 stored tanks, 1,500 stored artillery pieces, and 5,000 stored ATCs to the aforementioned NATO totals; all of these would be subject to reduction. More to the point, the Pact proposals would give the Soviets a much greater entitlement to stationed TLE, all of which could be maintained in active Soviet forces. Finally, limits on stationed aircraft and helicopters were also very much a part of the initial pact proposals.

Beginning in October 1989, however, when the WTO revised its aircraft and helicopter proposals to reflect the 4,700 and 1,900 limits, the WTO also ceased pressing for sublimits on stationed aircraft or helicopters. That said, the official WTO proposal still remains:

Nor more than 350,000 personnel, and no more than 4,500 tanks, 4,000 artillery pieces, 7,500 AFVs, 350 strike aircraft, and 600 helicopters permitted in the stationed forces (active or stored) on either side.[10]

Obviously, hard negotiating will be required to resolve the differences and ambiguities that continue to separate Alliance and Pact proposals governing stationed forces. At their most fundamental level, the Pact proposals are still designed to preserve a Soviet entitlement to ground forces stationed in Eastern Europe far in excess of what NATO members would prefer. At the same time, because NATO defenses greatly depend on the contributions of U.S. ground and air forces—which could not reasonably be stationed in the United States and still perform the missions for which they are required—the WTO proposals are also aimed at requiring a large portion of the U.S. contribution to NATO to be withdrawn from Europe.

Given NATO's manpower proposal, and given also the defense budget reductions announced by the Bush administration, a substantial reduction in U.S. ground and air forces would seem likely in any case. Because of this probability, however, NATO has been more determined than ever to reduce Soviet force levels. As noted previously, this has meant Alliance insistence on a low ceiling on only U.S. and Soviet stationed forces. And, consistent with the objective of constraining the potential for a post–CFE Soviet domination of the European force balance, NATO has also insisted that no one country be permitted to have more than 30 percent of the total (active and stored) tank, artillery, ATC, helicopter, or combat aircraft holdings of all the participating WTO and NATO states. This rule, which is known as the sufficiency rule, would cut deeply into the Soviet force levels. No other country on either side (NATO or WTO) would be affected.

THE NATO AND WTO COUNTRIES WITH THE LARGEST HOLDINGS IN THE ATTU

	TANKS	ARTY	ATCS	HELOS	AIRCRAFT	MANPOWER
USSR	37,000	33,400	36,200	2,800	10,500	2,800,000
U.S.	6,200	2,800	6,500	819	754	305,000

NATO proposed that no one country have more than 12,000 tanks, 10,000 artillery pieces, 16,800 ATCs, 1,140 helicopters, and 3,420 combat aircraft (active or stored) in the ATTU region.[11]

The WTO accepted the principle on which this Alliance proposal was based, but not the ceilings. The Pact countered with a proposal that no country be permitted more than 14,000 tanks, 17,000 artillery pieces, 18,000 AFVs, 1,200 strike aircraft, 1,350 helicopters, or 920,000 personnel.[12]

Once again, the higher ceilings in the WTO proposal would permit the Soviets to retain more TLE than they would be entitled to under NATO's proposal. The evolving Soviet/WTO position did, however, imply Pact acceptance of NATO's entire negotiating framework—parity at levels below the levels of the lowest side, restrictions on TLE in stationed forces and in the holdings of any one country, and, as will be discussed, additional regional subceilings prohibiting the concentration of TLE in geographic areas where they would be most threatening.

It is well worth repeating that the lack of mutually acceptable counting rules also remains a major potential stumbling block. Pact data released in January 1989 identified NATO's equipment holdings as 30,700 tanks, 57,000 artillery pieces, 47,000 armored fighting vehicles, 5,270 helicopters, and 4,075 strike aircraft. Even allowing for Pact counting rules, NATO claims to possess less than 24,000 tanks, 20,000 artillery pieces, 30,000 ATCs, 3,000 helicopters, or 3,000 aircraft of this type. Thus, any perception of agreement on ceilings needs to be tempered by a recognition that the two alliances have serious differences over both counting rules and the magnitude of NATO's current holdings. Fortunately, given Pact counting rules, the WTO data do seem generally consistent with Alliance estimates of Pact weapons holdings in the ATTU region.[13]

The counting rule problem is particularly challenging for aircraft, helicopters, and ATCs/AIFVs. NATO's "look alike, count alike" approach to aircraft has already been discussed. This approach, while eminently sound in theory, is difficult to apply equitably. For example, Soviet spokesmen point to the inequity of including all Soviet land-based naval aircraft while excluding all sea-based U.S. and other allied aircraft. In a similar vein, both sides are experiencing difficulty with the application of "look alike, count alike" rules to helicopters and ATCs. Both sides have a large number of unarmed transport helicopters of the same types that they are proposing to constrain. Equally important, they have had—and in some cases, still do have—small numbers of the same types of armed helicopters as the transport helos that they want excluded from the combat helicopter category. Finally, both sides have large numbers of ATC look-alikes, which they employ as ambulances, transportation for engineers, and command and control vehicles. Both sides have also expressed some concern about excluding reconnaissance vehicles and light tanks, neither of which are currently captured under NATO's tank or ATC definitions. NATO is not opposed to the inclusion of any combat vehicle but has not been prepared to capture them under the agreed ATC ceiling.

The two sides also have differences over timing. The WTO has called for reductions in two phases, in order to achieve parity by 1997. NATO has proposed that the sides concentrate on achieving an agreement within one year (by September 1990), and that all required reductions and TLE eliminations be completed within two to three years thereafter. WTO spokesmen have applauded NATO's willingness to seek rapid results, but they have expressed misgivings about the ability of the WTO to achieve these optimistic deadlines.

NATO has called for reductions to the equal, lower ceilings by 1992 or 1993.[14] The WTO has proposed reductions to levels 10-15 percent below the levels of the lowest side in all categories (tanks, artillery, ATCs, helicopters, aircrafts, and manpower) by 1994, and reductions of an additional 25 percent by 1997.[15]

REGIONAL SUBCEILINGS

Residual force levels in the aggregate, even as supplemented by constraints on stationed and single country holdings, would need to be further refined if the potential for security and stability were to be maximized. Of particular concern to NATO are possibilities for offensive concentrations of WTO forces in Central Europe, and especially in the areas closest to the IGB. To address this potential, NATO has proposed a set of zonal subceilings that would require both sides to eliminate the presence of inordinately large number of tanks, artillery, and ATCs in active units located in these areas. The WTO has responded with similar proposals of its own.

NATO's package of zonal subceilings is focused first and foremost on reducing the active force levels that the WTO currently maintains forward deployed along the IGB. However, for salient political as well as military reasons, NATO is also committed to retaining Alliance force levels sufficient to prevent the Pact from achieving a deep, rapid penetration of the border. Such a penetration would threaten Western Europe's largest industrial and population centers. From almost any perspective, the WTO has concentrated ground forces in this limited geographic area far in excess of essential defensive requirements. NATO, on the other hand, is at most only modestly in excess of the bare minimum active force levels essential to the immediate forward defense of the 750-kilometer IGB.

For its part, the WTO has also long recognized a requirement to limit damage to Eastern urban-industrial centers, but it has heretofore done so by maintaining concentrations of conventional forces sufficient to seize the offensive, thereby forcing NATO to fight deep in allied territory. Reducing Pact capabilities for such an offensive thrust, while nevertheless retaining Alliance capabilities for a forward defense of the IGB, are complementary objectives of Alliance participation in CFE.

NATO has proposed that each side retain only 8,000 tanks, 4,500 artillery pieces, and 11,000 ATCs in "active units" forward deployed in the Inter-German Border area.[16] See Map 6.2 for a breakdown of current NATO and WTO holdings in the IGB area.

The aforementioned subceilings on TLE in active units along the IGB, when combined with the subceilings NATO has proposed for TLE in active, stationed forces, would virtually eliminate the threat of an unreinforced Warsaw Pact attack in this region. That is, with only 3,200 Soviet tanks available to spearhead

Map 6.2
The Inter-German Border Area

**CURRENT HOLDINGS
IN THE IGB AREA**

	TANKS	ARTY	ATCS
NATO	8,500	4,800	11,500
WTO	19,800	12,300	20,000

(NOTE: The IGB Area includes the FRG and
Benelux for NATO, and the GDR, Czechoslovakia,
and Poland for the WTO).

such an undertaking, and with no more than 8,000 tanks in all WTO ground forces concentrated in proximity to the IGB, it is highly unlikely that the Warsaw Pact would attempt to threaten NATO with a surprise attack, or that such an attack would succeed if the Pact were foolhardy enough to attempt such a risky course of action. Rather, it seems very probable that the Pact in general, and the Soviets in particular, would feel compelled to reinforce before initiating any hostile activity. Constraining the potential for rapid Soviet reinforcement is, therefore, also an objective of the Alliance zonal reductions proposals.

NATO has further proposed that no more than 10,300 tanks, 7,600 artillery pieces, and 18,000 ATCs be permitted in active units located anywhere in Europe's Central Region.[17] See Map 6.3 for a breakdown of current NATO and WTO holdings in the Central Region.

Assuming that the Warsaw Pact maintains active forces along the IGB up to the full TLE entitlement proposed by NATO, the subceilings on TLE located in the Central Region would limit the number of Soviet tanks, artillery pieces,

Map 6.3
Europe's Central Region

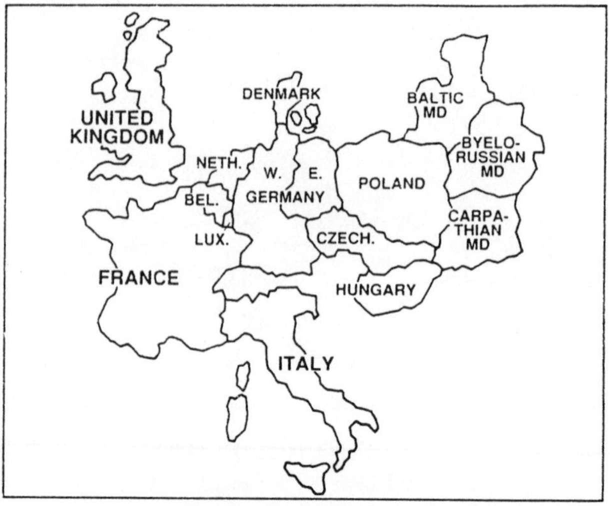

CURRENT HOLDINGS IN THE
CENTRAL REGION

	TANKS	ARTY	ATCS
NATO	11,000	8,100	19,100
WTO	32,200	23,700	33,200

(NOTE: The Central Region includes the FRG, Benelux, France, Italy, the U.K., Denmark, and the Netherlands for NATO, and the GDR, Czechoslovakia, Poland, Hungary, and the Soviet Baltic, Byelorussian, and Carpathian Military Districts for the WTO).

and ATCs in active forces that could be located in the three Westernmost military districts of the USSR. That is, the Soviets would only be entitled to a number of tanks, artillery, and ATCs in the Carpathian, Byelorussian, and Baltic MDs equal to the difference between (1) what the WTO maintains along the IGB, and (2) the numbers permitted in the Central Region. For example, assuming that the WTO has 8,000 tanks in the IGB region, the Soviets could only have 2,300 more tanks in the rest of the Central Region. Such limits would significantly impede the ability of the Soviet Union to reinforce rapidly and substantially the forces that the Soviets and other WTO members could concentrate rapidly at the IGB.

Finally, NATO has proposed a cap on TLE in active ground forces located anywhere in Central Europe from the Atlantic to the Urals. While perhaps less militarily significant than the other zonal ceilings, the Central European ceilings establish a basis for further distributing the TLE in active Pact forces. The difference between the total entitlement (e.g., 20,000 tanks) and what would be permitted in the center (11,300) would have to be positioned on the flanks or put in storage.

NATO has proposed that each side retain no more than 11,300 tanks, 9,000 artillery pieces, and 20,000 ATCs in active units located anywhere in Central Europe.[18] See Map 6.4 for a breakdown of current active force levels in Central Europe.

The NATO CFE reductions proposals, to include the subceilings envisioned by NATO for each of the three successive zones (Central Europe, Central Region, and IGB—see Map 6.5) are summarized and portrayed graphically in Figure 6.1. Collectively, these ceilings should eliminate any realistic possibility that either alliance could execute a successful surprise attack in Central Europe. Force levels sufficient for forward defense would, however, be maintained. Point defenses of critical nodes (garrisons, depots, airfields, headquarters, critical transportation and communication nodes, etc.) throughout Central Europe would also remain adequate to prevent an attacker from achieving a decisive advantage in the initial hours of combat. Furthermore, each side would retain reserve forces sufficient to bolster its forward defenses in the event the other side mobilized and concentrated its total force for a fully reinforced attack.

Obviously, the regional subceilings proposed by NATO have remained focused only on tanks, artillery, and ATCs. It is worth reiterating NATO's position that regional subceilings on aircraft, helicopters, and manpower would be inappropriate: that they could not be effectively verified and that, in a crisis or transition to war, the Warsaw Pact could very rapidly or clandestinely put back into any subregion the helicopters, aircraft, or manpower it had previously reduced. Moreover, given the operational ranges of aircraft and helicopters, NATO has maintained that regional reductions would be militarily irrelevant in wartime, whereas the peacetime restationing of such weapons to meet subceilings could be very expensive. It is equally worth repeating that these Alliance views were not initially shared by the WTO, and unless the WTO position is formally changed, they will remain among the most difficult challenges for the CFE negotiators to resolve.

Critics of NATO's proposals are, of course, also technically correct in claiming that NATO's preoccupation with equipment in "active" forces tends to disguise the fact that much of NATO's equipment in Central Europe is kept in storage. The often implied criticism that NATO is seeking an unfair advantage is not, however, even remotely accurate. In September 1989, NATO proposed that both sides be equally constrained by ceilings on equipment in active units located anywhere in the ATTU. Under NATO's proposal, both sides would be required to place a minimum of 4,000 tanks, 2,000 artillery pieces, and 2,500

Map 6.4
Central Europe

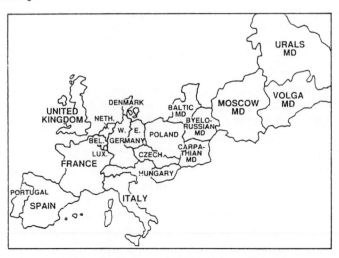

ACTIVE FORCE LEVELS IN CENTRAL EUROPE

	TANKS	ARY	ATCS
NATO	12,000	9,400	21,000
WTO	37,000	28,000	37,500

(NOTE: "Central Europe" includes Belgium, the
Netherlands, Luxembourg, the Federal Republic of
Germany, Denmark, France, the U.K., Italy, Spain,
Portugal, the GDR, Czechoslovakia, Poland, Hun-
gary, and the territory of the Soviet Union west of
the Urals comprising the Baltic, Byelorussian, Car-
pathian, Moscow, Volga, and Urals Military Districts.
It does not include Turkey, Greece, Norway,
Iceland, Bulgaria, Rumania, or the Soviet Leningrad,
Kiev, Odessa, North Caucasus, or Transcaucasus
MDs).

ATCs in storage in the IGB area, or in "cadre-manned" units located elsewhere
in the ATTU.[19] Furthermore, each side would be permitted to monitor the other
side's stored and cadre-manned equipment to ensure that it could not be activated
without immediate detection.

The possibility of both sides storing large quantities of equipment should not
be seen as a flaw or a deception, but rather as a constructive aspect of the NATO
proposals for greater stability and security. That is, when combined with deep

Map 6.5
NATO Zones

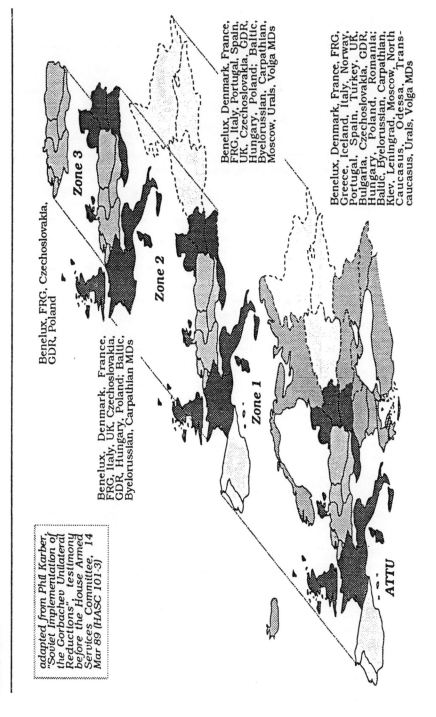

adapted from Phil Karber,
"Soviet Implementation of
the Gorbachev Unilateral
Reductions" testimony
before the House Armed
Services Committee, 14
Mar 89 (HASC 101-3)

Benelux, FRG. Czechoslovakia,
GDR, Poland

Zone 3

Benelux, Denmark, France,
FRG, Italy, Portugal, Spain,
UK, Czechoslovakia, GDR,
Hungary, Poland: Baltic,
Byelorussian, Carpathian,
Moscow, Urals, Volga MDs

Zone 2

Benelux, Denmark, France,
FRG, Italy, UK, Czechoslovakia,
GDR, Hungary, Poland: Baltic,
Byelorussian, Carpathian MDs

Benelux, Denmark, France, FRG,
Greece, Iceland, Italy, Norway,
Portugal, Spain, Turkey, UK:
Bulgaria, Czechoslovakia, GDR,
Hungary, Poland, Romania;
Baltic, Byelorussian, Carpathian,
Kiev, Leningrad, Moscow, North
Caucasus, Odessa, Trans-
caucasus, Urals, Volga MDs

Zone 1

ATTU

Figure 6.1
NATO Proposal

RULES SYSTEM	ATTU CEILINGS — OVERALL (RULE 1)	30% RULE (RULE 2)	STATIONED FORCES — ACTIVE TOTALS (RULE 3)	ZONAL CEILINGS (RULE 4) — TOTAL	ACTIVE FORCES — CENTRAL EUROPE	CENTRAL REGION	IGB AREA
MBT	40,000	12,000	3,200 (3,400) <10,800>	20,000 (22,600) <51,500>	11,300 (12,000) <37,000>	10,300 (11,000) <32,200>	8,000 (8,500) <19,800>
ARTY	33,000	9,900	1,700 (1,800) <6,600>	16,500 (17,700) <46,200>	9,000 (9,400) <28,000>	7,600 (8,100) <23,700>	4,500 (4,800) <12,300>
ATC	56,000	16,800	6,000 (6,400) <10,800>	28,000* (28,800) <53,500>	20,000 (21,000) <37,500>	18,000 (19,100) <33,200>	11,000 (11,500) <20,000>
HELOS	3,800	1,140	—	1,900 (2,200) <3,500>	—	—	—
AIRCRFT	11,400	3,420	—	5,700 (6,700) <13,500>	—	—	—
MANPWR (US/SOV)	—	—	.275M (.305M) <.600M>	—	—	—	—

NOTES:　* – OF 28,000 TOTAL, NO MORE THAN 12,000 CAN BE AIFV
( ) – NUMBERS INDICATE CURRENT NATO INVENTORY
< > – NUMBERS INDICATE CURRENT WARSAW PACT INVENTORY

reductions to parity, a storage requirement could significantly complicate the ability of either side to gain an advantage through surprise. An aggressor would have to choose between initiating an attack with much of his equipment still in storage (and therefore subject to easy destruction), or removing the equipment from storage, thereby exposing an aggressive intent, and enabling the defender to take timely countermeasures.

The absence of NATO proposals for regional subceilings applicable specifically to either of the flank regions is also not an oversight, flaw, or quest for unfair advantage. Given the geographic proximity of the Soviet Union to (especially) Turkey and Norway, and because the Soviets will remain better able than Alliance members to rapidly reinforce the flanks, legal subceilings on Soviet force concentrations would not necessarily provide a meaningful impediment to Soviet aggression or intimidation. On the other hand, NATO's ability to deter such possibilities could require Alliance members to reinforce the flanks in peacetime, unfettered by any treaty prohibition. Thus, the absence of flank subceilings in NATO's proposals was deliberate.

WARSAW PACT PROPOSALS FOR REGIONAL SUBCEILINGS

The WTO has put forward two distinct sets of regional reductions proposals. However, only the second set of proposals is receiving serious consideration in the negotiations, and even this set includes elements unacceptable to NATO. Specifically, the WTO proposals include regional subceilings on aircraft, helicopter, and manpower, and they make no distinction between equipment in storage and equipment in active units; these are omissions that would seriously prejudice the outcome in favor of Pact retention of a large asymmetry in active forces.

As depicted in Map 6.6, the most current WTO proposals divide the ATTU region into four distinct zones: North, Center, South, and Rear.[20]

The subceilings proposed for each of these zones, as portrayed in Figure 6.2, would not require NATO (or the Pact) to undertake a vastly disproportionate share of the overall ground force TLE reduction in any one zone. Rather, reductions could be distributed in a manner roughly proportional to the quantities of such TLE that currently exist in each zone. And inasmuch as the WTO appears to have dropped its initial insistence on regional manpower, aircraft, and helicopters subceilings (these subceilings are, however, still depicted in the figure inasmuch as they remain a part of the official Pact proposal), this may not prove to be an insurmountable obstacle either. Finally, the Pact proposals to cap combat aircraft at 4,700 and helicopters at 1,900 (which are not depicted in the figure because the details have not yet become a part of the formal Pact proposal) must also be seen as honest attempts by the WTO to speed the negotiation.[21]

As of this writing, the WTO has not tabled any proposals concerning TLE in storage. They have, however, indicated tentative acceptance of storage requirements provided that (1) NATO agree to a ceiling on the amounts of TLE that could be counted as "in storage," and (2) TLE held in low strength (cadremanned) units on national territory be counted the same as TLE in storage. NATO has agreed to the first provision and is considering the second.

On one hand, it is remarkable indeed that the negotiations have progressed to a point where so many differences have been narrowed or resolved. On the other hand, as spectacular as the progress in CFE has been, it should be kept in proper perspective. Clearly, WTO leaders made a conscious decision before the negotiations had even begun that the structure of the Pact proposals would mirror NATO's negotiating framework. The Pact was apparently also predisposed to telegraph

Map 6.6
ATTU Regional Zones

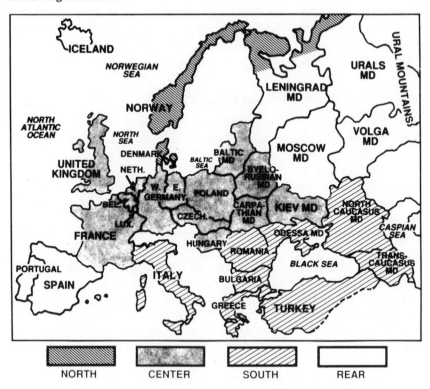

immediately WTO acceptance of what many in the West had believed impossible: Pact reductions to numerical parity with NATO in tanks, artillery, and armored troop carriers. As the quid for this quo, however, Alliance leaders had to overcome their initial hesitance to include helicopters, aircraft, and manpower as prospective TLI.

Both sides met the challenge. However, the two sides have nevertheless remained wed to some significantly different positions. The remainder of this chapter, then, is devoted to the task of highlighting the key differences that separate the sides, and to recommending possible—which is to say, potentially "mutually acceptable"—solutions.

THE PROSPECTS FOR A CFE AGREEMENT:
A TENTATIVE APPRAISAL

As noted previously, both NATO and the WTO have proposed that each side reduce to no more than 20,000 tanks and 28,000 ATCs in the ATTU area. Such ceilings would require the WTO to reduce more than 35,000 tanks and 30,000

Figure 6.2
Pact Proposal #2 (NATO Hltf Data—Pact Counting Rules)

RULES / SYSTEM	ALLIANCE CEILINGS	SUFFICIENCY (ONLY IMPACTS ON SOVIETS)	STATIONED FORCES	REGIONAL CEILINGS			
				NORTH	CENTRAL	SOUTH	REAR
TANKS	20,000 (23,600) <52,600>	14,000	4,500 (8,000) <10,600>	200 (200) <900>	13,300 (15,800) <35,700>	5,200 (6,600) <10,300>	1,300 (1,000) <5,700>
ARTY	24,000 (17,700) <42,800>	17,000	4,000 (3,400) <6,700>	1,000 (500) <1,000>	11,500 (8,500) <27,300>	8,500 (7,200) <9,200>	3,000 (1,500) <5,300>
ATC	28,000 (28,600) <55,800>	18,000	7,500 (9,000) <10,900>	150 (100) <1,600>	20,750 (19,000) <35,700>	5,750 (7,500) <13,100>	1,350 (1,950) <5,400>
HELOS	1,700 (2,600) <3,600>	1,350	600 (950) <1,300>	30 (20) <70>	1,250 (2,000) <2,700>	360 (400) <600>	60 (160) <300>
AIRCRFT	1,500 (2,900) <3,100>	1,200	350 (700) <600>	30 (30) <130>	1,120 (2,020) <2,100>	290 (720) <640>	60 (150) <200>
MANPWR	1.35M (2.93M) <4.08M>	.92M	.35M (.47M) <.60M>	.02M (.034M) <.093M>	.91M (1.47M) <1.98M>	.27M (.97M) <1.633M>	.15M (.45M) <.374M>

( ) – NUMBERS INDICATE CURRENT NATO INVENTORY
< > – NUMBERS INDICATE CURRENT WARSAW PACT INVENTORY
TANKS: INCLUDES MAIN BATTLE AND LIGHT TANKS
ARTY: INCLUDES TUBE, MORTAR AND MRL GREATER THAN 100MM
ATC: INCLUDES APC AND AIFV
MANPOWER: EXCLUDES PARAMILITARY FORCES

HELOS: INCLUDES ATTACK AND ASSAULT; EXCLUDES 130 PACT TRAINING AND 1,700 NATO TRAINING AND OTHER HELICOPTERS

AIRCRAFT: INCLUDES AIR FORCE AND NAVAL BOMBERS AND FIGHTER/BOMBERS; EXCLUDES 6,500 PACT AND 2,500 NATO TRAINERS, RECCE AND FIGHTER/INTERCEPTORS.

ATCs, whereas NATO's reductions would amount to no more than about 2,500 tanks and 1,000 ATCs if NATO's definitions and counting rules were adopted. Under these circumstances, it is inconceivable that NATO could continue to refuse persistent Pact demands for the inclusion of less than 2,000 allied light tanks under the 20,000 tank ceiling. It is conceivable, however, that the WTO will simply elect to not press the issue. As a practical matter, the WTO has more than twice as many light tanks as NATO. In either case, the WTO will probably get what it wants.[22]

The prospect for an agreement on artillery is also bright. By mutual agreement, the WTO and NATO dropped anti-tank weapons from the artillery category.[23] This movement seemed to portend imminent agreement on other differences as well. However, eliminating the gap between NATO's proposal for a ceiling of 16,500 and the Pact's own proposal for a ceiling of 24,000 remains a potential challenge. NATO has less than 18,000 pieces of "accountable artillery," whereas the WTO has more than 50,000. NATO has not been prepared to permit the WTO to have more artillery than the Alliance (even if both sides were entitled to the same number). Alternatively, the WTO has not been prepared to accept a substantially smaller ratio of artillery to tanks and ATCs than Pact doctrine and force structure have heretofore demanded. Finding a solution to this problem has been difficult.

Having made a great deal of the principle that both sides should reduce to TLE levels below the levels of the lowest side, the WTO will continue to have difficulty explaining why this should not be the case for artillery. On balance, it seems likely that a compromise will emerge. NATO will probably have to find a way to accept an artillery ceiling higher than 16,500; perhaps as a quid pro quo for Pact acceptance of the 30 percent sufficiency rule ceilings on Soviet tanks, ATCs, etc. And for its part, the WTO will have to agree to a ceiling lower than 24,000. For example, a ceiling of roughly 18,000 for all artillery (tube, MLRS, and mortars) might be made to appear slightly below current NATO levels (with a little creative counting), but it would at least meet Soviet doctrinal parameters for defensive sufficiency. This level would obviously be higher than NATO would prefer, but it would also be well below the artillery density Soviet doctrine suggests is required for a successful attack.

Differences over the ATC definition and counting rule may not be all that difficult either. Here, however, the differences have had less to do with finding a level that both sides could live with, and more to do with applying the definitions and counting rules that either side has proposed. Both NATO and the WTO have large numbers of ATC look-alikes (i.e., vehicles that look similar or identical to ATCs, but which are not used to transport infantry). Despite NATO's insistence on a "look alike, count alike" rule for helicopters and aircraft, neither alliance has been prepared to accept the inclusion of ATC look-alikes under the agreed-upon 28,000 ceiling. Raising the proposed ceiling on ATCs is, of course, one possibility. Putting ATC look-alikes into a new category of TLE is also a possibility, especially inasmuch as a requirement to also capture other Armored Combat Vehicles (ACVs) is receiving the attention of both sides.[24]

Whereas NATO had sought initially to reduce only the combat vehicles that it perceived to be the most threatening (tanks, artillery, and ATCs), both sides have more recently become concerned about the circumvention potential extant in any types of armored vehicles that might be left totally unconstrained. An ACV category has, therefore, begun to receive serious consideration both as a means to constrain such a potential and as a means to deal with the ATC look-alike problem.

Neither NATO nor the WTO has been eager to take the lead in proposing a higher ceiling on ATCs. Furthermore, NATO has been loath to abandon entirely its position on "look alike, count alike," and neither alliance has been prepared to undertake the politically contentious task (within its own alliance, and with the other side) of proposing a ceiling and subceilings for a whole new category of TLE (i.e., ACVs). One possible solution might be to include ACVs (and ATC look-alikes) under a stabilizing measure. This would require both sides to report the numbers and locations of all such vehicles and—potentially—also limit the gross number that could be in active units located anywhere in the ATTU. Such a *droit de regard*, if combined with a strong "noncircumvention" provision, might satisfy the concerns of both sides. It would, however, also soften NATO's position on "look alike, count alike."

NATO's insistence on a subceiling of 12,000 for AIFVs in the ATC category is also likely to complicate the ATC issue. Whereas NATO currently has far less than 12,000 ATCs that fit the AIFV definition, the WTO has more than twice that number. From the perspective of some NATO members, it was important to keep open Alliance options to eventually acquire a substantially greater number of AIFVs than NATO has already fielded. Other NATO members were insistent that NATO's ATC proposal deny the WTO an option to retain all of the Pact's existing, very modern, and very potent BMP model AIFVs. Twelve thousand simply emerged as a compromise between these different Alliance perspectives; Pact interests were not considered.

A logical case can be made, however, that the WTO will not elect to retain an ATC force composed only of BMPs. To be sure, the BMP is a superior offensive weapon system, but it lacks cargo space suited for support to infantry in the defense. Thus, like NATO, the WTO may simply elect to retain a mix of AIFVs and less sophisticated but more versatile ATCs of other types. If so, a WTO counterproposal for some AIFV ceiling (e.g., 14,000) may be forthcoming and acceptable to NATO, especially if ACVs and/or look-alikes were included.[25]

Helicopter definitions and counting rules do not appear to be quite so complex, although the look-alike problem is prominent here as well. NATO has proposed a definition that includes only armed helicopters, and the reduction proposal is equitable in its treatment of the helicopters on both sides. That is, although the WTO would be required to take somewhat larger reductions in order to meet NATO's proposed ceiling of 1,900 (which the Pact has now agreed to), both sides will gain a much desired cap on the other side's ability to field much greater numbers of these potentially important weapon systems. Furthermore, by excluding transport helicopters, each side will achieve greater certainty that the other could not in the future substitute attack helicopters for much less threatening transport types.

That said, both sides have large numbers of helicopters that, while designed and utilized primarily for transport requirements, could be armed and employed as combat helicopters. In fact, both sides also currently possess armed helicopters of the same type(s) as their transport helicopters.[26] Although difficult, this problem should not be permitted to stall an agreement. These re-roled transport helicopters generally lack sophistication when employed in an attack configuration, and they do not present a major circumvention potential. The verification problem can also be resolved, either by counting only those that are armed (but with a reporting requirement for the transport variants as well), or by eliminating the combat variants and modifying all helicopters of that type to make it impractical to convert them rapidly into combat helicopters. At the same time, however, the WTO should have to agree that NATO's "look alike, count alike" rule will be applied strictly to all future helicopters.

Such an approach may help resolve an important difference concerning combat aircraft. From the very beginning of the CFE negotiation, an aircraft reduction was expected to be one of the most contentious issues that would have to be faced. Although NATO ended the initial suspense by agreeing to include aircraft in some form, this modest but important concession was followed immediately by NATO air proposals that bore little resemblance to the WTO's proposals. Specifically, NATO's definition and counting rule credited the Pact with 13,500 combat aircraft of all types, and NATO with only 6,700 comparable Alliance aircraft. The initial WTO definition, on the other hand, captured about 3,000 NATO and WTO "strike" aircraft on each side (if Western data were used; and fewer Pact aircraft if Pact data were used).[27] As noted above, other kinds of combat aircraft (fighter-interceptors, intermediate-range bombers, and combat-capable training aircraft) were not included by the WTO. Nor were land-based naval aircraft of any kind.

Since October 1989, WTO leaders have been sending signals that an expansion of the accountable aircraft types to embrace all types of "frontal aviation" might be possible. If so, the Pact was prepared to accept a common ceiling of 4,700. What the Pact is still not prepared to accept, however, is the inclusion of land-based naval air without the inclusion of NATO's sea-based aircraft. The Pact has also been adamant that its training aircraft and its strategic forces (not only its long-range bombers, but also its PVO fighter-interceptor aircraft) not be subject to negotiated reductions or ceilings of CFE. NATO's current proposals are nowhere compatible with these Pact positions as of this writing.[28]

It remains to be seen whether the differences can be bridged. NATO is very unlikely to agree to Pact proposals for a limit of 1,500 on "strike" aircraft; nor is the subsequent Pact proposal for aircraft in frontal aviation likely to find much favor either. Despite the fact that both sides currently have roughly the same number of aircraft in units and designed to perform ground attack and tactical air defense functions, no Alliance member is prepared to consider seriously deep cuts if all NATO aircraft are included, and especially if large numbers of Pact aircraft are excluded. NATO has depended heavily on the quality, quantity, and versatility of its aircraft both for Alliance conventional roles (ground attack and air defense) and for nuclear deterrence. Moreover, NATO is most unlikely to accept the WTO contention that the very large advantage enjoyed by the WTO in other types of aircraft (not to mention offensive surface-to-surface missiles and surface-to-air air defense missiles) would not leave the WTO in a commanding position following a deep reduction in NATO's premier air defense and ground-attack assets.

On the other hand, the WTO is certain to reject NATO's air proposals, which would leave the WTO at a self-perceived qualitative disadvantage without the quantitative offset the Pact has heretofore viewed as the sine qua non of the air balance. As a practical matter, NATO and WTO air forces are structurally very dissimilar. The majority of NATO aircraft are "multi-role"; that is, they are capable of performing both air defense and ground-attack missions. Many WTO aircraft, on the other hand, currently tend to be single-role types; this accounts in part for the larger number of Pact airframes.[29]

Single-role distinctions will be difficult for the WTO to sustain in the future. Not only are multi-role aircraft more efficient and cost effective, the potential for multiple capabilities will simply be hard to avoid for technological reasons in future, state-of-the-art aircraft. This fact could make the WTO's proposal both highly subjective and difficult to sustain in practice. And while NATO's most modern aircraft probably do have a qualitative edge over most current WTO aircraft, the qualitative gap has been closing rapidly. Thus, there is a natural reticence on the part of Alliance members to agree to anything other than an across-the-board parity in the numbers of combat aircraft of all types.

The solution, if there is one, will demand that both sides make major concessions, not just to the other side, but—far more important—toward what will have to be practical, vice legalistic, compromises. A Pact proposal for a modest reduction in NATO's combat aircraft, in exchange for the exclusion of only the older types of training aircraft on both sides, might, for example, be negotiable. In return, however, the WTO would have to accommodate NATO's concerns about the asymmetry in other combat-capable aircraft and, in particular, in the Soviet PVO air defense aircraft. If the Pact is unable to do this by agreeing to a comprehensive air ceiling, both parties might have to consider less traditional compromises. For example, a Pact proposal for reductions to something less than strict numerical parity, overall, but requiring only very modest reductions to NATO's aircraft, might be acceptable to both sides if the de facto ceilings on all types of aircraft "evaporated" at a specific date—for example, the turn of the century. Such an outcome would at least ensure (1) that most of each side's immediate concerns were met, and (2) that neither would have to sign an agreement that it would later find legally binding and permanently disadvantageous.

A path to the more traditional kind of solution may, however, also exist. Were the WTO able to demonstrate that its trainer aircraft could not be refitted for combat roles, the quantitative disparity between the two sides could at least be narrowed. And if each side could also be assured (e.g., in a "side letter," such as that proffered in SALT II) that the number of the other side's naval aircraft would remain stable, the potential for some artificial, offsetting compensation for sea- and land-based naval aircraft on both sides might offer a further reduction in the current asymmetry. Finally, NATO might be able to agree that current types of PVO aircraft be excepted, provided of course that all "future" fighter aircraft (of any type) were included under the agreed-upon ceiling.

Suffice it to say that a not very different approach has already been accepted for anti-tank weapons that have a potential to be used as artillery. In order to resolve the artillery definition and counting rule, both sides agreed that existing anti-tank weapons with a caliber greater than 100 millimeters would be excluded, but that future weapons of a type that could be used as artillery would count under the artillery ceiling. It is hoped that this precedent will not be forgotten during the negotiation of the combat aircraft and helicopter definitions and counting rules.

Manpower ceilings are unlikely to be as contentious as aircraft. NATO's proposal for a cap of 275,000 on only U.S. and Soviet manpower "stationed" outside national territory in Europe may, for example, be addressed seriously by the WTO. There have already been indications that the Soviets intend to reduce their force levels this much anyway. Also, most Eastern European governments would welcome such an outcome. Furthermore, there appears to be a growing possibility that the Soviets may even propose a lower ceiling (perhaps 200,000) on stationed U.S. and Soviet forces.[30] Ironically, during his State of the Union Address, President Bush seized the initiative and proposed lowering the ceiling of U.S. and Soviet forces to 195,000 in the Central Region, with the allowance of 30,000 additional U.S. forces outside the zone to account for geographical symmetry.

Concerning the regional subceilings, while much could also be said of the similarities and differences between NATO and WTO proposals to regionally constrain the distribution of permitted TLE, three aspects are of major importance. First, the WTO proposals seeking to regionally constrain aircraft, helicopters, and manpower (as well as tanks, artillery, and ATCs) are going to be rejected totally by NATO. Fortunately, the WTO does appear ready to concede its position on this issue. Next, the WTO's proposal to include Italy in the Southern Region is also unacceptable.[31] It is inconsistent with the actual orientation of Italian forces (i.e., they are oriented on the Central Region) and quantitatively self-serving (i.e., NATO would be required to take reductions in the South, even though NATO is below the proposed Pact ceilings for ATCs and artillery in the Center). Thus, the WTO will also need to concede its position on this aspect of any regional outcome. Finally, there are the WTO regional reduction proposals that seek to cap the total number of active and stored TLE located in each of four subregions— in the center, rear, and on the northern and southern flanks. Both sides may have to give a little in order to resolve the storage issue. That is, the WTO proposals for combined ceilings on active and stored TLE can probably be combined with NATO's proposals for ceilings only on TLE in active ground force units.

The Pact concern is that NATO, and in particular the United States or FRG, might exploit the absence of any constraint on stored TLE, and that this could give NATO a huge reinforcement advantage in the Center Region. A secondary concern is, of course, that allied intentions to store TLE in Germany will be perceived as an implicit requirement for the Soviets to store equipment in Eastern Europe (a possibility that the Poles, as well as various members of NATO, would like to prevent, and about which the Soviets do not appear all that enthralled either). That said, if the WTO can accept NATO's proposals for regional ceilings on TLE in active ground forces, NATO should be prepared to accept limitations on the amount of ground force TLE that could be counted as "stored" in Central Europe (or anywhere else in the ATTU). And provided the two sides can also agree on the minimum quantities that would have to be stored, and on the maximum that could be counted as stored, this should satisfy the first Pact concern.

This solution assumes, of course, that the WTO will not persist in its demand for TLE ceilings so low as to prevent NATO from retaining its POMCUS holdings and very modest quantities of war reserve stocks (WRS) either in the Central Region or under the ceiling applicable to "stationed" TLE. While NATO and, in particular, the United States can afford to reduce substantially the quantities of tanks, artillery, and ATCs currently maintained in WRS, the WTO should not expect NATO to agree to POMCUS/WRS limits that would preclude the Alliance from achieving a mobilizable and sustainable forward defense of the IGB. Room for compromise exists. As an illustration, the overall ceilings on tanks in active units in the Central Region could be 10,300 (NATO's proposal for the Central Region), with NATO agreeing that no more than 3,000 (the difference between the active ceiling and a total ceiling of 13,300 tanks in the WTO proposal) could be counted as stored.

The Central Region problem would appear to disappear, provided the storage issue is resolved and Italy is included. If this were indeed the case, either side should be able, with only modest adjustments, to accept the remainder of the other side's regional proposals for ground force TLE. The ceilings on TLE in the WTO's "rear region" do not appear substantially different from NATO's proposals for all of Central Europe. And although the Turks have expressed some initial concern, the option to retain cadre-manned units (vice stored TLE in the IGB Region) should not present an insurmountable problem either. Thus, the only remaining issue could be some form of constraint on TLE located on the flanks.

This may or may not remain an important sticking point. That is, given the size of the Soviet reductions under CFE, the flank reinforcement problem may be a canard. On the other hand, the principle behind NATO's proposal could still be difficult to concede politically. Clearly, the Pact's very low proposed ceilings for the northern flank would leave Norway exposed, and some fig leaf of a Pact concession may be required. For example, if the sum of the regional subceilings were greater than the overall ATTU ceilings on TLE, NATO might be able to strike a compromise that would satisfy all Alliance members and the WTO.

This also assumes, however, that Turkey will not continue to take strong exception to the Pact's inclusion of the Kiev MD in the Central Region.[32] The Turks view Soviet forces in Kiev as a threat to Turkey and insist that the Kiev MD be included in the Southern Region. Issues like these may not appear major, but they are frequently among the most difficult to resolve. Furthermore, the Turks also remain concerned about providing the Soviet Union an option to retain the WTO's entitlement to stored equipment in cadre-manned units that the USSR would be free to locate on the southern flank. Suffice it to say that these Turkish concerns are real to the Turks, and they will need to be taken seriously by other members of the Alliance if NATO is to resolve the remaining regional distribution and storage issues.

That said, the significant point to derive from this discussion of regional zones and ceilings is that the Pact's evolving set of zonal proposals seems to be coming progressively closer to meeting most of NATO's concerns. The Italian issue still has to be resolved with the WTO, but most of the other issues tend to be more concerned with intra-Alliance differences than with NATO–Pact differences. If Turkish concerns can be satisfied, for example, the raw numbers in the WTO's regional proposals for ground force TLE ceilings might be made acceptable to NATO. Alternatively, NATO's regional proposals, if supplemented to resolve Pact concerns about TLE in storage, should be acceptable to the WTO.

A final issue that will nevertheless require resolution is NATO's proposal for destruction of excess TLE within 2-3 years of active treaty enforcement. For the moment at least, the WTO does not appear to be contesting NATO's proposal for mandatory TLE destruction. On the other hand, much of the equipment being removed from Eastern Europe as the result of Pact unilateral reductions is also being removed to facilities east of the Ural Mountains. NATO will undoubtedly attempt to hold the WTO accountable for destroying the difference between what the Pact purported to have in the ATTU in January 1989 (59,000 tanks) and what it has agreed to have at the end of the reduction period (20,000 tanks).[33] It is entirely conceivable, however, that the WTO will claim that the tanks it removed from the ATTU prior to a CFE agreement should not count. Were this to occur, the prospect of an agreement might be dashed. Despite the number of Pact tanks that would remain (and still be subject to destruction), an act of bad faith on the part of the WTO would probably jeopardize treaty ratification by the U.S. Senate, not to mention other NATO governments. One can only hope that both sides will avoid the temptation to circumvent the destruction provision by preemptively removing TLE already declared and currently subject to negotiation.

The other destruction issue is, of course, concerned with timing. The WTO may not be able to destroy in two to three years the more than 80,000 TLE items that it would potentially have to destroy. Much will depend on a determination of what constitutes "destruction" for treaty compliance purposes. If total destruction were required, or if there were agreed-upon provisions for "converting" certain TLE in ways that would make them unusable for military purposes, the process could be very time-consuming. In any case, both sides would do well to consider interim destruction provisions that could be carried out quickly, while permitting each side to salvage usable parts (like engines, expensive electronic components, etc.) prior to commencing the more laborious and time-consuming process needed to achieve full elimination.

CONCLUSION

It has not been difficult to describe CFE measures that could substantially enhance military security and stability in Europe. As noted, NATO's current CFE proposals would go a long way toward achieving these ends, and the WTO's counterproposals seem to indicate WTO willingness to endorse most if not all of the NATO initiatives. Clearly, the equal lower ceilings on TLI would bound the gross quantitative offense-defense relationship. NATO's proposed 30 percent sufficiency rule, and the proposed limitation on TLE in "stationed, active" forces would further ensure that this balance could not be upset suddenly by the Soviet Union (or, for that matter, by any other state). Early warning could be enhanced through the placement of a sizable portion of the residual equipment in monitored storage. And the subceilings on ground force TLE in active forces in each of the geographic regions would constrain offensive capabilities, backed by capabilities for rapid reinforcement, sufficient to deter or defend against either a surprise attack or a more fully generated large-scale offensive. Finally, the reductions and constraints on combat air forces, helicopters, and manpower proposed by NATO would complement reductions to tanks, artillery, and ATCs.

In short, reductions to levels adequate for deterrence and defense, complemented by appropriate stability measures to ensure the inadequacy of those levels for offensive operations, could substantially improve the security of both NATO and Warsaw Pact. However, armament ceilings will probably not be sufficient to sustain a stable balance unless force modernization is also tempered, albeit by mutual self-restraint. As a practical matter, military capabilities will change constantly due to new technologies employed in new organizational arrangements, using new techniques. A process that weds modernization and change to evolutionary mutual adjustment should be sought. CFE proposals for greater transparency, effective verification, and periodic consultation would seem the best available means to this end.

As alluded to at the beginning of this chapter, stability and security will also ultimately depend on more than the military dimension of the East–West situation. In the final analysis, both alliances must reach out politically, economically, commercially, and socially in ways that will cement the potential for new, and much more cooperative, relationships. Only then will lasting security and stability be assured.

On May 30, 1989, the heads of state from all of NATO's member countries issued a joint declaration in which they pledged to match progress in arms control with, among other things, expanded economic and trade relations, exchange in technological and managerial fields, integrated efforts to address common environmental and social problems (like terrorism and drugs), and initiatives to expand scientific cooperation, resolve long-standing disputes, and stem the uncontrolled spread of dangerous military technologies. In short, NATO's leaders provided a clear statement of their vision of a more cooperative and less confrontational world. Furthermore, the military, political, economic, social, and other dimensions of NATO's proposals for achieving that vision were made explicit.[34]

As suggested by this chapter, the first step toward the objectives described in this vision can and should be taken by the Warsaw Pact. Pact acceptance of the large, asymmetrical reductions called for in NATO's CFE proposals is precisely what is required. Much greater military security and stability in Europe would be achieved, and this achievement would unquestionably remove the current most difficult impediment to constructive political, economic, commercial, and other relationships.

NOTES

1. Phillip A. Karber, "Strategic Significance of the Western Conventional Arms Control Proposal: In the Context of the Gorbachev Unilateral Reductions and the CFE Negotiations in Vienna," Testimony before the Senate Armed Services Committee, April 6, 1989, pp. 1–6.

2. Phillip A. Karber, *NATO–Warsaw Pact Force Levels in a Conventional Arms Control Context*, Vol. 2, *Atlantic-to-the-Urals Summary*, Washington, D.C.: BDM Corporation, August 11, 1989, passim.

3. "Negotiation on Conventional Armed Forces in Europe: NATO Objectives," in *United States Arms Control and Disarmament Agency (ACDA) Arms Control Update*, March 1989, No. 12, pp. 4–5; and Phillip A. Karber and John H. Milam, "Conventional Force Reduction in Europe: A Comparison of NATO and WTO CFE Proposals," Presentation before the New Alternatives Workshop: Arms Control and Technology, May 25, 1989, pp. 1–8. The proposed subceiling on Armored Infantry Fighting Vehicles (AIFVs) is intended to cap the number of more sophisticated and lethal turretted fighting vehicles that could be retained as a part of each side's total entitlement to ATCs, which would also include armored personnel carriers. For the United States and others in NATO, the distinction is between our Armored Personnel Carriers (APCs), most of which are of the M113 variety, and AIFVs like the U.S. Bradley fighting vehicle and German Marder. On the Pact side, the BTR is considered an APC, whereas the BMP is considered an AIFV. The 1,200 ceiling on AIFVs would not require NATO to reduce any AIFVs, but the WTO would be required to eliminate roughly half of its current AIFV holdings.

4. Karber and Milam, "Conventional Force Reductions in Europe," pp. 10–11. The Pact's Armored Fighting Vehicle (AVF) definition appears to be roughly coincident with NATO's definition of Armored Troop Carriers (ATC). The one notable difference appears to be NATO exclusion of armored reconnaissance vehicles.

5. "Declaration of the Heads of State and Government Participating in the Meeting of the North Atlantic Council in Brussels (May 29–30, 1989)," Press Communiqué M-1 (89) 21, NATO Press Service, May 30, 1989, p. 4.

6. Briefing by Mr. Thomas Marshall and Dr. Charles Bailey, "CFE: Overview and Status," July 20, 1989, Science Applications International Corporation, 1710 Goodridge Drive, McLean, Virginia 22102.

7. "Declaration of the Heads of State and Government," pp. 4–5.

8. Several allied nations, to include especially the FRG, have indicated an intent to take manpower reductions (e.g., Bundeswehr 2000) and were willing to be included in a broader NATO manpower reduction proposal in order to justify these reductions politically.

9. *ACDA Arms Control Update*, pp. 4–5; and Karber, *NATO-Warsaw Pact Force Levels*, p. 9.

10. Karber and Milam, "Conventional Force Reduction in Europe," p. 14.

11. Ibid., pp. 15–16.

12. Ibid.

13. NATO's "Conventional Forces in Europe: The Facts," Brussels, Belgium: NATO Press Information Service, November 25, 1989, passim; and Warsaw Pact's "Correlation of Forces In Europe," Moscow, USSR: Novosti Press, 1988, passim.

14. "Declaration of the Heads of State and Government," pp. 4–5.

15. March 9, 1989 Proposal by the Delegation of the Warsaw Pact to the CFE Negotiations, Vienna, Austria, "Conceptual Approach to the Reduction of Conventional Armed Forces in Europe," translation by USIS, March 9, 1989, pp. 2–6.

16. *ACDA Arms Control Update*, pp. 4–5; and Karber and Milam, "Conventional Force Reductions in Europe," pp. 10–11.

17. Ibid.

18. Ibid.

19. The destruction of equipment in excess of agreed-upon limits was included as an explicit element of the "Declaration of the Heads of State and Government," p. 5.

20. Michael Gordon, "Warsaw Pact Offers Details of Its European Arms Proposal," *The New York Times*, May 31, 1989, p. 15.

21. Ibid; and discussions with members of the North Atlantic Assembly, June 13. Also see FBIS-EEU-89-128, July 6, 1989, p. 1. Translated from *Rude Pravo*, "CSSR Delegate Outlines Pact CFE Proposal" (in Czech), June 30, 1989, p. 7.

22. Karber, *NATO-Warsaw Pact Force Levels*, passim.

23. The definition and counting rule for artillery was agreed upon in Vienna in October. Current types of anti-tank weapons of a caliber greater than 100 mm were not included; however, any future weapons of this type that have the potential to be employed as artillery will count against the ceiling and subceilings applicable to artillery. Those ceilings have not yet been established.

24. The WTO first raised the issue in March 1989. The Pact's definition of AFVs included reconnaissance vehicles, whereas NATO's proposal was only for limiting troop (i.e., infantry) carriers. In response to NATO's proposal, the WTO frequently cited the circumvention potential that would exist if only some of the major armored vehicles were captured. In December 1989, NATO tabled a proposal that is intended to address this Pact concern, but which would require that the ATC ceiling (28,000) also be adjusted.

25. This idea was, in fact, raised for discussion on December 13, 1989, when NATO tabled its proposal to include ATCs in an expanded ACV category. "Declaration of the Heads of State and Government," passim, but especially pp. 7–10.

26. Karber, *NATO-Warsaw Pact Force Levels*; and per discussions with Brigadier Robin Grist, British Military Attaché in Washington, and Colonel Claus Oldhausen, his West German counterpart, in November 1989. NATO's members are continuing to struggle with a helicopter definition that does not prevent Alliance members from acquiring attack helicopters in the future. The Turks are concerned about being left out, and the French are concerned about the impact on the French helicopter industry.

27. Michael D. Scanlon, "Conventional Armed Forces in Europe (CFE) Negotiations: Facts and Figures," CRS Report to Congress, Congressional Research Service, Library of Congress, October 30, 1989, p. 14.

28. Ibid.

29. United States Government Memorandum U-427/DI-5, "NATO CFE-Related Aircraft Reference Aid," July 17, 1989; and discussions with British Vice Air Marshal (Retired) Tony Mason in July 1989.

30. Molly Moore and George C. Wilson, "Pentagon Drafts Major Cuts in Forces, Weapons," *The Washington Post*, November 28, 1989, p. 1; and John D. Morrocco, "Defense Department Grapples with Massive Spending Cuts," *Aviation Week and Space Technology*, November 27, 1989, p. 16.

31. March 9, 1989 Proposal by the Warsaw Pact, "Conceptual Approach to the Reduction of Conventional Armed Forces in Europe," translation by USIS, March 9, 1989, pp. 2-6.

32. Ibid.; and discussions with Vladimir Kulagen, Soviet Foreign Ministry, in April 1989.

33. The destruction of TLE in excess of agreed-upon limits was an explicit element of the "Declaration of the Heads of State and Government," p. 5. In October 1989 the destruction proposal was tabled in Vienna.

34. "Declaration of the Heads of State and Government," pp. 7-10.

7

Verification

In October 1989, at the beginning of round three of the CFE negotiations, both NATO and the WTO presented (tabled) proposals for information exchanges, stabilizing measures, and verification. (See Figures 7.1 through 7.3). Both indicated an intent to insist on effective verification through measures that would include the detailed reporting of TLE quantities by unit designation and geographic location. And both proposed intrusive On-Site Inspections (OSI) at all reportable locations. Finally, each side tabled proposals to constrain activities that might be perceived as threatening to the other side. These constraints are known as stabilizing measures.

The final CFE verification regime is probably the single most important element of the round three proposals. In addition to OSI, the final regime might include monitors at storage sites (a NATO proposal) and at exit–entry points (a WTO proposal), observer teams to verify adherence to the stabilizing measures (much as is already being done under the Stockholm agreement), and remote sensors and aerial overflights (similar to the President's Open Skies proposal, which is also under consideration by NATO and the WTO). The important similarities and differences between the verification proposals tabled by NATO and those tabled by the WTO will be discussed at greater length. For now, suffice it to say that Pact insistence on continuous monitoring at exit-entry points (EEPs) could become very contentious. The other differences appear to be more negotiable.

With respect to the information exchanges and stabilizing measures, there were many similarities and few differences. There do not appear to be any "treaty-stoppers"; however, the proposed constraints on exercises, reporting requirements for transit of TLE through the ATTU region, and prior notification requirements for the call-up of reservists could present significant difficulties. These and other aspects of the proposals tabled in round three can be summarized as follows:

Figure 7.1
Exchange of Information

MEASURE	NATO	PACT	REMARKS
REPORT OF INFORMATION ON LAND, AIR AND AIR DEFENSE TO INCLUDE:			NOTE: PACT PROPOSAL EXCLUDES AIR DEFENSE UNITS
● UNIT ORGANIZATION	✔	✔	NATO: BATTALION/PACT: REGIMENT
● PERSONNEL STRENGTH	✔	✔	NATO: ONLY FOR UNITS WITH TLE PACT: ALL REPORTABLE UNITS
● TLE (#, LOCATION, UNIT DES)	✔	✔	
● TLE IN: STORAGE DEPOTS TRAINING REPAIR FAC	✔ ✔ ✔ ✔	✔ ✔ ✔ ✔	
ALSO PROVIDE INFOR ON: ● PARAMILITARY FORCES ● BRIDGING (AVLBs) ● U.S./SOV STATIONED FORCES	✔ ✔ ✔	✔ ✔	PACT DOES NOT ADDRESS

- Limitations on Military Exercises. NATO proposed a limit of one exercise per nation every two years for exercises involving more than 40,000 troops and 800 tanks. Notification would have to be given one year in advance. By contrast, the WTO's proposals are more stringent. The WTO has proposed that each alliance limit the number of its large-scale exercises to one per each three-year period. The WTO also wants a two-year prior notification. In addition, the WTO wants a prohibition on more than three simultaneous exercises of over 25,000 troops, and it wants each alliance to limit itself to no more than six exercises per year involving more than 25,000 troops. The WTO has yet to specify what ceilings would be placed on TLE densities in such exercises, but it has indicated an intent to add such ceilings later. These may or may not prove to be a problem for NATO. What seems likely to be a problem, however, is the included requirement that NATO apportion the permitted exercises among its 16 members. For France, which is not a member of the military command structure, the WTO proposals also imply its subordination to NATO's structure, which the French do not now accept.

- Limitations on the Call-up of Reservists. NATO proposed that any nation intending to call up more than 40,000 reservists notify all other participants of its intent 42 days in advance. The WTO did not specify the levels that would require notification, but did indicate that call-ups by either alliance above some unspecified level should not only be notified in advance, but also should be limited to once every two years. Furthermore, the WTO wants a limit on the number of simultaneous call-ups by the individual members of either alliance. For the same reasons that Warsaw Pact proposals for exercise constraints were a problem for NATO, these proposals may also present problems.

- Limitations on the Movements of Forces. NATO proposed that any nation intending to move more than 600 tanks, 400 artillery pieces, or 1,200 ATCs from one zone to another (within the ATTU) be required to give 42 days advanced notification. By contrast, the WTO wants limits as well as notifications for movements of TLI (to include

Figure 7.2
Stability Measures

MEASURE	NATO	PACT	REMARKS
NOTIFICATION OF CALL-UP OF RESERVISTS	✔	✔	NATO: 40,000/PACT: TBD
NOTIFICATION OF MOVEMENTS • THRESHOLDS • ADVANCE NOTIFICATION • DURATION • PROVISIONS FOR EEPs • SPECIFY ROUTES, TIME, ETC	 ✔ ✔ ✔ 	 ✔ ✔ ✔ ✔ ✔	 E.G., NATO: 600 MBT/PACT: TBD 42 DAYS IN ADVANCE REPORT IF GREATER THAN "X" DAYS MOVEMENT ACROSS REGIONS THRU EEPs PACT PROVISIONS EXTREMELY DETAILED
MONITORED STORAGE • LIMITS ON ACTIVE FORCES • REMOVAL PROVISIONS • MAINTENANCE PROVISIONS	 ✔ ✔ ✔		NO PACT PROVISIONS FOR STORAGE 16,000 MBT/14,500 ARTY/25,500 ATC E.G., 600 MBT - 42 DAYS NOTIFICATION 10% REMOVAL FOR MAINTENANCE
LIMIT ON BRIDGING EQUIPMENT • LIMIT ON ACTIVE UNIT AVLBs • REMOVAL FROM STORAGE	 ✔ ✔	 ✔ ✔	 NATO: 700/PACT: TBD 42 DAYS NOTICE/NO MORE THAN 50
CONSTRAINT ON SIZE OF MILITARY ACTIVITIES	✔	✔	NATO: 40,000 TROOPS/800 MBT PACT: 40,000 TROOPS/ "X" TLE
INFO EXCHANGE ON MILITARY SPENDING		✔	INFO ON VOLUME AND STRUCTURE
RESTRUCTURING OF FORCES		✔	

aircraft, helicopters, and manpower) above some unspecified level, regardless of whether that movement is into or out of the ATTU, through the ATTU (e.g., en route from the United States to the Middle East), or between zones. And the WTO would restrict all such movements to specified exit and entry points. These proposals are not likely to be accepted by NATO. The requirement to report transits of the ATTU is unacceptable to the United States.

• Monitored Storage. NATO's basic proposal was discussed in Chapter 6. Not discussed, however, were the related stabilizing measures, to include inspection rights, and rules related to the temporary removal of TLE from storage. NATO's proposal calls for monitored storage but does not specify how this will be accomplished. The WTO has called for permanence of regular inspections of stored TLE. NATO has further called for 42 days prior notification of any removal of TLE from storage, and limitations of 600 for tanks, 400 for artillery, and 1,200 for ATCs. Also, the NATO proposal would require that TLE removed from storage be returned within 42 days (except that up to 10 percent could be removed as necessary, and without prior notification, in order to accomplish essential maintenance functions, etc). Similar rules were implied for TLE in low strength (cadre-manned) units—which NATO has agreed to in lieu of storage—but details were not provided. The WTO has yet to formally agree to NATO's storage proposals, nor has the WTO tabled storage proposals of its own. On the other hand, the measures tabled by the WTO do specifically call for the verification of TLE located at permanent storage sites.

• Restructuring of Forces. The WTO proposals included a vague proposition that both sides restructure their forces to make them less capable of offensive action. Over the

Figure 7.3
Verification Measures

MEASURE	NATO	PACT	REMARKS
DECLARED SITES			
● OSI W/NO RIGHT OF REFUSAL	✔	✔	QUOTAS TBD/LIMITS ON DURATION
● OSI MEANS - GROUND	✔	✔	
AERIAL	✔	✔	NOT SPELLED OUT FOR NATO
EEPs MANNING	?	✔	MAJOR PACT PROVISION
NTM	✔	✔	NO USE OF CONCEALMENT TO IMPEDE NTM
NON - DECLARED SITES (OSI W/RIGHT OF REFUSAL)	✔		NOT RECOGNIZED BY PACT - ALL SITES DECLARED (CBT, CS, CSS)
MONITORING STORAGE SITES	✔	✔	NATO ESTABLISHED MODALITIES PACT PLACEHOLDER LANGUAGE ONLY
MONITORING OF REDUCTIONS			
● ELIMINATION/DISTRUCTION	✔	✔	INCLUDES DISBANDMENT OF UNITS
● CONVERSION OF EQUIP		✔	NATO ONLY RECOGNIZES DESTRUCTION
● RIGHT TO INSPECT	✔	✔	NATO: NO QUOTAS/PACT: QUOTAS TBD
MONITORING STABILITY MEASURES	✔	✔	PACT REFERS TO MONITORING RESIDUAL FORCE ACTIVITES
AERIAL INSPECTION	✔	✔	PLACEHOLDER LANGUAGE FOR NATO
MEASURES FOR VERIFICATION FOR HELO AND AIRCRAFT			
● MEASURE INCLUDED	✔	✔	PLACEHOLDER LANGUAGE FOR NATO
● NTM/OSI	✔	✔	PACT: RIGHT TO USE ELECTRONIC/OPTICAL MEANS AT AIRFIELDS
● FREE ACCESS TO AIRCRAFT		✔	COCKPIT AND ARMAMENT INSPECTION
COOPERATIVE MEASURES FOR NTM	✔	✔	NO OBSTRUCTION OF NTM
CONSULTATIVE FORUM	✔	✔	TO RESOLVE AMBIGUITIES
OTHER NATO MEASURES:			
EXIT/ENTRY POINTS (EEPs)	✔	✔	PLACEHOLDER LANGUAGE FOR NATO EXTENSIVE USE OF EEPs BY PACT
PRODUCTION MONITORING	✔		PACT DOES NOT ADDRESS ISSUE
OTHER PACT MEASURE:			
DATA VERIFICATION	✔	✔	ON SIGNATURE, COMING INTO FORCE OF TREATY, FOLLOWING REDUCTIONS AND YEARLY

last year, Pact spokesmen have floated the idea of a "thin-out zone" of 50–100 kilometers along the Inter-German Border; this idea may be at the core of what the WTO has in mind. As tabled in Vienna, however, the WTO's restructuring proposals only mention (1) limiting military activities and mobile attack formations in forward areas, (2) withdrawing bridging equipment from forward units, (3) changing the permanent locations of land forces with attack weapons, and (4) refraining from construction of new facilities or expanding old ones for stationed forces. NATO has no comparable proposals and is highly unlikely to agree to any of the aforementioned WTO propositions.

- Exchange of Information. Both sides have called for an exchange of detailed information on land and air forces. NATO proposes that the location of all TLE in units, in storage, and at other temporary but frequently utilized locations (e.g., maintenance facilities) be declared. Unit identifications, the authorized personnel levels in TLE-holding units, and the geographic coordinates of each unit headquarters would also have to be provided down to battalion (land) and squadron (air) level, along with a declaration of the quantities of TLE in those units. The WTO has tabled similar proposals but has suggested that the data be disaggregated only to regimental level (for land and air forces; but for air forces, the WTO would provide data only on aircraft in "frontal aviation" units). The WTO proposal would, however, require reporting on the locations and personnel strength of all units—combat, combat support, and combat service support—whereas NATO's proposal does not require reporting on the location or personnel strength in units other than those with TLE holdings.

Furthermore, the WTO proposal does not include a separate provision for reporting on manpower, to include U.S. and Soviet manpower levels in stationed forces. Given NATO's proposal to limit only U.S. and Soviet stationed manpower, NATO has included a provision requiring an exchange of information on the manning of U.S. and Soviet stationed forces. Finally, both sides have similar proposals concerning the frequency with which the exchanged data should be updated, the means of communicating the information (i.e., through diplomatic channels), requirements to prenotify changes in organizational structure 42 days in advance, and requirements to immediately notify changes of 10 percent or more in the troop strength of reportable units. (It should be noted that the WTO has not agreed to 10 percent as the trigger for this provision, and it wants five days in which to submit the report). Also, NATO has proposed that data on TLE not in military units—for example, ATCs in police and/or paramilitary units—be governed by the same rules that govern the data exchange on accountable TLE. The WTO's proposals have not mentioned the issue of TLE in units other than military units; thus, neither is there a WTO proposal for a reporting requirement.

Readers interested in the details in these and other, less important NATO and WTO proposals are encouraged to read Appendix D and Figures 7.1 through 7.3. Issues such as the WTO's proposal to exchange information on military spending, NATO's noncircumvention provision, and proposals tabled by both sides for limits on Armored-Vehicle-Launched Bridges (AVLBs) are discussed there. Suffice it to say that the AVLB constraints are trivial, the WTO's proposal for an exchange of information on defense budgets is mostly propaganda, and the noncircumvention provision tabled by NATO, while important, is not likely to present a problem for the WTO (unless, of course, the Soviets refuse to count the tanks and other TLE already removed from the ATTU to areas east of the Ural Mountains).

VERIFICATION

In general terms, the verification regime advanced by NATO, and that which was tabled by the WTO, have much in common. Both sides view verification as a national (vice alliance) responsibility, but with a possibility that collective verification efforts could be pursued at the discretion of either side. Areas of significant disagreement are relatively few, and they can be summarized as follows:

- Declared Sites, without Right of Refusal. NATO has proposed that declared sites be subject to on-site inspection without right of refusal. Other sites that might contain TLE would also be subject to on-site inspection; however, both sides would retain a right to limit or refuse such inspections. The WTO does not mention undeclared sites; on the other hand, the WTO proposals for a comprehensive information exchange (all combat, CS, and CSS units) would increase the number of accountable and, therefore, inspectable sites. Both sides have proposed that there be quotas for on-site inspections. NATO has called for limiting the number of inspection days that each nation must accept (a "passive" quota), and that this quota be based on the quantity of TLE in that country's forces and on the size of its geographic area. The WTO has proposed that the quota be equal for each alliance, that the inspecting alliance be permitted to determine who will do the inspecting, and which of the other alliance's members will be subject to the inspection. Neither side has specified how many inspections each side will be permitted to conduct (the active quota) or any one nation required to receive (the passive quota). The active quota will probably be between 100 and 200 inspections, with a slightly higher number available for the conduct of an initial baseline inspection (in the first 90 days after treaty entry-into-force).

- Baseline Inspections. Both sides want a right to conduct a baseline inspection of the other side's military facilities in order to determine the accuracy and sufficiency of the data that were exchanged upon entry-into-force. The WTO has further proposed that a second baseline inspection should be conducted at the conclusion of the reduction period, and that locations emptied of all TLE should also be subject to separate closeout inspections (above and beyond the number of inspections permitted by the quotas already discussed). By contrast, NATO envisions accomplishing these latter inspections in conjunction with routine inspections, and within the agreed-upon quotas.

- Elimination Monitoring. Whereas NATO demands a right to continuously monitor the "destruction" of TLE, without quotas, the WTO proposals call for "elimination or conversion," and quotas for the presence of inspection teams at elimination sites and at "temporary armament storage areas." The latter are clearly envisioned by the WTO as essential to the temporary storage of the large quantities of TLE that the WTO must eventually eliminate (or convert), and they indicate WTO estimates that the process may take longer than the three years called for in NATO's treaty implementation proposal (see Chapter 6). While NATO may, and probably will, accept the WTO's concept of temporary storage, NATO's members are likely to insist on the right to continuously monitor elimination activities and any storage sites that are required incidental to the elimination process.

- Exit–Entry Points and Production Facilities. NATO inserted language in its October proposals to the effect that provisions would be required for monitoring TLE entering the ATTU either from production facilities located in the region or at an entry point (e.g., a port, rail or road crossing, or airport). Similarly, monitoring might also be required at exit points in order to ensure that the "count" of TLE located within the ATTU was kept accurate. Since October, however, NATO's members have come to realize the enormity (and probably futility) of such a massive bookkeeping undertaking. That is, the expenditure of human and dollar resources would be unlikely to prevent or even deter cheating if the other side were of a mind to cheat. And if the other side were not of such a mind a periodic exchange of historical data would suffice, at least for those occasions where the quantities of TLE entering or leaving the ATTU were small (e.g., amounting to less than one battalion or squadron). Furthermore, NATO's European members were chary about the idea of any permanent or semipermanent on-site presence of inspectors either at EEPs or at production facilities. Such inspections might provide the other side opportunities for military and industrial espionage.

Many of the Soviet production facilities (which are the arsenals of the WTO) are located east of the Ural Mountains; a fact that also dissuaded NATO from pursuing the concept of on-site production monitoring. That said, the WTO has not proposed production monitoring at all, and NATO is not likely to propose monitoring the output of production facilities at any place more sensitive than "holding areas" located in proximity to those facilities.

EEP monitoring remains a major concern, however. The WTO proposals tabled in October are replete with passages specifically calling for a continuous or regularized on-site presence at EEPs. Furthermore, the WTO apparently envisions many such points, not only at the boundaries of the ATTU but also at the boundaries that separate the several zones within the ATTU. Thus, although NATO has abandoned the idea of EEPs as an important component of its verification regime, the WTO has given EEPs considerable emphasis. This has only raised Alliance concerns about the espionage potential that any massive presence of WTO inspectors would create for the European members of NATO.

- Verification of Aircraft and Helicopters. Alliance concerns about the potential of Pact verification proposals to also entail intentions to conduct espionage were further heightened when the WTO tabled its optical and electronic means of observation. The WTO also proposed that each side be permitted a quota of opportunities (which might be accomplished either on-site or from the air by aerial inspectors and cameras).
- Aerial Inspections. Both sides have alluded to the possibility of aerial inspections. So far, however, only the WTO has proposed that such inspections be subject to quotas, with "no right of refusal." In all probability, serial inspections will become a part of NATO's proposal when it is fully tabled. Furthermore, the two sides will probably use the on-going negotiation of President Bush's Open Skies proposal as a means to also establish the modalities of aerial inspections conducted as part of a CFE verification regime.

VERIFICATION: THE LARGER PICTURE

The preceding discussion of the individual elements of the WTO and NATO proposals for an effective verification regime cannot be divorced from what must be verified. In addition to the reductions and ceilings (and regional subceilings) discussed in Chapter 6, both sides will want to verify the compliance of the other side with the constraints (stabilizing measures) and the information-reporting requirements discussed previously. That said, the "verification regime" (the combination of the cooperative measures—like the data exchange—and the opportunities for on-site and aerial inspections and monitoring activities) must also be concerned with more than the technical compliance of the other side. It should, for example, be equally concerned with promoting security and stability in Europe, and with eliminating the threat of surprise attack and of large-scale offensive actions. In this regard, it must also entail "transparency."

Along with transparency, both sides should obtain the means to rapidly and unambiguously detect changes by the other side that might indicate an aggressive intent, or an intent to alter the military balance in some decisive manner. At the same time, however, the level of transparency should not be permitted to compromise the security of sensitive information, to include industrial secrets. The WTO is unlikely to become confused about the relative intelligence value of the various Warsaw Pact "verification" opportunities. Thus, if NATO enters into a CFE agreement, to include an agreement on verification, Alliance members must ensure that the potential intelligence costs and benefits of the verification regime are in NATO's net interest.

This admonition may appear self-evident and, therefore, of little consequence to the idle reader. It is, however, at the very heart of Alliance problems in deciding on the details and modalities of NATO's verification proposals. That is, NATO must chose between verification measures that will enhance the probability that NTM, complemented by on-site inspections, will detect and confirm any irregularity in the quantities of TLE in the ATTU and/or in any of the regional zones; or, alternatively, NATO might choose instead to place emphasis on achieving greater transparency. If the latter, Alliance members—to include especially the United States—must, however, be confident in NATO's ability to detect WTO cheating or circumvention at levels below those that might be militarily significant.

Recognizably, technical verification during the period in which both sides accomplish force reductions, to include the elimination of large quantities of TLI, will focus on monitoring the accomplishment of these reduction obligations. This does not appear to present difficult verification tasks, or requirements for much intrusiveness. Following the reductions, however, the focus on both sides will probably shift from strict numerical accountability of TLE to a concern instead with accurately and confidently assessing the evolving composition and operational capabilities of the other side's remaining conventional force structure.

For NATO this will translate into requirements for allied Intelligence Communities (ICs) to monitor the size, location, composition, and activities of WTO units, by type (e.g., tank regiments and divisions). Considerable intrusiveness will probably be required. By also intrusively monitoring TLI in storage, and by accounting for TLI production and unit movements into and out of the ATTU regions, the ICs should be able to accurately assess WTO treaty compliance. In this regard, it is important to recognize that allied intelligence organizations are already engaged in nonintrusive intelligence collection and assessments. Their task can, however, be made much more achievable by a CFE transparency regime that will require the WTO to report accurately on the location, unit designation, and composition of all unit and storage holdings, any changes to those holdings, large-scale training activities, production, and TLE transfers. It can be further enhanced by opportunities to observe WTO activities more extensively and to actually inspect intrusively.

An argument is frequently heard that the application of OSI at reportable locations will deter WTO noncompliance at those locations, but that an inability to inspect intrusively at other locations will still enable the Pact to cheat massively. This argument needs to be dealt with on its merits. TLE not associated with unit equipment sets (active or stored), and left unsupported by sufficient CS/CSS infrastructure, does not pose a significant military threat to either side. Even assuming that large quantities of TLE and other equipment could be produced and pooled secretly, without detection by either NTM or CFE inspectors and monitors, it is unlikely that whole regiments or divisions could be manned and trained in militarily significant numbers without being rapidly and unambiguously detected.

The combination of current U.S. and allied intelligence collection activities, and the application of intrusive OSI, permanent monitors, aerial overflights, and other possible CFE verification measures should put the possibility of militarily significant cheating with respect to quantities of TLE well within the range of acceptable risk.

If verification requirements are approached from the perspective of a trade-off between the levels of risk that might be involved in various hypothetical TLE cheating scenarios, and the utilization of scarce intelligence collection resources, the case for focusing CFE verification efforts on achieving transparency (vice "accountability" of individual TLI) becomes even more apparent. Achieving verifiable transparency with respect to Warsaw Pact force structure, modernization rates and directions, training activities, and readiness levels will provide NATO with high confidence in its ability to ensure Alliance security. TLE accountability, on the other hand, is only likely to be of significant value during the period in which excess TLE must be eliminated.

Following the required TLE eliminations, Alliance verification efforts will nevertheless be necessary to deter, or if deterrence fails, to detect the generation of offensive capabilities potentially threatening to NATO. Capabilities for WTO aggression could, for example, be enhanced through an abrogation of the zonal limits in the CFE agreement (through prohibited force concentrations), through a large-scale mobilization and/or reinforcement from outside the ATTU region, or as the result of either legal or illegal quantitative or qualitative force adjustments (e.g., through threatening modernization rates, and/or adjustments to the residual CS/CSS force structure). Furthermore, the possibility that the Soviet Union and/or other members of the WTO might attempt to enhance substantially the combat potential of paramilitary forces must also be monitored adequately. It is with respect to monitoring these kinds of possibilities, and not clandestine tanks, that NATO can achieve the greatest security benefit.

This conclusion may not be entirely obvious. However, if one considers that the WTO has 39,000 more tanks today than it will have following reductions, it is difficult to imagine a scenario in which even a small fraction of the eliminated tanks could be restored without unambiguous detection. Furthermore, it is not at all clear that the Soviet Union could achieve any significant advantage through modest, hard-to-detect cheating scenarios, or that a large, quasi-legal restoration of force structure in areas east of the Ural Mountains would not provide a much more effective, and less risky, avenue for gaining such an advantage. Finally, it seems far more likely that any future Soviet/WTO threat to NATO, if it materializes at all, will result primarily from qualitative vice quantitative enhancements.

NATO's primary CFE verification objective should be to enable Alliance members to determine very early, and with high confidence, whether the Warsaw Pact were preparing for hostilities or otherwise engaged in militarily significant treaty abrogation or circumvention activities. The detection of minor discrepancies in the quantities of permitted TLE would be of little or no probable military significance.

To be sure, NATO's Indications and Warning (I&W) systems already provide a high level of confidence in NATO's ability to detect with no less than several weeks of strategic warning any Soviet/Pact preparation for war. If explicitly tied to the current I&W system, however, the CFE reduction and stability measures, complemented by a robust NTM and OSI monitoring regime, could enhance substantially the ability of Alliance members (especially the United States) to provide much earlier and much more accurate and unambiguous warning of mobilization, reinforcement, and other potentially threatening Pact activities. Ideally, NATO's proposed monitoring regime should also enhance intelligence sharing among NATO allies and facilitate prudent, responsive decisions by U.S. and allied leaders.

It is with this challenge in mind that NATO must come to grips with the task of specifying what can be inspected, and through what means. Some level of intrusive OSI will undoubtedly be proposed. Equally important, both sides can probably tolerate the continuous presence of monitoring teams in areas outside the perimeters of sensitive areas and facilities. Beyond such means, a number of other verification measures are also under consideration. For example, airborne sensors may have great utility in terms of providing an inexpensive supplement to NTM (e.g., if NATO aircraft were permitted to overfly and photograph Warsaw Pact installations and production facilities).

Some of the measures under consideration do not, however, appear consistent with the magnitude of the verification task, or with the need to keep the verification regime focused on the forest, not on the individual trees. Schemes such as the placement of identification tags on each piece of TLE will, for example, be expensive and might do very little either to improve NATO's ability to monitor units, TLE in units or in storage, or illegal TLE located at some unknown, hypothetical stash. Similarly, extensive sensor fields implanted throughout Eastern Europe are virtually certain to be inordinately expensive and of dubious military value should the Warsaw Pact make a conscious decision either to attack NATO or to deliberately violate the agreement. It is with respect to militarily significant circumvention that NATO must focus its verification proposals.

Intrusive OSI of declared units/facilities, complemented by more frequent, but less intrusive, observation through aerial overflight and mobile monitoring teams could significantly enhance the ability of NTM to monitor both Warsaw Pact treaty compliance and activities that might not be treaty violations but that might nevertheless pose a threat to Alliance security.

There are, of course, still other verification means and modalities under consideration by NATO and the WTO. These include the establishment of manned exit and entry points through which all TLE entering or leaving the ATTU or any of the regional subzones would be required to pass. Exit–entry points have obvious heuristic appeal. Were both sides required to transport TLE across borders only at such points, each could maintain accountability of the quantities of TLE entering or leaving an area at the agreed-upon points. Furthermore, any TLE observed entering or leaving that area at other than a declared exit–entry point would obviously raise doubts about treaty compliance. On the other hand, before insisting on an exit–entry regime, the WTO would be well advised to consider the potential costs as well as the alleged benefits. It is far from clear that permanently manning a large number of such points would be cost effective. Posting guards 24 hour per day, 365 days per year, at potential road and railroad junctures, ports, and airfields seems unlikely to be at all productive. Were the other side to cheat, it is not difficult to imagine that the guards could be rapidly circumvented. And if accountability is all that is desired, a more efficient regime could certainly be devised.

In this same regard, care must also be taken with respect to the verification inspections. For example, both NATO and the WTO would do well to reject any requirement that all units and TLE "freeze in place" as soon as an intent to inspect has been announced. If adopted, such proposals could seriously impact on the cost and effectiveness of military training. If unavoidable to ensure adequate verification, the costs would need to be borne; however, this is not the case. Even when on training maneuvers, ground force units and TLE are readily available for inspection by the other side. Accounting for helicopter and air forces absent from garrison locations would, of course, be more difficult. Even here, however, it is the presence of accountable units, and not the number of TLE physically present in those units at the exact time of an inspection, that will provide the best measure of compliance.

Furthermore, given the potential of NTM and/or mobile monitoring teams to continuously observe an airfield prior to an inspection, the removal of a significant number of helicopters or aircraft would be subject to detection. Were this to occur, the onus would be on the inspected party to explain to the satisfaction of the inspectors the relationship of those aircraft to the unit force structure and supporting infrastructure at the inspected airfield.

As these illustrative examples are intended to suggest, verification of a CFE agreement may not be possible in terms of strict, continuous accountability of all TLE. On the other hand, as discussed previously, it should be entirely possible for both NATO and the WTO to verify with high confidence that the other side was not engaged in noncompliant or circumvention activities that could potentially undermine its security, or the stability of the military balance in the ATTU region. And it is with respect to this objective that any judgment about the verifiability of a CFE agreement should be made.

8

Current CSBM Negotiations

Perhaps the most important of all multilateral talks are the Negotiations on Confidence- and Security-Building Measures (CSBM). These talks take place simultaneously with the CFE talks, and both are colocated in the Hofburg Palace in Vienna. For most delegations, the negotiators are the same people for both talks. In earlier chapters we presented snapshots of what the CSCE and CDE processes are, as well as explaining what CSBMs are and their significance to European security. In this chapter we will examine more closely the actual process involved and current proposals under discussion.

THE MANDATE

All negotiations have objectives or desired outcomes. The objectives of the CSBM talks are published in the CSCE Concluding Document, dated January 15, 1989, commonly called the Vienna Mandate. This charter contains five major concerns:

- That the 1986 Stockholm CSBM agreement "was a politically significant achievement and that its measures are an important step in efforts aimed at reducing the risk of military confrontation in Europe."
- That the full effect of the Stockholm measures will depend on their implementation, although initial implementation was encouraging.
- That the Negotiations on Confidence- and Security-Building Measures will "build upon and expand the results" of Stockholm by adopting "a new set of mutually complementary (CSBMs) designed to reduce the risk of military confrontation in Europe."
- That these negotiations will take place in accordance with the 1983 Madrid CSCE follow-up conference concluding document.

- That the next CSCE follow-up conference, to commence in Helsinki in March 1992, "will assess the progress achieved in these negotiations."[1]

The CSBM negotiations' objectives will include expanding existing measures approved in Stockholm and developing new measures. Stockholm CSBMs that include notifications of major military maneuvers, alerts, and other exercises as well as permitting OSI have been largely successful. When we sum the number of notifications, OSI, and observations, we have had 139 such acts since 1987 without one violation. In fact, according to the North Atlantic Assembly:

There have been no indications that any country has cheated; no evidence that any of the exercises inspected have been threatening to any nation; [and that] all countries actually participating in inspections have mounted a significant effort to demonstrate compliance with the verification provisions of the Stockholm Document.[2]

The key note of importance here is that, although the objectives of the Stockholm Document, when agreed upon, are only politically rather than legally binding, the results are notable and in fact have served as a de facto treaty among the 35 participating nation-states. The CSCE forum produces results and is the Europeanwide security forum most favored by all participants.

There are at least eight good reasons why this forum has produced results. According to U.S. Ambassador Jack Maresca, these are:

- This forum is what Europe is—complex, yet manageable.
- This forum results in agreements (not years of frustrating stalemate).
- This is the forum where new ground is broken.
- This is the model forum to challenge conventional alliance-to-alliance talks in new directions such as "Open Skies."
- The Warsaw Treaty Organization breaks down in this forum reflecting the greater degree of autonomy achieved under Gorbachev (since each nation is accountable only unto itself).
- The Neutral and Nonaligned Nations have more interest in this forum and serve as a buffer between alliance viewpoints.
- The forum dilutes the Greece-Turkey problem because Cyprus is represented.[3]

After the autonomous CFE negotiation is concluded, this forum will continue to serve European security issues in the future.

Even with its many successes and its uniqueness among negotiating fora, the CSBM talks do present the appearance of overlap between CFE and the Stockholm agreement, which may become a conceptual blur to readers and the Congress—a major concern of Ambassador Maresca and other delegation members. Keep in mind, however, that the CSBM talks are intended to increase security through data exchanges, on-site inspections, exercise notifications, and the like to make the military forces of Europe more visible and transparent to their neighbors. Perhaps in this trust-building environment of openness true European security may evolve.

THE CURRENT PROPOSAL

In this chapter we will examine the West's proposal formally presented in Vienna. Although five proposals were formally presented in 1989, the Western proposal has been the basis of all discussion in Vienna. Thus, a modified version of the Western proposal ultimately will be agreed upon. The Western CSBM package consists of 12 measures and one "nonmeasure," which is the establishment of the Seminar on Military Doctrine mentioned in Chapter 1. (For a full text of the Western proposal, see Appendix E.) The West's proposal is subdivided into three separate categories:

- Transparency of Military Information.
- Transparency and Predictability of Military Activities.
- Contacts and Communications.[4]

Under the general heading of Transparency of Military Information, there are three separate measures designed to create more openness and confidence.

Measure 1. Exchange of Military Information: Provides for annual information exchanges by the participants concerning their military organization, manpower, and equipment in the whole of Europe. Specifically, the measure requires data on all brigade/regiment level ground combat units and wing, air regiment, or equivalent air force units—for example, peacetime locations, strength, and number of major weapons systems. The measure also includes mandatory notification of unit transfers to new locations, if for more than 30 days, and notification of reserve call-ups of more than 40,000.

Measure 2. Information Exchange on Major Conventional Weapon Deployment Programs: Provides for annual information exchange on the total number of major weapons systems on hand and anticipated fielding of new equipment by equipment model number.

Measure 3. Establishment of a Random Evaluation System Related to the Exchange of Information: Provides a framework for mandatory evaluation visits to check on information submitted in Measures 1 and 2. The number of evaluation visits is the higher number of a minimum of three or a number that equals 10 percent of the number of reported brigades and wings (for larger forces).

Under the general heading of Transparency and Predictability of Military Activities, there are six measures that build upon the CSBMs previously agreed upon in Stockholm.

Measure 4. Enhanced Information in the Annual Calendar: Addresses additional information to be included in annual calendars of military activities. The additional information includes military activity/exercise location, duration, size, and unit designations to operational command level.

Measure 5. Enhanced Information in Notification: Is similar to Measure 4 but includes mandatory information on number of reservists and fixed-wing aircraft sorties by mission function to be used during exercises.

Measure 6. Improvements to Observation Modalities: Builds upon the existing observation CSBM, which lays out how observers will be accommodated. In effect, this measure standardizes the scheduling, briefings, and provisions to be furnished by the host nation.

Measure 7. Changes to Thresholds: Requires notification of activities whenever the number of troops meets or exceeds 13,000 or if more than 300 tanks are participating. Airborne and amphibious operations are also subject to formal notification requirements when troop numbers meet or exceed 3,000.

Measure 8. Improvements to Inspection Provisions: Improves upon existing inspection procedures by including the conduct of a preliminary aerial survey of the area to be inspected as well as inspection team composition requirements that limit the team's size to no more than six members.

Measure 9. Lowering the Threshold for Longer Notice of Large-Scale Activities: Simply reinforces the notification requirements concerning military activities involving more than 50,000 troops.

Under the general heading of Contacts and Communication, there are three final measures to the Western proposal that seek to improve the principle of military openness:

Measure 10. Improved Access for Accredited Personnel Dealing with Military Matters: Seeks to ease normal travel restrictions imposed within a nation-state for duly accredited military observers and inspectors.

Measure 11. Development of Means of Communication: Provides for use of normal diplomatic communications channels, with a designated point of contact on a 24-hour basis, but allows for additional means of communication such as public telex lines.

Measure 12. Equal Treatment of Media Representatives: Encourages states to grant foreign media representatives access to the observation/inspection activity on an equal basis with host nation media access.

OTHER PROPOSALS

The authors have elected not to reproduce the texts of the six other proposals from the East, the Neutral and Nonaligned Nations, and combinations of individual states. In essence these proposals, with the exception of the East's inclusion of naval forces, are variants of the Western proposals or are self-serving in nature. The Eastern naval CSBMs, though, are significant and are summarized below.

MEASURES COVERING NAVAL FORCES

— Notification within an agreed period of time of naval exercises involving 20 or more combat ships (1,500 or more tons displacement each); or 5 or more ships of which at least one has a displacement of 5,000 or more tons and is equipped with cruise missiles or aircraft; or over 80 naval aviation (including carrier-based) combat aircraft.

— Notification of transfers of naval forces involving entry into or movement for agreed-upon distances within the zone of application for CSBMs of groups consisting of ten or more combat ships (1,500 or more tons displacement each); of five or more ships of which at least one has a displacement of 5,000 tons or more and is equipped with cruise missiles or aircraft.

— Notification of marine force transfers (by sea or by air) to the territory of another State starting from a level of 2,000 men.

— Notification of naval aviation transfers to the territory of another State starting from a level of 30 combat aircraft.

— Invitation of observers to naval exercises involving 25 or more combat ships (1,500 or more tons displacement each) or 100 or more combat aircraft.

— Limitation of major naval exercises to a level of 50 combat ships.

— Limitation of the duration of naval exercises to 10-14 days.

— Limitation of notifiable exercises conducted by each State (including cases of its participation in joint exercises) to a level of 6-8 exercises in a calendar year.

— Prohibition of notifiable naval exercises in zones of intensive shipping and fishing as well as in straits of international significance.

— Inclusion of information on notifiable naval activities in annual calendars of notifiable military activities to the extent determined by the relevant provisions of the Document of the Stockholm Conference.

— Conclusion of an agreement on measures to prevent incidents in the sea area and air space adjoining Europe.

EDITORIAL COMMENTS

It is clear from the definitions used that the U.S. Navy is the principal target of the East. The fact is that the U.S. Navy has been less than enthusiastic, and our Vienna CSBM and CFE negotiators immovable, concerning the inclusion of naval forces. Political pressure on the Bush administration from other Western political leaders may force a "cave-in." We think that the Navy is correct in refusing to enter the CSBM business because international law in general is "messy" at best, and such limits on naval operations may ill serve broader U.S. interests. Also, we should not disregard the Madrid mandate, which excludes independent naval operations, and thus remember this functional link to be fair in our argument.

The CFE Mandate (Appendix A) excludes nuclear weapons, naval forces, and chemical weapons. Since we have a forum for discussing chemical weapons and have declared that SNF talks will start upon successful conclusion of the CFE talks, only naval disarmament remains as a subject for a future mandate. The United States may, at some future date, agree to negotiations on naval forces; however, such conditions would surely be driven by unilateral, U.S. budget constraints, or by a shift in public opinion, and not by any clear strategic objective.

Prior to the development of the CFE Mandate, defense analysts were wondering what bargaining chips were available to NATO to induce the Warsaw Pact to agree to large, asymmetrical reductions. On December 7, 1988, President Gorbachev announced the now famous unilateral withdrawal of troops and tanks from Eastern Europe. It became suddenly clear that NATO did not have to concern itself with offering up concessions on the Strategic Defense Initiative or other important bargaining chips such as naval forces. Mr. Gorbachev's rationale for wanting arms reduction was deduced as economic necessity. While the U.S. Navy breathed a sigh of relief, the Soviets have continuously spiked current, rather smooth, negotiations with insistence that naval operations be limited with a Confidence- and Security-Building Measure, or that naval forces be reduced through disarmament talks. Many nations in Europe are also in favor of some kind of constraint to naval operations. How long we can keep the U.S. Navy away from the "cutting" room is anyone's guess, but since we have been successful to date, we should continue to exclude the U.S. Navy from arms reduction talks.

PROSPECTS FOR SUCCESS

The prospects for success are very favorable for adoption of the Western proposal. While the French persisted in delaying progress in CFE, an alliance-to-alliance forum they never liked, they have been quite constructive in the mini-caucuses held weekly by the West. All 35 nations in the CSBM talks sit in French alphabetical order in a forum that France has always championed. Agreement may come in 1990, which would finish these CSBM negotiations. Perhaps the only true impediment to successful agreement is the reluctance of the NNA to end the talks, and thus end their influence, at least temporarily, in European security affairs. The second part of the CDE process, disarmament, is another matter. With the expected CFE treaty in 1990, the participating nations will have to decide whether or not to pursue conventional arms reductions in some form of alliance-to-alliance CFE model, or in the CDE. Should we fail to reach a CFE agreement in 1990 or 1991, the CFE Mandate states that the whole CFE process will become subject to review at the March 1992 full CSCE in Helsinki. Sooner or later we are going to have to readdress our position in CSCE and on multilateral conventional arms reductions overall. It is our opinion that follow-on negotiated reductions should take place within the CSCE process, provided that agreement takes the form of treaty (as in the CFE) and does not remain as politically binding only (as in the CSCE). The CSCE process may be the alternative forum or organization that could replace future political versions of NATO and WTO that are currently being discussed. The group of 35 may very well continue breaking new ground as its 16-year history indicates. This process is successful, remains inviolate, and offers an acceptable alternative to continued alliance-to-alliance talks.

Surely, we will seek to achieve further reductions to improve security at lower levels of forces, at lower levels of cost. NATO's declaratory policy is to immediately initiate Short-Range Nuclear Forces (SNF) negotiations upon successful conclusion of the CFE treaty. This policy was declared by President Bush on May 29, 1989 as a consensus-building compromise to satisfy growing political pressure for such talks in the Federal Republic of Germany. Like other declared policies such as "the reunification of Germany," the United States will find that this one cannot be disregarded or further "qualified" in the name of caution. Preparations and planning for SNF talks have been initiated within the Interagency Group. Unlike the multilateral negotiations in CFE and in CSBM, the nuclear talks will most likely take place on a bilateral basis in the framework established by the successful Intermediate Nuclear Forces (INF) treaty, since France and the United Kingdom have obstinately refused to cooperate in such talks. Furthermore, U.S. declaratory policy states that we will not negotiate to a 100 percent withdrawal of SNF (i.e., a third "zero" option). SNF negotiations will take place after successes in START, CFE, and with or without agreement in CSBM. On the other hand, significant delays in CFE or in START will delay initiation of SNF talks.

NONNEGOTIATED DISARMAMENT

Events in Eastern Europe may have more impact than arms negotiations. Political changes in Poland, Hungary, East Germany, Czechoslovakia, Bulgaria, and Rumania have turned the East into a chaotic quagmire of political counterrevolution. Prior to these breathtaking developments, many non-Soviet Warsaw Pact countries announced their own unilateral arms reductions in consort with those of the USSR. Independent unilateral actions from Eastern and Western nations may well continue in the turbulent times ahead, which will greatly strain the organizational concept of both treaty organizations. The difference between the dissolution of NATO and the dissolution of the Warsaw Pact is "bricks and mortar." NATO was constructed as a political alliance and is managed as such. Its physical plant in Brussels and in other cities in Europe is a fixed asset that can continue to support a variety of Western diplomatic concerns and thus may easily remain in service.

The Warsaw Pact is not anchored in such a concrete foundation. The shutdown of the Warsaw Treaty Organization seems more probable in the intermediate term than the dissolution of NATO. However, a potential solution for the long term rests in utilization of NATO's political structure as a permanent, political Western caucus for further discussions within the CSCE process, the European Economic Community, and other regional organizations and/or processes—a vision shared by the Bush administration.[5]

NOTES

1. Johann Einvardsson, *Draft Interim Report of the Subcommittee on Confidence- and Security-Building Measures*, published by the Internal Secretariat, North Atlantic Assembly, Amsterdam, May 1989, pp. 8–9.

2. Ibid., pp. 2–3.

3. Interview with Ambassador Jack Maresca conducted by co-author Colonel David E. Shaver on September 20, 1989, in Vienna, Austria.

4. All formal proposals are provided a number. NATO's proposal was originally submitted as an outline in March 1989 and later fleshed out or amplified with more substantive explanation. The current number of the Western proposal is CSCE/WV.1/Amplified, dated June 9, 1989. The measures presented in this chapter were transcribed from the original documents.

5. James A. Baker III, Secretary of State, from a speech at the Berlin Press Club; excerpts reprinted in *The Washington Post*, December 13, 1989, p. A18.

9

Future Environment

In the following chapter we will discuss the future environment to bound the role of conventional arms control in national security strategy. To this point we have presented the significant background, objectives, procedures, issues, definitions, and current negotiations in order to prepare the reader for a more academic discussion of "where are we going" in the post–CFE 1990s.

ON STRATEGY

Since the United States and its major NATO Alliance partners have relied heavily on a threat-driven strategy to support military planning, programming and budgeting, the diminishing threat (perception) may logically lead to diminishing military budgets. This in turn leads to diminishing force structure, and the budget spiral continues downward unabated as the threat continues to diminish.[1]

The movement from a threat-driven strategy to a resource-driven strategy has already occurred. Military planners are shifting from worst case global scenarios to multiple, lower-case scenarios, which are more compatible with lower-case budgets and, perhaps, more realistic in application. Of what will this kind of an environment consist? And what can we do now to prepare for this changing national security environment?

The following section, "After Containment: International Changes through a Nonauthoritarian Looking Glass," was written for and presented at the International Studies Association meeting in London on March 29, 1989. The author, Dr. Regina Gaillard, prepared this analysis, prior to the President's "beyond containment" series of speeches, for a panel on "East–West–South Relations into the 1990s: Chaos, Conflict, Containment, or Cooperation?" Put on your thinking cap to grasp this nonauthoritarian world environment envisioned by the contributing author. The thoughts presented herein unlock the mystery of the world of the 1990s and, thus, point the way to the national security strategy most appropriate for the United States.

AFTER CONTAINMENT: INTERNATIONAL CHANGES THROUGH A NONAUTHORITARIAN LOOKING GLASS

by Regina Gaillard

The bedrock of international relations for over 40 years, East–West polarity and its companion, the Western strategy of containment, is being shattered with breathtaking regularity. World reality is changing so quickly and so dramatically that many of yesterday's hypotheses about politics among nations will be invalid tomorrow.

The international relations theory of realism, as introduced concurrently with the era of the Cold War, propounded a view of relations among nation-states based on national interest defined as power.[2] In a case of art imitating life, neorealism, introduced after three decades of cold war,[3] viewed the most favorable international situation as a system dominated by two great powers,[4] and it essentially negated the possibility of structural transformation.

Neorealist power politics is overly dependent on its definition of the action of states in the international arena as "anarchic," without rule, as opposed to hierarchic, implying authority. If we question that the nature of states is simply power struggling, and if we perceive other moral or economic goals of states, we can assume that inter-state alliances formed and sustained by mutual consent between stronger and weaker powers acknowledge a hierarchy. Therefore, over a finite period of time, states acknowledge an authoritarian relationship "whose rightness and legitimacy both (states) recognize and where both have their stable and predetermined place." Furthermore, Hannah Arendt insists that "since authority always demands obedience, it is commonly mistaken for some form of power or violence. Yet authority precludes the use of external means of coercion.[5]

The hypothesis that nation-states acknowledge a hierarchy of authority suggests that U.S. relations with its World War II allies in Western Europe and U.S. and Soviet relations with independent states of the Third World were based on authority rather than power. If these relationships were authoritarian, it follows that their disintegration produces nonauthoritarian relations between states.

This section reviews changes taking place in the East–West and North–South axes of the international system (the arena in which nation-states act) and changes in world dynamics (those areas excluded from the neorealist power equation), and it juxtaposes a nonauthoritarian view against continuing assumptions and expectations by policymakers biased by realism's restricted power orientation. The section concludes that theory based solely on power is, in fact, increasingly unrealistic and not a wholly productive base on which to judge present change or strategies for the future. Rather, the thesis suggests that contemporary change can be better understood through a hierarchical framework of which emerging nonauthoritarian relationships among nations are only a part.

CONFRONTING THE STATUS QUO

International politics, international theory, and international themes developed since World War II have, even if unconsciously, been influenced by the superpower struggle for dominance. We hold dearly to our core beliefs and to what is familiar. The majority of our life experience (for our older readers), if not our entire life experience (for our younger readers), has been a world perceived almost exclusively through the East–West prism.

During this period the lingua franca of international relations and national politics became weighted with a jargon implying agendas rooted in the East–West axis of hostility. "Containment" and "cold war" are the more obvious examples. When the Cold War was extended to the southern arc and became increasingly "hot," we coined a "Third World,"[6] which came to mean the South between East and West.

"National security policy" meant "international security" against the world Communist threat, "global commitments" and "credibility" of the "will" to sustain the war between East and West. In the southern parts of the world, international security became the framework for "national security doctrine" entailing "professionalization" of local militaries and enhancement of their ability to counter insurgencies and "wars of national liberation." Theories of development, underdevelopment, and dependency became weapons in the ideological war between East and West, and between Marxism–Leninism and capitalism. By the 1970s, many shifted their faith to more neutral and optimistic theories of international interdependence and transnational relations.

As we enter the 1990s, the underpinnings for theories developed over the past 40 years are being swept away, and for the most part, we find ourselves running only on the fumes of a vocabulary outdated by real world events. The United States and USSR have made astounding approaches toward further cooperation. Confronted with the new jargon, if not the faits accomplis of Gorbachev—that radical red Russian reformer in Moscow—it is no wonder that after 40 years, many on both sides are fearful of retiring a familiar threat (or perhaps of personally being retired). "Caution" has become the watchword of the status quo.[7] The message is that the war is still on—only the rules of engagement have changed.

THAW ALONG THE EAST–WEST AXIS

The rules of engagement in the East–West relationship are changing, indicating world release from superpower struggle and setting the stage for the new nonauthoritarianism. The thematic clue that a new relationship is emerging is that certain mutually hostile jargon defining the relationship has been changing and a new terminology is being coined. President Bush has tentatively suggested that we should move "beyond containment."[8] Containment as a term meaning conflict has long since been changed to "deterrence."[9] "Peaceful coexistence," a term invented by Lenin connoting ongoing war, was dropped from the lexicon before and after Gorbachev used it again in 1987.[10] It is a reminder to the United States of the collapse of "détente," a word that breathes life into warnings of caution as the United States continues to sit down with the Soviets at the arms control bargaining table.

A joint study prepared over the course of three years by U.S. and Soviet scholars proposed that this new era of U.S./USSR cooperation be delineated by the concept of "sustainable peaceful competition."[11] Robert Legvold, a leading U.S.-Soviet scholar, claims that for the first time in over two decades the United States and USSR are "in phase—both preoccupied with domestic difficulties and both wiser about the limitation of power."[12]

A myriad of East–West meetings have given strong signals that the superpowers are receptive to reducing mutual tensions. They have pledged to continue conventional arms control negotiations, now known as CFE (Negotiations on Conventional Armed Forces in Europe), in Vienna, and U.S. and Soviet leaders can now sit down and discuss regional conflicts as they did at recent summit meetings.[13] The U.S. and Soviet military establishments have not spent thousands of hours looking in on-site observations of each other's training and weaponry and discussing each other's strategy and military doctrine.[14] Brigadier General Hopkins of the U.S. Marines stated that the Soviets have promised to reorganize their forces to assume a defensive posture.[15] Former President Reagan took a giant step toward future cooperation with the East when he signed up the United States to attend the International Human Rights Conference scheduled to be held in Moscow in 1991.

Elsewhere, former U.S. Secretary of State George Shultz commented that "the Soviets have played a remarkably constructive role" in peacekeeping efforts in southern Africa and the other conflict hot points throughout the Third World.[16] It appears that the Soviets told the Angolans and Cubans that "a military solution wasn't in the cards."[17] Since 1983, the USSR has reduced from 22 to 7 the number of African countries receiving its military aid.[18] In El Salvador, the FMLN rebels "are said to have been told by Moscow that even if they did win, the Soviets couldn't become their patrons and they would have to look to the West for help."[19] The Soviet ambassador to Nicaragua announced last November that the Soviet Union had no intention of establishing a military base in Nicaragua or anywhere else in Central America, and that perestroika meant that there are limits to Soviet aid.[20] Moreover, the Soviets agreed in principle, and presumably put pressure on Vietnam, to remove their estimated 100–120 thousand troops from Cambodia.[21]

It is significant that the Soviet Union has been calling on the United Nations (UN) for help in solving its international problems. Questions concerning the Sino-Soviet rapprochement were discussed at the UN under the auspices of Secretary General Perez de Cuellar,[22] and the UN has assumed a larger role in brokering peace agreements in Afghanistan and between Iran and Iraq.[23]

Even as the Soviet Foreign Minister travels through the Middle East to assure the USSR of a diplomatic role in possible peace negotiations, it is apparent that both superpowers have restrained their clients in that area.[24] Moreover, there is a growing mutual conception of the Middle East as the "tar baby" of international politics.[25]

In the far East, a recent study on the Philippines suggests that superpower concepts of spheres of influence "could be turned into a device for international understanding and peace rather than for conflict and war."[26]

U.S. and USSR domestic events have contributed to "a framework of peaceful competition which necessarily envisages cooperation."[27] U.S. deficits in budget, trade, and the national debt, and Soviet economic deterioration have resulted in economic reassessments in both East and West. Political elections and economic democratization in the Soviet Union have been perceived to blur old themes of contention between the superpowers. A late 1988 poll in the United States, reflecting a bipartisan research project, found that 64 percent of Americans agreed that "the U.S. should try harder to reduce tensions with the Russians."[28]

TROUBLES IN THE TRILATERAL WEST

In 1973, the Japanese were invited to join North Americans and Western Europeans in founding the Trilateral Commission. The inclusion of Japanese members in a private, transnational attempt to influence the management of the world economy acknowledged the growing importance of the Japanese in international economic affairs and fostered sanguine ideas of tripartite cooperation and equally sanguine theories of the benefits to be derived from trilateral leadership of an "increasingly interdependent world."[29]

By 1982, the year of the onslaught of the Third World debt crisis, the annual Trilateral Commission meeting was reportedly punctuated by "heated discussions" on mutually antagonistic trade, financial, and national security policies among the Japanese, U.S., and EEC members.[30]

The heated discussions within the Western Alliance have become hotter. "Trade wars," "protectionism," "competitiveness," and "burdensharing" have become the new themes of conflict. "Decline theory" has emphasized the economic dimensions of security.[31] With "peace breaking out" all over the world, "the new ascendency of economic power, rather than simply military strength" is apparently becoming a true measure of national security and well-being. "If military conflict is receding, economic warfare seems to be on the rise."[32] In addition, John Gaddis has warned that "wars most often arise among nations that are economically interdependent."[33]

In *The Political Economy of International Relations*, Robert Gilpin echoed U.S. and European accusations that the Japanese have been using the international capitalist system and its markets with impunity since 1971, when it became apparent that the dollar could no longer support "free-riders.[34] But he claims that at the present time Japanese investment of their record surpluses in U.S. bonds and securities represents more than their fair burdensharing.[35] On the Japanese side, there are increasing signs of restiveness as they play a secondary role in Alliance security decisions and endure increasing criticism.[36]

While the European community looks forward to becoming the world's preeminent economic power after becoming one market in 1992, it also has been flexing its intra-Alliance muscle. High protectionist barriers have been erected against Japan and the United States, and while the United States played the traditional mutual security theme, "Gorbymania" seized Europe. NATO resistance to deployment of the replacement Lance missile system increased as "theological cold warriors" insisted that the Alliance "bargain from strength" in arms control negotiations.[37] Tradition-sundering Gorbachev initiatives and themes of glasnost and perestroika bred not only international differences, but also intra-national political debates on "whither the Alliance?"

DELINKAGE ALONG THE NORTH–SOUTH AXIS

Along the southern arc, theories of "development toward democracy," "underdevelopment," "dependency," and "national liberation" have proved bankrupt. Latin America has turned theory on its head by initiating "democracy without development" of a rational capitalist economic structure. Nor has any form of Marxism–Leninism proved a viable economic model for the Third World.[38]

Development has lost force as an international issue. Third World calls to the North for a New International Economic Order are no longer heard. In the face of mounting debts and sharpening social inequities, the Third World calls for "cooperation rather than confrontation."[39] Third World predilection for the traditional economic theories of development and dependency now translate "cooperation" into "debt relief" and obscure the reality that the Third World is unwilling or unable to help itself. A U.S. study by the Agency for International Development declared that after spending billions of U.S. dollars, developmental aid to the Third World never achieved its objectives.[40] The Soviet Union has reprimanded Third World allies and friends for "economic inefficiencies."[41] In reality, the Third World has become the world's permanent underclass.

Contrary to public repetition by the superpowers of themes recalling "spheres of influence" and "hemispheric security," the United States and USSR have been withdrawing from untenable alliances. Clients of the Soviet Union have been pressured to move from military to political action,[42] and the United States, bowing to its own human rights policy, has withdrawn support from most authoritarian regimes. These tentative steps toward superpower "delinkage" from their clients created a nonauthoritarian international environment in which Syria, Afghanistan, and five Central American presidents, for example, demonstrated that the Third World is able to execute successful end runs around the flanks of the superpowers. The joint Central American decision to disassemble the Contras, made without consulting U.S. authority, not only proved that the South can "brush aside the argument that a policy of containment can be applied" to the the the Third World,[43] but also that the South can exercise power diplomatically within the framework of nonauthoritarian international relations.

In turn, international business has brushed aside the Third World. Multinationals, the ogres of the 1970s, are no longer a Third World issue since many subsidiaries were linked to the deteriorating economies of their host countries.[44] High technology, miniaturization, and changing tastes in the North have increasingly reduced demand for the resources, low technology, and agricultural products of the South, precipitating a worldwide competition for shrinking markets. This negative economic scenario shatters the theories of North–South interdependence that were propounded in an era of expansionary world political and economic policies.

During the next century, world population will double—90 percent of that growth will be in the Third World,[45] widening the gap between the rich and poor nations and exacerbating the already apparent crises of starvation, urbanization, unemployment, environmental waste, and disease. Third World countries have demonstrated that very few of them have the "state-like qualities" to sustain or implement coherent economic and domestic political policies in order to manage the standard responsibilities of the modernizing nation-state.[46]

Internal chaos in the South and its spillover effects on the North have been a subliminal international issues throughout the Cold War. The Nuclear Non-Proliferation Treaty was a remarkable cooperative effort by the United States and USSR to limit the spread of nuclear weapons technology, especially to "unstable and adventurous" Third World countries.[47] Recently, the U.S. Chief of Naval Operations, Admiral Trost, pointed out, although still within a Cold War context, that U.S. concentration on the East–West axis has caused Americans to ignore threats from the South.[48] Former Secretary of State Shultz, speaking at the UN last year, warned that "the spread of weapons in the Third World is not an East–West issue,"[49] particularly at a time of superpower disarmament talks and cooperation in peacekeeping efforts throughout the Third World.

Democratization of the Third World, according to the old theories, would firmly plant the newly developed countries in the world capitalist system. Countries choosing the socialist path would become part of COMECON, the Eastern trading bloc. But today democracy has spawned economic and domestic political chaos throughout much of the Third World, particularly in Latin America, and the chief economic tie of a majority of Third World nations to the world system is through the negative umbilical of their international debt. Similarly, the Soviet Union has denied COMECON membership, in reality a guarantee of Soviet aid, to hopeful satellites—those which, along with their capitalist brethren, are the equally bankrupt and mismanaged socialist states of the Third World.

It is important to note here two positive and possibly mitigating factors in the negative scenario of Third World deterioration and delinkage. First, regardless of whether democracy works in the Third World, there is widespread acceptance of domestic ideals among Third World masses and an expectation that democracy must eventually work for them. Nondemocratic forms of government or at least nonelected governments are increasingly perceived as unacceptable. Second, the phenomenal spread of knowledge of human rights values, not necessarily to or through governments, but directly to people in the Third World and elsewhere, has created what I call a Second Revolution of Rising Expectations.

Both sets of knowledge—democracy and human rights—might be examples of "political learning on a transnational scale."[50] However, the assimilation of these values at lower ranges of national societies, combined with the high expectation level, might initiate a "trickle up" effect from the societal level to, or bypassing, national governments and back into the structure of the international system, creating a positive reinforcement of desirable international values.

At the present time, however (and back to reality), Shahram Chubin, an Iranian security analyst living in Geneva, claims that the United States and USSR have reached what he calls "symmetrical disillusionment with globalism" in the Third World, and that the Cold War there "has perhaps ended,"[51] lessening Northern interest in the South. Whether the cause is superpower economic strains or "Viet-Afghan Syndrome"; or deterioration, debt, or democratization in the Third Word; the chaotic regimes of the South have increased their independence from Northern—both Eastern and Western—political and economic dominance.

EAST-WEST-SOUTH IN THE INTERNATIONAL HIERARCHY

As the possibility of superpower confrontation diminishes in the Third World, the last gasp of the international security theme is expressed in calls for "regional stability" and a "peaceful international order." "Stability" and "international order" indicate rigidity in the face of rapid world changes and a preference for the status quo. In the metaphor of a life, we have spent the majority of it wedded to one all-encompassing theme—containment—simple and familiar. Now that we are in the "passages," we are forced to accept changes over which we have very little control—if we intend to move on to a constructive future.

The demise of the simple, power-structured world as we knew it, and the theories developed from it, are inappropriately termed in negatives of "decline" and "disorder" rather than in terms of change. The systems connoted by the bipolar structure have already been changing. Our old theories and themes are holding us back from objectively contemplating a nonauthoritarian world.

Economic stress within the superpowers and in the South has been the condition most conducive to change. Both the United States and USSR retain their military power while seeking firmer footage in the changing world economic system. The Western alliance—the United States, Japan, and Europe—increasingly see each other as economic rivals rather than military allies, while the South, reeling from the debt crisis, seeks any economic alliance in a desperate search for foreign exchange. Robert Gilpin suggests that we are embarking on an era of bilateralism, regionalization, sectoral protectionism, minilateralization, and nationalization of the world economy.[52] International trade and economic regimes, treaty systems and multilateral alliances formerly dominated by the superpowers are barely holding together, signifying a massive breakdown in bipolar authority even as the United States and USSR retain military power.

Significantly, emerging nonauthoritarian relationships among nations have focused attention on the authority of non-state international institutions, indicating existence of a supra-national hierarchy acknowledged, at least when convenient, by even the most powerful nations. The UN might well move to fill the "peace gaps" as the superpowers extricate themselves from regions of decreasing interest or from areas in which there are no perceived rewards from confrontation. The trend for a greater UN role is being set as the UN "pursues peace" in Cyprus, Lebanon, Afghanistan, Iran-Iraq, the Western Sahara, Southern Africa, and Cambodia.[53] Most important, activist Secretary General Perez de Cuellar plans to attempt an overall Middle East pact, which would effectively eliminate a major source of bipolar conflict and increase diplomatic or economic options regarding that area.

A nonauthoritarian view of international changes can examine power and dynamic factors objectively. Even as many in the West declare themselves vindicated over the bankruptcy of Soviet Marxism, they ignore that Marxism, as applied in the USSR, only catapulted the Russians into the position of world power vis-à-vis the United States that de Tocqueville foresaw in 1832 without benefit of ideology. The United States and the USSR are great territorial and military powers. Similarly, reality in a nonauthoritarian world demands awareness that Western Europe and Japan are, potentially, the third and fourth most powerful military entities.[54] The enormous military capability of the great powers and the proliferation of sophisticated weaponry throughout the Southern arc, particularly to nations with regional power pretensions, suggest the continuation of reliance on hints of force in international relations. Trade wars within the Western Alliance and the need to counter European and Japanese economic infiltration might promote further U.S.-USSR cooperation. Mutual experiences with nuclear accidents and growing Soviet awareness of the nonmilitary impact of industrialization suggest the environment as a major functional area for U.S.-USSR cooperation. Since the Soviets and Americans are increasingly becoming the receivers of investment, goods, and services from the European and Japanese economic giants, the two "dogs of war," leashed together by their nuclear capabilities and economic disabilities, and possibly unleashed from their mutual hostility, might look together elsewhere to exercise their military power and influence.

Nonauthoritarian theory can include in its analyses those circumstances above or below the international nation-state level. Intrastate events such as human rights conditions, overpopulation, drug problems, and insurgency can rationally be opened to scrutiny and enlarge the basis for prediction of future conflict in the world system. The spillover effect in the North of seemingly unsolvable Third World problems and the subtle but long-standing inclination to Northern cooperation on these issues indicates a trend toward containment of the South. Policing chaos within the South through a series of agreements on ad hoc spheres of influence suggests a certain equitable division of labor if U.S. capability for long-range projection of force could be considered a complement to Soviet continental power. However, this employment of force could be interpreted as international consensus on preserving values important to the system rather than enforcing a balance of power.

CONCLUSION

Stubborn adherence to theories of power politics obviates examination of change that could provide richer insights into unifying values and norms, or sources of international conflict within states, in the international arena, and supra-internationally. Retention of overarching military capabilities in the North, the delinkage of the South, and the international perception that competition for economic power is a zero sum game have elicited Hobbesian views of the future of international relations that may not be warranted. Without a nonauthoritarian world view, such dismal theorizing overlooks the learning capacity of humankind in a world of instant communications and possibilities for constraints on state power. Trends toward national democratization and widespread acceptance within societies of ideals of human rights and democracy, in addition to the renaissance of the United Nations, indicate the possibility of a continuation of non-power restraints on states. Combined with negative national economic conditions, these non-power constraints indicate sources of hierarchical authority extending from below to above the international level.

Conversely, axial realignments and delinkages demonstrate that states can maintain nonauthoritarian relations with each other while simultaneously acknowledging the higher authority of the international system as a whole. The mature behavior of immature, chaotic states in international relations, and the inability or unwillingness of strong states to exercise their capabilities, indicate that there are factors other than power that influence the behavior of states. This suggests that both powerful and weak nation-states acknowledge an authority of rules and norms rooted in the hierarchical structure of the international system itself. Whether this international structural authority represents the institutionalization of sovereignty, international law, or societal beliefs is a question for further study.

This section has reviewed contemporary changes and trends from the theoretical point diametrically opposed to the power politics position that the world system is—particularly when not balanced—anarchic. The view from a nonauthoritarian perspective demonstrates that intra-national changes below the level of the international arena and the authority of rules and norms for state behavior that are embedded in the international structure extend their influence vertically into the international system, thus demanding that a hierarchical framework be considered as a basis for future analyses of international relations.

(*Comment*: If we are indeed moving to a world environment that is nonauthoritarian—a world beyond containment—then we may need to develop alternative defense to implement this new national security strategy with its associated implementing policies of caution. With the death of containment as national security strategy, we are left with the justification of its implementing military strategy of forward deployment and associated military resources. In the next chapter we will explore alternatives to our current defensive posture in Europe.)

NOTES

1. Strategic Studies Institute, U.S. Army War College, *How to Think about Conventional Arms Control: A Framework*, Carlisle Barracks, Pa.: SSI, October 1, 1988, p. 80.

2. Hans J. Morganthau, *Politics among Nations*, New York: Alfred A. Knopf, 1963, p. 5.

3. Kenneth N. Waltz, *Theory of International Politics*, Reading, Mass.: Addison-Wesley, 1979.

4. John Gerard Ruggie, "Continuity and Transformation in the World Polity: Toward a Neorealist Synthesis," in *Neorealism and Its Critics*, ed. by Robert O. Keohane, New York: Columbia University Press, 1986, p. 137.

5. Hannah Arendt, "What Is Authority?" in *Between Past and Future*, New York: Viking Press, 1968, p. 93.

6. French demographer and former president of the UN Commission on Population, Professor Alfred Sauvy, writing in the early 1960s, lamented the political distortion of the term "Tiers Monde," or Third Estate, which he had first applied to the developing countries in an article in *L'Observateur*, August 14, 1952. See Alfred Sauvy, *General Theory of Population*, translated by Christophe Campos, New York: Basic Books, Inc., 1969, text and footnote, p. 204.

7. Frank C. Carlucci, *Report of the Secretary of Defense Frank C. Carlucci to the Congress on the FY 1990/FY 1991 Biennial Budget and FY 1990–94 Defense Programs*, Department of Defense, Washington, D.C.: U.S. Government Printing Office, 1989, p. 3. See also *The New York Times*, May 13, 1989, p. 1A, for summary of President Bush's message of caution.

8. "Transcript of Bush's Remarks on Transforming Soviet–American Relations," *The New York Times*, May 13, 1989, p. 6.

9. Paul F. Gorman, "Military Instruments of Containment," in *Containment: Concept and Policy*, Vol. 1, ed. by Terry L. Deibel and John Lewis Gaddis, Washington, D.C.: National Defense University Press, 1986, p. 219.

10. Arthur Macy Cox, "Mr. Gorbachev's Peaceful-Coexistence Ploy," *The New York Times*, June 25, 1988, p. 27. See also Department of Defense, *Soviet Military Power: An Assessment of the Threat 1988*, Washington, D.C.: U.S. Government Printing Office, 1988, p. 19.

11. Graham Allison, "Success Is within Reach," *The New York Times*, February 19, 1989, p. E19.

12. James J. Markham, "The Idea That Democracy Pays Helps Reshape East–West Ties," *The New York Times*, September 22, 1988, p. 1E.

13. Patrick Cockburn, "Third World: Stronger, Bolder," *The New York Times*, June 20, 1988, p. A19.

14. David Ignatius and Michael Getler, "The Great Non-Debate on American Foreign Policy," *The Washington Post*, October 23, 1988, p. C1.

15. Caleb Baker, "Marine Corps' Mission Debate Rekindles as Threat Changes," *Defense News*, September 12, 1988, p. 4.

16. Strobe Talbott, "Of Deficits and Diplomacy," *Time*, March 6, 1989, p. 26.

17. Robert S. Greenberger and Tim Carrington, "Peace Is Proliferating in Many Trouble Spots from Mideast to Asia," *The Wall Street Journal*, July 29, 1988, p. 1.

18. James Brooke, "Cuba Pulls 450 Soldiers Out of Angola," *The New York Times*, January 11, 1989, p. A10.

19. Paul Lewis, "Third World Must Stem Arms Flow, Shultz Warns," *The New York Times*, June 14, 1988, p. A15.

20. Julia Preston, "Soviets Raise Profile, But Not Aid, in Managua," *The Washington Post*, November 6, 1988, p. A37.

21. Ann Scott Tyson, "Moscow to Help Speed Vietnam Pullout," *Christian Science Monitor*, September 6, 1988, p. 11.

22. Ibid.

23. Frederick Kempe, "Perez de Cuellar Wins U.N. New Respect," *The Wall Street Journal*, September 26, 1988, p. 22.

24. Markham, "The Idea That Democracy Pays," p. 1E.

25. Ignatius and Getler, "The Great Non-Debate," p. C1.

26. Leif Rosenberger, "Toward a U.S.–Soviet Agreement in the Philippines," *SAIS Review*, Vol. 9, No. 1, Winter-Spring 1989, pp. 213–26.

27. George F. Kennan, "The Gorbachev Prospect," *The New York Review of Books*, January 21, 1988, p. 3. This is a quote from Mikhail Gorbachev.

28. Markham, "The Idea That Democracy Pays," p. 1E.

29. Regina Gaillard, "The Trilateral Commission; Its Goals and World Policy: Is There a Latin American Connection?" Unpublished dissertation, University of Miami, 1984, p. 70.

30. Ibid., p. 69.

31. The most popularized version of decline theory is contained in Chapter 8, the last, of Paul Kennedy's *The Rise and Fall of the Great Powers: Economic Change and Military Conflict from 1500 to 2000*, New York: Random House, 1987. Kennedy contends that the relative decline of the United States and other powers is caused by imperial overstretch and military spending, which destroys the national economy and, thus, national power. See also David Calleo's works that address U.S. decline, especially in relation to NATO, the most recent of which is *Beyond American Hegemony: The Future of the Western Alliance*, New York: Basic Books, 1987.

32. Ignatius and Getler, "The Great Non-Debate," p. C1.

33. John Lewis Gaddis, "Epilogue: The Future of Containment," in *Containment: Concept and Policy*, Vol. 2, ed. by Terry L. Deibel and John Lewis Gaddis, Washington, D.C.: National Defense University Press, 1986, p. 723.

34. Robert G. Gilpin, *The Political Economy of International Relations*, Princeton: Princeton University Press, 1987, pp. 224–27.

35. Ibid., pp. 337–38.

36. Susan Chira, "Japan Ready to Share Burden, But Also the Power, with U.S.," *The New York Times*, March 7, 1989, p. A1.

37. Stephen F. Cohen, "Centrists Lack the Guts to Respond to Gorbachev," *The New York Times*, September 19, 1988, p. A23.

38. Andre Gunder Frank, conversation at the International Studies Association Annual Meeting, St. Louis, April 1988.

39. Kempe, "Perez de Cuellar," p. 22.

40. David B. Ottaway, "Foreign Aid Largely a Failure, U.S. Report Says," *The Washington Post*, February 21, 1989, p. A5.

41. Preston, "Soviets Raise Profile," p. A37.

42. Douglas Farah, "Salvadoran Guerrillas Step up Armed Attacks," *The Washington Post*, October 20, 1988, p. A34.

43. Charles S. Robb, "Support the Peace Plan and the Contras," *The Washington Post*, January 24, 1988, p. C7.

44. Gaillard, "The Trilateral Commission," pp. 124–26.

45. Anastasia Toufexis, "Too Many Mouths," *Time*, January 2, 1989, p. 48.

46. Yale H. Ferguson and Richard W. Mansbach, *The State, Conceptual Chaos, and the Future of International Relations Theory, 1989*, in Lynne Rienner Publishers, Fall 1988-Winter 1989.

47. Gaillard, "The Trilateral Commission," p. 78.

48. Richard Halloran, "Navy's Top Officer Says Military Cannot Halt Influx of Latin Drugs," *The New York Times*, July 23, 1988, p. 10.

49. Flora Lewis, "Salvador at a Crossroads," *The New York Times*, February 19, 1989, p. E19.

50. Richard K. Ashley, "The Poverty of Neorealism," in *Neorealism and Its Critics*, ed. by Robert O. Keohane, New York: Columbia University Press, 1986, p. 293.

51. Markham, "The Idea That Democracy Pays," p. 1E.

52. Robert G. Gilpin, *The Political Economy of International Relations*, Princeton: Princeton University Press, 1987, Chapter 10.

53. Kempe, "Perez de Cuellar," p. 22.

54. Substantiating the author's argument that we are unconsciously influenced by familiar themes, the major open source for quantitative assessments of military forces, *The Military Balance 1988-1989*, published by the International Institute for Strategic Studies, London, lists individual European countries according to their East–West alliances, pp. 45–93. Even though China is listed as third in some categories (pp. 7, 146–51) and India is a power to consider, I have qualitatively discounted their ability to project extraregional military power.

10

Alternative Defenses

We should now see that new defensive concepts may be necessary in a future environment of "beyond containment." This logic may lead to a military strategy of gradual return of forces to the United States—one that is reversible—for the next decade. Out attention in Europe would turn to conceptual and resource alternative defenses as the drawdown occurs. Dr. Thomas L. Wilborn has provided an interesting survey of existing alternatives in the following section of this book.

NATO STRATEGY FOR POST–CFE AGREEMENT EUROPE: ALTERNATIVES TO FLEXIBLE RESPONSE AND FORWARD DEFENSE

by Thomas L. Wilborn

After a CFE agreement is implemented, flexible response and forward defense may or may not be militarily feasible strategic concepts for NATO, depending on the provisions of the treaty. It is at least possible that capabilities will be cut to such low levels and restrictions on deployments will be so confining that the necessary capabilities for flexible response and forward defense cannot be provided.[1] Whether that occurs or not, the political atmosphere, both in Europe and the United States, is unlikely to provide as strong a basis of support as now exists for the current NATO strategy. In Europe—especially West Germany—support for deploying nuclear weapons on the territory of the FRG already has waned, and the belief that there is a real, military threat from the Warsaw Pact is held by only a small minority of the population.[2] Moreover, annoyance and sometimes anger at the inconvenience of the presence of large numbers of foreign forces are increasing.[3] On both sides of the Atlantic, Gorbachev's initiatives and frustrations with high defense budgets have begun to dangerously erode support for national security programs that promise continuously rising expenditures. In West Germany, financial constraints are reinforced by anticipated serious manpower shortages to further mitigate against maintaining the present NATO force structure, which depends heavily on human resources provded by the FRG.[4] In this kind of political climate, the popular demand for a perceptibly less provocative and expensive force structure and doctrine may be impossible to resist. The nature of the terrain in the FRG, 60 percent of which is wooded, urbanized, or enclosed, also seems to mitigate against a NATO strategy heavily dependent on armor and mechanized infantry.[5]

An alternative approach to the defense of Western Europe, developed before the Gorbachev initiatives and the CFE talks but wholly compatible with them, has emerged in the FRG in the 1970s and 1980s through an extended debate on "nonprovocative," "nonoffensive," or "defensive" defense.[6] These proposals, which hereinafter will be referred to with the less emotional term "alternative defense," were initially motivated by concern for the credibility of the U.S. nuclear umbrella and for the consequences to the FRG of a nuclear war in Europe should deterrence fail. Given the nuclear arsenals of the superpowers, the authors of the proposals were all convinced that the defense of Western Europe following NATO strategy and doctrine would lead to the complete destruction of the territory that is supposed to be defended, especially that of the Federal Republic of Germany. Most of the analysts, who include academics and retired officers, also share a number of other perceptions and concerns. They are convinced that:

- A deliberate, calculated attack by the Warsaw Pact is highly unlikely—one would guess that most of them do not believe it is possible at all. One infers from their writing that a conflict in Europe, if it ever occurred, would probably be an outgrowth of a crisis in Eastern Europe, or possibly a reaction to a conflict elsewhere in the world.

- Interdependence between Eastern and Western Europe is as reliable a basis for long-term European security as military preparations.

- The United States should play a smaller role, and European NATO states a larger role, in the defense of Europe.

- The political divisions of Central Europe, including the potential reunification of Germany, are acceptable, if only because the consequences of trying to change them are too unpredictable to be acceptable.

- At least in Central Europe, "victory" or "defeat" are no longer legitimate military objectives.

- NATO's force structure does not make the most effective use of scarce demographic and financial resources.

As a result of these primary concerns, the FRG analysts of alternative defense focused on force structure and strategies forswearing the use of battlefield nuclear weapons by NATO, and they consciously avoided creating targets suitable for the enemy's nuclear or chemical weapons. The proposals are all explicitly defensive, to the extent of denying NATO the capability of launching a counteroffensive into WP territory at all. While there are differences in the various proposals, as the following descriptions will illustrate, most of them incorporate area defense by light infantry units exploiting the terrain and the capabilities of highly accurate Precision Guided Missiles (PGM).

SOME ALTERNATIVE DEFENSE PROPOSALS

While many alternative defense concepts have been proposed, a few by non-Germans, all of the important variations are represented by the ten listed below. Six are briefly described, followed by relatively detailed descriptions of four of the more influential proposals.

- Frank Barnaby and Egbert Boeker—Centers on a zone 50 kilometers wide along the Inter-German Border (IGB), saturated with sensors and a vast network of underground fiberglass cables for communications, and manned with infantry with sophisticated anti-tank, anti-aircraft, and anti-ship weapons. There would be no heavy armor or other offensively oriented weapons allowed.[7] Of course this concept is not current, given the strong potential for German reunification.
- Jonathan Dean—Features an exclusionary zone, 50 kilometers wide on the NATO side and 100 kilometers wide on the WP side of the IGB. Heavy armor, self-propelled artillery or missiles with more than 50 kilometers range, armed helicopters, and most aircraft would be banned. Otherwise, there are no limitations.[8]
- Norbert Hannig—The major feature is a "fire barrier" or "defense wall"—an uninhabited strip of land four kilometers wide along the IGB loaded with sensors. In time of war, it would be kept under constant fire. Behind the fire barrier, there would be a zone for anti-armor squads for the enemy who survived, and a rear defense farther back.[9]
- Alvin M. Saperstein—Frontier defense forces occupying light fortresses, tank traps, minefields, etc. Maneuver forces, strong enough to halt the enemy forces weakened by the frontier defense, but not strong enough to threaten WP territory, would defeat any enemy formations that survived.[10]
- Gene Sharp—Civilian-based defense, for which Mahatma Gandhi is the main inspiration.[11]
- Franz Uhle Wettler—Reduce the use of NATO armor to open country, and focus the main attention of defense to light infantry. The structure would range from a section to a brigade.[12]
- Horst Afheldt's Area Defense or Chessboard Model—Afheldt's original plan, altered in 1983, was presented in 1976. Its basis is a decentralized network of some 10,000 "technocommando" units, each with 20 men, that would be equipped with highly accurate anti-tank weapons, mines, and light infantry weapons designed for the specific purpose of repulsing the enemy's mobile heavy equipment. The system would cover all of the territory of the Federal Republic. In peacetime, each unit would be stationed and trained in the region of about 20 square kilometers in which it would operate if deterrence failed. As enemy forces advanced into the technocommando unit's jurisdiction, it would automatically go into action, wearing down any hostile advance, and providing intelligence to the other units of the system about the aggressor's capabilities

and the direction of his attack. The network would also be equipped with longer-range target-seeking missiles (but not long-range enough to threaten the territory of the enemy) to supplement the light, short-range anti-tank missiles organic to the technocommando units. Afheldt estimates that each unit would need to destroy three advancing tanks, so that the WP would have to pay a heavy price for conquest. The technocommando units would exploit the technological trends of automation and miniaturization, and also the personnel's intimate knowledge of the terrain being defended. The force would have no tanks, mechanized infantry, armored personnel carriers, attack helicopters, long-range artillery, combat aircraft, or even central headquarters, and thus would present enemy forces with no suitable targets for nuclear or chemical weapons. (Afheldt would accept a supporting air force, but only for the political purpose of deterrence, not warfighting.)

Because this network could prevent the Soviets from a fait accompli and would buy time for a U.S. sea-based nuclear response, even though it would not be capable of defeating or repulsing the advancing force, its author contends that it constitutes a credible deterrent.

Instead of the current force of 775,000 men, Afheldt estimated a need for 340,000 men.[13]

• Afheldt's 1982 Chessboard—Afheldt's 1983 refinement of his original model does not change the basic structure. It still consists of thousands of small infantry units spread over all of West Germany, although it requires more personnel because each squad unit would have 25 men with a 10 to 15 square kilometer area to defend instead of 20 men per unit with responsibility for 20 square kilometers. As before, the system was designed for each unit to slow down and attrit the invader in its area of responsibility, not stop or repulse him. But after going some 50 kilometers, the invader would have lost half his tanks. The light infantry would be backed up by engineer troops and communications specialists (approximately one and seven per square kilometer, respectively). The defense would be highly dispersed and well camouflaged with no movement under fire, thus presenting no suitable target for heavy and concentrated enemy fire. Each squad would destroy several enemy vehicles and report the character and movement of the attackers to the other units of the network.

The members of the squads would live in the neighborhood—they would be in position in a matter of hours. Anti-armor weapons, which could be fired by remote control to protect the defender's position, would be close by. Alternately, any squad could transmit the position of the attacking tank to a rocket launcher in the area of another squad. Troops farther back would be able to prepare barricades and obstacles, including prefabricated structures that may be deployed rapidly. The obstacles will make it easier to locate, bomb, and destroy the advancing vehicle.

According to Afheldt, the system's effectiveness depends upon the invulnerability of the communications system and the accuracy of the anti-armor weapons and rocket launchers. The first problem, he contends, can be solved by fiberglass cables buried underground and secured in peacetime. He believes that PGMs do not now have the accuracy to meet the requirement of each squad attriting three tanks. However, concentrating research on defensive weapons instead of tanks and long-range missiles should soon at least double their lethality, which should provide each squad with an adequate capability. The missiles would be the throwaway type with many redundant holes so that the attacker could not hit all of them even if he could locate them.[14]

- Jochen Loser's Area Covering Defense Model—Jochen Loser, a retired major general, accepts the basic orientation of most alternative strategists, giving special emphasis on effective use of terrain in conjunction with artificial barriers and the dispersal and concealment of the defender, and the exploitation of existing high technology solutions for target acquisition and communications.

Loser's network has three levels. The last, homeland defense area, will not be discussed because it has little relevance to the principles of alternative defense.

— A border defense zone of up to 60 kilometers from the border based on "hunter" forces, manned at two-thirds of authorized strength during peacetime;
— An area defense zone with a depth of 150 to 200 kilometers from the border manned at one-third of authorized strength during peacetime; and,
— A homeland defense area relying on reservists for the remaining FRG territory.

Hunter forces, which would defend the border zone, would be made up of three types of units:

— Hunter company: armed with four rocket systems for use against tanks and infantry, it would have responsibility for 90 square kilometers of territory.
— Combat hunter group: consists of three hunter companies, an assault company, and a blockade company. It would have responsibility for 270 square kilometers and rely mostly on heavy rockets.
— Hunter brigade: the highest level of organization, the hunter brigade would be composed of three combat hunter groups, a heavy rocket company, and an attack helicopter command. The brigade, which could assume division tasks, would work in the border zone and behind it, and could also be used for counterattacks to regain lost territory.

The fortified border zone requires 50 combat hunter units ("shield forces") or at least 30,000 men, all from the FRG. The area defense zone, behind the border zone, would be defended by existing German and allied armored and mechanized bridgades ("sword forces"). They would use terrain, obstacles, fire and hit-and-run tactics to halt a WP attack short of the Weser-Lech line.[15]

- The SAS "Spider and Web" Concept—SAS, the European Study Group on Alternative Security Policy, is composed of a number of military, political, and academic personnel from seven NATO countries and Austria, and its proposal reflects a wide variety of perspectives and interests. As a result, it may have less internal coherence and more complexity than some others proposed by single authors or more homogeneous groups. The proposal by Andreas von Bulow, which the West German Social Democratic Party adopted as part of its official defense policy, is very similar to the SAS scheme.

According to the SAS plan, the defense of NATO's central front would be based on three main elements:

— 450 battalions of network infantry, each assigned to a fixed area, covering a forward zone 50 miles in depth. This zone, approximately ten miles adjacent to the IGB, would be a "killing ground" into which nearby units would concentrate their fire. To reduce the possibility of surprise attack, 150 battalions stationed relatively close to the border would be fully manned in peacetime. The other 300 battalions would have 25 percent of wartime strength during peacetime. Mobilization to full strength would be decentralized, requiring less than a day. There would be no command level above battalion for the network infantry.

— A mobile, protected force of about 150 combat battalions positioned within and slightly behind the area covering scheme. To effectively exploit terrain conditions, the mobile element would break down into three components: armor, cavalry, and light mechnized elements. The mobile element would be organized hierarchically and would be manned at 90 percent of authorized wartime strength.

— The rear guard to protect infrastructure against airborne, commando, and other lower-level threats. It would be a light, interconnected object defense with some mobile formations. It would be formed almost entirely from the reserves. Replacements for all three elements would come from a well-trained pool of reservists in small coherent units.

The basic operational concept underlying the structure has been succinctly summarized by Lutz Unterseher, an influential advocate of alternative defense and the leading English language publicist for SAS, in his contribution to *Just Defence*.

The idea that underlies the cooperation of network infantry and mobile forces has been called the "spider-web" concept. It has also been called a case of "synergism" in which two structural elements of relatively robust simplicity are combined in such a manner as to present a potential invader with a deadly complexity. He would have to move in an environment against the resistance of the infantry network or the flanking threat of heavier mobile forces, or both. He would thus lose the initiative, being unable to adjust adequately to actual battlefield conditions.[16]

The network infantry—the web—would be well protected against concentrated artillery, have access to dispersed underground shelters (rapidly constructed from prefabricated parts) that would provide excellent concealment, and be provided an organic extrication capability. It would be expected to contribute toward four functions:

• The combat function: Network infantry units would execute delaying actions, gradual attrition, and the splitting up and channelizing of intruding forces. Accomplishing these tasks mainly required randomized obstacle systems and a flexible component of indirect fire.

- The covering function: The network infantry must be able to block or decimate rapid enemy assaults so that friendly mobile counterattack forces can advance unhindered and undetected. Such efforts can be facilitated by making extensive use of electronic countermeasures and dummy targets.

- The supportive function: Among other things, this includes continuously gathering and transmitting information, and operation and protection of a decentralized system of stationary depots, which serve both the infantry and mobile units.

- The political-military function: By delaying the enemy advance and maintaining current intelligence on the forces of both sides, the web would be able to provide the time and information for rational decision making (e.g., forbidding border-crossing adventures by mobile forces) and negotiation with the invaders.

The mobile element is to the infantry network as the spider is to the web. Unlike the network infantry, the spider forces are capable of massing for limited periods of time. Their role is to block, contain, counterattack, and ultimately destroy intruding formations. The web would hamper the invader's movements and cover its own maneuvers, so that spider forces may be much smaller than today's armored and mechanized forces. The spider forces also support the web by evacuating exposed infantry or "repairing the meshes," whichever is required.

Because of concealment and dispersion of the network infantry and the small size of mobile units, the "target profile" of this system is low. Mobile forces might be capable of crossing the border and attacking WP territory. But without the protection of the web, spider forces would be extremely vulnerable. According to Unterseher, this is the best possible pragmatic approximation to nonprovocation.

The defensibility of the Spider and Web Concept is derived from its structure, not the kind of weapons that are associated with it. The SAS weapons mix is not fundamentally different from that used by NATO for the conventional defense of the border belt, but there is a different emphasis. There would be fewer tracked and wheeled vehicles, self-propelled artillery, and multipurpose helicopters, and more semi-intelligent mines, remote-controlled direct-fire weapons, rapid-fire mortars, and soldier-fired SAMs. Weapons for deep-strike purposes would not be present for two reasons: first, they are destabilizing; second, they tend toward "high tech exoticism." That is, these weapons may not be cost effective, and there may be dangers in their sophistication.

Unlike some more "pure" alternative defense concepts, the SAS proposal explicitly deals with air defense, and it includes aircraft. Like the simpler schemes, it assumes that the low target profile will reduce any potential air threat to friendly troops, simplifying the air defense task. The emphasis of SAS air defense is therefore on protecting the civilian infrastructure from the potential threat of terror attack, and in conformance with the fundamental alternative defense idea, avoiding as much as possible air capabilities that could be viewed by the WP as offensive in nature. The air defense organization would consist of two elements:

— A surface-to-air missile network with clustered positions all along the border and several rearward clusters for the special protection of infrastructure and air bases to be used for the reception of transatlantic reserves, continuously modernized.

— The 400 to 500 air defense fighter force would have special characteristics. In Unterseher's words:

These planes, derivatives of existing models, should have STOL capability and be supported by a mobile base infrastructure that would, as a matter of course, make use of makeshift runways (stretches of roads) and club airfields. Abandoning our current huge air bases can be regarded as a major step towards a low target profile and, consequently, towards stability.[17]

Fighter bombers for deep penetration would be scrapped, but apparently there could be some close air support to back up the ground forces' forward defense.

The SAS proposal also includes a scheme for the defense of the Baltic coasts and exits, omitted in this discussion because it is not germane to the conventional arms control proposals now under consideration.

Afheldt's model, and many other proposals advanced by German strategists, either exclusively or mainly depend on German forces, with minimal roles by allied forces. The SAS model also places the principal burden on the FRG—all infantry web and rear guard units would be German—but allied forces would provide more than half of the spider formations. This would be less than half of NATO's current armored and mechanized forces on the central front. Even the German part of SAS land forces would be less demanding than current official army planning. In the air defense organization, FRG personnel would dominate the land-based missile shield, and NATO allies would be expected to provide the light fighters and CAS aircraft.[18]

ASSESSMENT

For the most part, the relatively few essays of mostly German proponents, published in reports of conference proceedings or "peace research" literature, have gone unanswered by mainstream defense analysts who do not attend the kind of conferences at which alternative defense proposals are discussed or read the journals of the peace movement. Most military planners know nothing of them. As a result, they have not been subjected to extensive criticism in English literature. Moreover, most criticism that does exist preceded Gorbachev's unilateral force withdrawal, the tabling of similar arms control proposals at Geneva by NATO and WP, and the increasing probability that, notwithstanding the complexities involved, a NATO–WP conventional arms control agreement will be concluded, sooner than most observers would have imagined several months ago.

Thus, in probably the most systematic critique to date of alternative defense in English, David Gates of Aberdeen University places emphasis on the sheer numbers of Soviet weapons and personnel that, he believes, could overwhelm the lightly armed soldiers envisioned by most alternative defense schemes. He notes the "devastating power" of artillery, which could not only cause great physical damage, but also attack the morale of NATO troops, many of whom would be imperfectly trained reservists.[19] In addition, there are other serious dangers implicit in any contest between the WP with its present capabilities and a NATO force fashioned in accordance with alternative defense principles. Other published criticism, including reports of computer analyses, have also assumed that an alternative defense structure would be established by NATO unilaterally, if at all.

These apparent vulnerabilities of alternative defense structures (especially the decentralized infantry units for the static area defense) probably will not be present in a post–CFE environment. With any agreement likely to be negotiated, the WP will not have any numerical advantages within the Atlantic-to-the-Urals region, and its armor and long-range artillery, among other weapons systems, probably will be reduced well below even current NATO levels. As long as the Soviets abide by such a conventional arms control agreement, the criticisms based on the present WP conventional force structure must be seriously questioned through analyses that explicitly assume a post–CFE, not pre–CFE, environment. One analyst who criticized alternative defense in the present European environment, Stephen Flanagan of NDU,[20] did advocate a version of alternative defense in the context of a future conventional arms control regime with stringent limitations.[21]

However, other criticisms relate to the intrinsic characteristics of alternative defense schemes, whatever the size and capabilities of enemy forces. The most fundamental criticism relates to deterrence.

A basic principle of all alternative defense concepts is that as far as conventional force structure is concerned, NATO must renounce provocative capabilities and doctrines: it denies itself the possibility of deterrence by the threat of punishment. Deterrence, then, will be based only on NATO's ability to deny the WP its military objectives. Critics contend that this posture could encourage military adventures, because the enemy would know that if military intervention failed, he could merely retreat across the IGB and be no worse off than before the attack, because NATO's force structure and doctrine would always guarantee the attacker the status quo ante. The possibility of punishment on the territory of the enemy, not just on the battlefield, is the surest deterrent, the critics argue.[22]

Alternative defense strategists answer such arguments mainly by challenging the assumption that a threat of punishment is necessary to deter. The only conceivable way in which the Soviet Union/WP may believe that they could "win" in a conventional or nuclear battle in Europe, they argue, is if they can present the West with a fait accompli in a very short time; otherwise they would have to consider the possibility of U.S. intervention.[23] The static defense of most alternative plans would prevent rapid breakthroughs, they contend, better than present NATO formations. In any case, the losses of human and material resources would be substantial, and the possible political implications of failure would inhibit any national leader.[24] The threat of punishment is logically effective as a deterrent against intentional attacks and, logically, self-denial of the capability to punish may weaken deterrence to a degree as far as the least likely scenario for Central Europe is concerned. On the other hand, because the enemy has little incentive to preempt when confronted with an alternative defense structure, it provides more stability and therefore greater deterrence in times of crisis, the more likely scenario for the beginning of a NATO–WP conflict.[25]

Alternative defense strategists tend to discount the possibility that the Soviet Union might escalate to nuclear weapons to prevent failure because they assume that U.S. nontheater nuclear forces, as well as the *force de frappe* and Britain's fleet of ballistic nuclear submarines, would remain effective deterrents against nuclear war, even though they question the utility of these capabilities to deter conventional war. They assert this position even though most alternative defense proposals would significantly reduce the number of U.S. troops in Europe, and all would eliminate U.S. theater nuclear weapons, the two elements that most orthodox observers believe are necessary to link the conventional battle in Europe and U.S. strategic nuclear forces.

On the other hand, it is arguable that the U.S. nuclear commitment to NATO will have greater credibility, and thus be a better deterrent of Soviet nuclear escalation, in the context of a conventional arms control regime. With conventional arms control, a Soviet conventional attack would represent the end of détente and the beginning of a new, more dangerous cold war than the one that would have been considered ended with the signing of conventional arms control and other agreements in the first place. Escalation to the use of nuclear weapons because the objectives of its aggression had not been achieved, especially when NATO Europe had become a nuclear free zone (clearly a goal of the West German alternative defense strategists), would in all probability be viewed as an extremely serious threat to the most vital interest of the United States. It would have enormous political significance. Certainly, cautious adversaries could not assume that U.S. leadership would not respond in kind, even if the U.S. military presence in Europe had been substantially reduced.

Defenders of Flexible Response, the basis of current NATO strategy, also charge that alternative defense schemes would be less effective deterrents because they would not provide the WP military planner with uncertainties; he would know exactly what to expect, and he could estimate outcomes and develop countermeasures with confidence.[26] While this charge has more validity against some proposals (e.g., Afheldt's) than others (e.g., SAS's), it is one that alternative defense strategists cannot fully answer. Indeed, eliminating the uncertainty about NATO attacks into Eastern Europe is the purpose of their plans.

Since deterrence is a factor of the perceptions of the opponent, it will never be possible to determine, at least without conflict, which theory of deterrence is correct. Both views are plausible, and neither can be eliminated on the basis of logic alone.

Most alternative defense schemes are highly dependent on high technology, and often emerging technology, solutions. Moreover, their success is closely tied to PGMs, some of which represent immature and untested technologies. Even if the weapons systems are efficient and do not malfunction with changes in weather or become extremely sensitive to dust, etc., they will require highly skilled, well-trained technicians.[27] In a period of decreasing manpower reserves, the personnel requirements of alternative defense will be extremely difficult to fulfill. Being heavily committed to a technological monoculture, alternative defense structures are vulnerable to countermeasures, and as noted in the discussion of deterrence, are highly predictable. The area defense schemes that are the foundation of most alternative defense plans benefit from all of the advantages of decentralization, but also suffer from the problem of a weak command and control system. Yet, if command and control centers became prominent, they would become targets for enemy attacks, including preemption, and violate a fundamental principle of the alternative defense idea.

Several alternative defense proposals, such as four of the six plans briefly described previously, contain provisions for special zones along the IGB. In the case of Hannig's and Saperstein's, the zone would probably be a permanent barrier between East and West Germany. Such ideas would probably never have had widespread political support; in the expected atmosphere of détente in a post–CFE environment, they would have been completely unacceptable, and surely so now.

Largely ignored by U.S. planners and analysts, alternative defense strategies and force structures deserve increasing attention, especially for post–CFE Europe. Although they adhere to principles that run counter to the strategy and doctrine of the last several decades, they may contain concepts that are more suitable for a time when resources committed to national security are expected to be extremely limited, and the character of the enemy of the Cold War is, for better or worse, undergoing fundamental change.

EDITORIAL COMMENTS

In co-author David Shaver's opinion, an additional alternative defense plan for Europe after large reductions are concluded in a CFE agreement is one that reduces U.S./FRG heavy divisions to fully reinforced cavalry regiments. The mobility and firepower in the small organization is offset by what the author terms the cavalry mentality. A cavalry officer, like no other, is trained well in reconnaissance, tactical creativity, and boldness of action. He is a true combined arms leader. The multitude of weapons systems and combat support systems available within a fully reinforced cavalry regiment and the regiment's varied missions make this organization and its leaders the perfect choice to provide the necessary offensive character to any prescribed "defensive defense."

Co-author Ralph Hallenbeck feels strongly that defensive restructuring advocates discussed by Dr. Wilborn seek to "have their cake and eat it too." In the following section, Colonel Hallenbeck recognizes honest effort to improve defensive capabilities without contributing to improved offensive capabilities, but he challenges restructuring advocates to consider the implications of a static defense vis-à-vis a mobile defense, the limited depth of the battlefield, the vulnerability of barrier systems, and need for combined arms in modern warfare, the reality of Soviet force regeneration capability, and the importance of logistical and sustainment capabilities. Should we be indifferent to the other side as we restructure, or should we embrace a restructuring regime that is compatible with them?

ASSESSING PROPOSALS FOR DEEP REDUCTIONS AND DEFENSIVE RESTRUCTURING FOLLOWING CFE

by Ralph A. Hallenbeck

Since the beginning of the Negotiation on Conventional Armed Forces in Europe (CFE), much has been said and written about the need to do more than just reduce to parity the military forces of the Warsaw Pact and NATO. From Western as well as Eastern academicians there have been repeated calls for really deep reductions on both sides, and also for restructuring the remaining forces to make them capable only of defense, or at least much less capable of offense. Various defensive restructuring concepts have also been advanced by Warsaw Pact political leaders and by the leaders of opposition parties in the West. Western governments and most military leaders on both sides, however, have tended to remain wary of calls for a massive reduction or restructuring of their forces and derisive of academic prescriptions for exclusively defensive military force structures.

To be sure, the idea of reduction and restructuring as separate but complementary means to enhance defensive capabilities has received some favorable military attention. For example, WTO and NATO military leaders have generally agreed that the unilateral reduction and restructuring currently ongoing among Soviet and Non-Soviet Warsaw Pact (NSWP) forces in Eastern Europe will decrease the WTO's capabilities for a blitzkrieg attack against NATO. Military leaders on both sides have also endorsed the reductions and extrareduction, stability, transparency, and verification measures under consideration in the CFE negotiations. From a military perspective, the questions have not been about whether military forces could be rendered less threatening through a combination of reduction and restructuring measures; the concerns have instead been with how, to what extent, and with what level of cost and risk.

What follows, then, is an attempt to sort through the more important ideas advanced to promote defensive dominance, and to distinguish or identify the ideas that appear to have substantial promise from those that should be viewed only in terms of their tactical utility (and both kinds from those that, for any combination of reasons, seem to lack much utility at all).

(1) *Reductions to parity at 10-15 percent below NATO's current levels of tanks, artillery, armored troop carriers, helicopters, and combat aircraft.*

In an effort to avoid an exegesis on the pros and cons of NATO versus WTO proposals for CFE force reductions, suffice it to say that the common objective of achieving quantitative parity in the weapons most associated with offensive warfare is an obvious place to begin the search for a "defensive" offense-defense balance. While wars have been fought and won by the smaller side, the attacker, with no known exception, would have preferred to have had a quantitative advantage. Thus, the real issue is not concerned with the goodness of parity for mutual defense, but with the force levels at which parity might be most advantageous to the defender.

The proposals tabled by both sides in the CFE negotiations seek a balance between a substantial reduction in the numbers of tanks, artillery, armored troop carriers, combat helicopters, and combat aircraft (the prospective Treaty Limited Items—TLI) on one hand, and the maintenance of combined-arms forces (and a mix of weapons) on the other hand, at levels sufficient for defensive and counteroffensive operations. Following reductions (and restructuring) by both sides to parity at TLI levels of 0–15 percent below current NATO levels (i.e., roughly what has already been proposed in CFE), analysis suggests that neither side will retain any decisive advantage over the other side. Neither NATO nor the WTO will have forces in position to launch and sustain a successful attack against the other side's comparable force, nor will either side have a realistic prospect of suddenly gaining a decisive advantage through any probable combination of mobilization, reinforcement, concentration, and/or qualitative arms race activities. Furthermore:

- The forces on both sides will remain sufficiently robust hat even an all-out preemptive attack will probably not be a death blow to the defender.
- Like NATO, the post–CFE WTO will have to choose between spreading forces laterally (in order to defend the Inter-German Border) or concentrating them in depth for an attack.
- If once side does choose to concentrate its forces and TLI for an attack, the other side will still have forces and TLI sufficient for a robust forward defense of its terrain, with enough left over for a modest but sufficient reserve.
- CFE proposals for supplementary regional, stationed force, and single country subceilings on Treaty Limited Items (TLI) should further deprive either side of an ability to rapidly, clandestinely, or efficiently generate and concentrate forces without providing early, unambiguous warning.
- With sufficient early warning, the defender should be able to mobilize for a robust, well-prepared defense; one that even a quantitatively superior attacking force will be unable to penetrate.
- Complementary stabilizing, transparency, and verification measures should also add to the stability of the military balance and the mutual security of the sides.

In short, the achievement of reductions and geographic restructuring along the lines of the proposals that have already been advanced in CFE should do a great deal to ensure the defensive sufficiency (and offensive insufficiency) of both NATO and the WTO. The question is, "Is there more than can and should also be done?"

(2) *Reductions to force levels much lower than those envisioned by either the WTO or NATO in the current CFE negotiations.*

Defensive restructuring advocates quite properly question why it is that TLI reductions by the Warsaw Pact to parity with NATO cannot be followed by further reductions on both sides to equal levels much lower than those currently proposed in CFE. Those who ask are, of course, familiar with the answer that is invariably provided: that there is a requirement for NATO (and the WTO) to maintain a certain "force minima" in order to implement a successful forward defense of the IGB. It is not a superficial answer. On the other hand, in the judgment of defensive restructuring advocates, this answer is and will remain wholly inadequate. They are determined to find an alternative through restructuring that will permit both NATO and the WTO to reduce the costs, risks, and aggravation of maintaining such inordinately large military establishments.

In fact, a strong case can be made that deep reductions on both sides (e.g., to 50 percent below current NATO levels) would almost certainly make NATO (and the WTO) incapable of a "layer cake" or "static" forward defense of the IGB, as NATO currently employs. The reasons for this are not hard to describe. First and foremost, both the WTO and NATO have to defend or attack over terrain that will remain relatively constant. Urban areas may spread, and highways may be made more or less useful as high speed axes of advance; however, the fundamental defensive requirement to prevent deep penetrations across the 750- 900-kilometer international border separating East from West in Central Europe will not change. Large (50 percent) reductions, even to parity, would leave both sides woefully lacking in forces sufficient to establish a robust defensive line all along the IGB. Even after deep TLI reductions, however, the attacking side would retain a formidable combined-arms force, fully capable of achieving penetrations of the other side's forward defenses at locations of the attacker's choosing.

The defender's reserves would necessarily be very modest if the defender utilized his depleted force primarily to man forward defensive positions all along the border. And under this circumstance, even armor-heavy reserves would almost certainly be incapable of moving laterally fast and deftly enough to prevent an attacker from finding and exploiting gaps in the depleted defensive line. Strategically significant objectives could be seized by a fast-moving attack, and the fabric of the defense could be decisively undermined before forces in forward defensive positions could even begin to regroup and respond. Given a paucity of mobilizable as well as active defensive forces (due to constraints on TLI), the additional warning time that might be available to the defender would probably not compensate for the unfavorable force-to-space ratio with which the defending side would be required to contend.

It is important, however, to appreciate that these judgments assume that the defender would continue to utilize the bulk of his forces to occupy a more or less static forward defensive line. A more prudent defender might elect to establish what can most accurately be termed a "force-on-force" defense, based primarily on capabilities for highly mobile warfare. Only a small fraction of the defending force would be used to conduct covering force operations in the immediate border area. The remainder would remain in reserve, ready to respond when and where attacks occurred.

- Following deep reductions, the defender could optimize his Command, Control, Communications, and Intelligence (C^3I) capabilities to locate and attack the other side's forces before they could penetrate to strategic depths and unhinge his defense.
- Such a defense would require the political will (and military flexibility) to risk trading space for both time and maneuver room (a requirement that has heretofore been anathema to West German and other NATO allies).
- Most important, a mobile defense would depend on retaining a competitive edge in terms of agility, mobility, target acquisition, command and control, and firepower/lethality of the defending force.
- The possibility of preemptive attacks, reinforcement from outside the ATTU, and qualitative advantages on the part of the aggressor might also tend to loom large in the calculus of a strategy for defending with a relatively small mobile force.
- And such a strategy would entail retaining in the reduced force structure a high level of peacetime manning and training readiness (Force-on-force operations are substantially more difficult to execute than the relatively static forms of defense currently employed by NATO. Thus, they would probably be beyond the means of forces manned largely by reservists).

Note: Unlike a mobile defense, a static defense is not necessarily dependent on maintaining the high training readiness of a full complement of defending units. Given a long warning time (as seems probable in a post–CFE environment), a static defense might still be achievable with a relatively high proportion of reservists. Partially for these reasons, NATO's military leaders have been slow to abandon the relatively high TLI force levels, derivative mobilization base, and static defensive strategies to which they have become accustomed. Even when pushed to accept reductions in the past, they have elected to take reductions largely in the quantities of active military manpower and in readiness. Thus, a case can be made that deeper reductions in active manpower (vice deep reductions in TLI) should be possible without abandoning NATO's forward defensive strategy. Such reductions have not, however, been a discernible objective of defensive restructuring advocates.

While a more mobile defense poses an alternative to NATO's current commitment to forward defense, it is problematic whether a force designed for mobile warfare could be differentiated from a force optimized for the offense. Precisely with this challenge in mind, defensive defense advocates have continued to search for other solutions in their prescriptions for deep TLI reductions. These have most frequently revolved around proposals to restructure all or most armor-heavy formations into a much larger number of infantry and anti-tank units, to emplace elaborate, technologically sophisticated barriers, and to denude the existing forces on both sides of armored vehicles, longer-range artillery, air power, and other weapons that could potentially give either side a combination of speed, range, mobility, and lethality.

(3) *Restructuring as a means to enhance defense while economizing on the TLI and force levels in NATO and WTO forces.*

From a perspective of critical military professionals, the defensive restructuring advocates have sought to "have their cake and eat it too." Almost all of the proposals to radically restructure NATO and Pact forces have rested on one or more of three precepts. First, that new, sophisticated barrier technologies would permit both sides to restructure their forces in ways that would and should also permit them to take much deeper TLI reductions than those contemplated in CFE. Second, that in combination with barriers, infantry equipped with an abundance of anti-tank weapons could so disrupt an attacking force that even very modest levels of armored and air forces held in reserve could defeat and expel what was left of the attacking force. And third, that tanks, artillery, ATCs, attack helicopters, and combat air forces in large numbers are required only for the offense and should be reduced substantially to levels appropriate only for the defense. In at least this final case, the benefits of restructuring would, to one extent or another, depend on the mutual participation of both NATO and the WTO.

At their worst, concepts for restructuring have naively assumed that neither side would dream of attacking, and that the only impediments to lasting peace are the size, armament, and structure of modern military forces. At their best, however, the concepts were offered as an honest attempt to improve defensive capabilities without also contributing to improved offensive capabilities. Somewhere in between these highs and lows are still other proposals. For example, the WTO has proposed "thin-out zones" along the IGB; while not linked to deeper ATTU-wide reductions, these do allege defensive enhancement in close proximity to the border. Were NATO to accept such zones, both sides would be left only with barriers and infantry, whereas all armored, artillery, attack helicopter, and other forces capable of mobility, firepower, and shock action would have to be kept to the rear.

The idea of substituting barriers for armored formations is, of course, not new or even untested. Despite the ultimate failure of the Maginot Line, for example, there is no empirical evidence to suggest that it was not a very formidable barrier to a direct attack, or that it offered any potential for offensive operations. As an historical point of fact, the Maginot Line held until France and, in particular, France's more mobile forces had been soundly defeated. The problem with the Maginot Line was that it was inordinately expensive, and the costs were borne by reducing France's mobile reserve forces. Thus, when the Line was outflanked, the defender's reserves were inadequate to the task of either repelling or defeating the Axis attack.

To be sure, defensive restructuring advocates have never, to my knowledge, proposed that NATO (or the WTO) build a fortification anything like the Maginot Line. On the other hand, short of such elaborate fortifications it is not entirely clear what they are proposing. That is, a call for more formidable barriers is all well and good, but NATO at least (and, in all probability, the WTO as well) already has (NATO) or intends to have (WPO) very elaborate barrier plans for their newly forward defensive areas.

To be sure, greater attention to the early emplacement of barriers—and the installation of more sophisticated types of barriers—may permit a modest reduction in the mobile forces on both sides. On the other hand, it is far from clear that more or better barriers will transform the calculus of modern warfare. It is difficult, for example, to envision a war on the scale of a world war that would suddenly come to a halt because the attacker could not cross anti-tank ditches, or traverse mine fields, or overcome dragons' teeth, wire, or some other affordable impediment to crosscountry maneuver.

A truly balanced assessment of the potential for barriers to replace maneuver forces does, however, require that some mention also be made of the political impediments in the West to the emplacement of more effective obstacles. Despite the validity of everything that has been said above, NATO has heretofore refused to build extensive barriers in peacetime for fear that they would solidify the political division of Germany. Thus, in fairness to advocates of more and better barriers as an alternative to large quantities of TLI, more could be done by NATO—at least on the tactical level—if the political will were there.

Furthermore, it may also be true that NATO (and WTO) defenses could be enhanced by a greater reliance on infantry. Defensive restructuring advocates make a well-reasoned argument that much of the terrain along the IGB is forested, mountainous, or urban, and that armored and mechanized forces are not optimally suited for such terrain. Here again, however, they have taken a tactical truth and attempted incorrectly to turn it into a finding of strategic importance.

NATO's military leaders readily acknowledge the importance of light infantry to the conduct of modern warfare. There are numerous indications that WTO commanders are equally aware of the potential contributions that infantry can and will be called upon to make. On the other hand, the military leaders on both sides have been unwilling to reduce their armored and mechanized infantry forces in order to acquire more light infantry. The reasons for this are manifold. First, because both sides are concerned most about the potential of the other side to achieve very rapid and deep penetrations, neither side has been structured to deal with the possibility that the other side will conduct its primary attack through terrain that would substantially impede armored movement. Second, given the versatility of mechanized infantry, both sides have felt confident that dismounted mechanized infantry could deal effectively with a secondary attack through formidable terrain. Third, NATO (and in a post–CFE environment, the WTO as well) will probably feel that its reduced quantities of armor, artillery, ATCs, combat helicopters, and combat aircraft are at or near the minimum essential for forward defense of the entire IGB (i.e., the open as well as the more difficult terrain). And fourth, because light infantry can be generated faster than TLI, both sides have stressed in peacetime the kinds of forces that would be the most difficult and time consuming to generate in a transition to war (i.e., forces equipped with sophisticated armored vehicles and modern combat aircraft are difficult to create rapidly). For example, the United States intends to rapidly reinforce NATO with at least one light infantry division if hostilities should commence or appear imminent.

All of the above notwithstanding, it remains problematical whether NATO (and the Pact) could not be equally well served by more light infantry and barriers, and with fewer heavy forces. Not to beat a dead horse beyond death, but the question of the utility of infantry and barriers may depend in large part on a determination of the defensive strategy on each side. That is, light infantry and obstacles covered by fires from small arms, artillery, and anti-tank weapons would be most effective if the strategy were to continue to be based on a more or less static, forward defense. Almost by definition, light forces are ill suited for highly mobile forms of warfare. They lack the mobility, armored protection, and firepower to survive if called upon to relocate over large distances, or to fight on the move. To be sure, infantry forces would probably remain capable of conducting guerrilla warfare against lightly defended enemy lines of communication after the enemy main attack had passed them by. On the other hand, once penetrated and bypassed by an armored attack, infantry lose their ability to influence the overall outcome of a war fought to the strategic depths of a continental battlefield.

Suffice it to say that the potential benefits of the current CFE proposals, as discussed previously, provide a useful "base case" against which alternative and/or supplementary proposals for further reducing and restructuring can and should be measured. Deeper reductions, especially in manpower, are certainly possible (in fact, at least on NATO's side, they are inevitable for political, economic, and demographic reasons). And provided that NATO's European members were prepared to increase substantially the quantities of rapidly mobilizable infantry, and provided also that the FRG did an about-face on the alleged political unfeasibility of more substantial barriers along the IGB, a reduction to smaller numbers of TLI in highly mobile, armored reserves would appear within the realm of the possible.

On the other hand, despite the potential defensive value of infantry and barriers, the full combat potential of infantry is only optimized when infantry units are employed as elements of a combined arms team. Infantry alone can usually be defeated rapidly when left unsupported by adequate artillery, armor, and air. Moreover, the same can also be said of the other elements of the team (i.e., armor alone is not the threat that nonprofessionals often assume). In this regard, any concentration of infantry along the IGB should not require them to be completely separated from armor and artillery (as has been proposed in various thin-out zones proposals); nor should concentrations of infantry along the border come at the expense of infantry support to armored reserves poised to counterattack. A dearth of infantry could very much limit the effectiveness of any armored operation.

Quantum reduction and restructuring advocates also need to consider the possibility that their proposals could greatly enhance the offensive potential of the side most able to reinforce rapidly with forces from outside the ATTU. More than 40 percent of the Soviet army is, in fact, located east of the Urals, and up to 20 Soviet tank divisions could be moved from the Ural Mountains to the IGB in a matter of a few weeks. Moreover, while Soviet/WTO forces located within the ATTU area in peacetime might remain structured in a treaty-compliant manner, the Soviet divisions reinforcing from east of the Urals would not necessarily be in a "restructured" condition. Thus, given the relatively long lead times necessary for NATO to reinforce from CONUS, really deep CFE reductions and requirements for massive restructuring could be an ephemeral condition on which to base Alliance security.

Finally, really deep reductions and restructuring could increase the military utility of preemptive attacks, qualitative arms racing, and/or cheating in ways that might provide the attacker greater mass (e.g., by increasing suddenly and dramatically the density of armor, artillery, and close air support in the attacking echelons). Of these potential threats, the one that is most likely to be significant, and yet most often overlooked, is the potential for a qualitative arms race "break out." Not only is such a possibility likely to be of special importance when the quantities of TLI are relatively small, but the peacetime costs of maintaining hedges against such a possibility could impose a substantial economic burden on both sides.

As a final note, NATO's military commanders have been opposed to the WTO's thin-out zone overtures on the basis of the asymmetrical impact of geography on NATO's defensive potential, and because of the issue of the political division of Germany. Unlike the terrain east of the IGB, the terrain on the western side of the border tends to favor the defense only in the areas closest to the border. Thus, a requirement to withdraw armor, ATCs, and artillery to even a distance of 50 kilometers from the IGB would be a major strategic concession. If the WTO were to attack, the zone would not provide any impediment to the swiftness or mass of the Pact attack. In fact, a blitzkrieg attack could be initiated more efficiently from attack positions to the rear than it could were the WTO required to withdraw from linear forward positions in order to concentrate for such an attack.

(4) *Other potential avenues for restructuring.*

The NATO and WTO proposals tabled so far in CFE clearly assume that the organizational structure of the forces on both sides will remain relatively constant. To be sure, the asymmetrical reductions called for in NATO's proposals will degrade what has been a very tank-heavy and artillery-heavy—and very quantitatively superior—Pact ground force. Substantial Pact restructuring will also be unavoidable even under the WTO CFE proposals, and it would appear to already be under way as the result of announced Pact unilateral reductions. On the other hand, the restructured Pact tank, artillery, and air forces—which, following unilateral and CFE reductions, should be organizationally similar to NATO's forces—will still be capable of offensive (or counteroffensive) operations to the full width and depth of the European battlefield. NATO will, of course, also retain a full range of combined-arms capabilities.

What is often overlooked even by the most ardent restructuring advocate, however, is that the offensive potential of both sides is as much dependent on logistical sustainment as it is on the combat power of the lead echelons. Modern ground and air forces consume enormous quantities of fuel, ammunition, and other supplies. Thus, they highly depend on transportation, maintenance, and supply units to provide the logistical wherewithal for their operations. This is not to say that defensive units do not also depend on substantial logistical stockpiles and "service support" infrastructure; they are very, but not necessarily equally, dependent.

For example, the attacker must, in general terms, expect to consume substantially larger quantities of ammunition, fuel, and other supplies than the more static, reactive defender. Furthermore, in anticipation of achieving a penetration, the attacker must position his logistical bases farther forward, whereas even if the defender is dislodged from his initial fighting positions, he is invariably required to fall back on his supply lines. Thus, the defender can neither afford to risk losing key supply bases by positioning them in forward areas, nor would he want to do so.

Suffice it to say that the attacker's preparations for war normally include building up and moving forward a substantial logistical tail. This task can be made more difficult and more time consuming if the attacker lacks adequate supply pools located in forward areas in peacetime, and if he also lacks the service support infrastructure (especially transportation and handling units) to accomplish the additional work load. The defender, on the other hand, can usually sustain defensive operations with lesser levels of supply, transportation, and other service support infrastructure, especially in forward areas.

There are theoretically obvious but hard to specify limits within which these "truths" apply; for example, there would appear to be an undeniable limit to the capability of either alliance for large offensive operations if logistical depots and service support force structure could be quantitatively and geographically constrained. This potential has not gone entirely unnoticed. In CFE, the French have pushed within NATO for reduction measures that would constrain the amount of tank and artillery ammunition that could be located by either side in forward storage areas. Other proposals have sought to also limit the quantities of mine-clearing and military bridging equipment that could be retained in active units. Finally, the U.S. Army has been strongly pushing its proposals for reducing service support force structure to levels roughly commensurate with the ATTU ceilings (and regional, stationed, and single country subceilings) on TLI. In the Army view, the key to a sound CFE agreement is a reduction in force structure (combat, combat support, and combat service support), not just TLI, and an ability to maintain visibility over all force structure changes that might occur following the reductions.

To date, none of these proposals have received the attention they appear to deserve. The principal problems with the French proposals are (1) that bulk ammunition and individual pieces of equipment are not readily amenable to verifiable, difficult to circumvent arms control limits, and (2) that there is a dearth of accurate information about the current holdings of either alliance on which to base a specific proposal. On the other hand, there is a growing recognition that the on-hand quantities of such material are potentially very important.

Although fixed treaty limits on logistical materiel may not be possible to achieve in this round of CFE, a case can be made that information on NATO and WTO ammunition holdings, and on the holdings of military bridging and mine-clearing equipment, should be included in the data exchanges that have already been agree to (in principle) by the two sides. Such exchanges would carry with them an opportunity for each side to validate the accuracy of the data provided, and by implication, to monitor on-hand levels. As a practical matter, the data exchange and validation processes would tend to focus attention on ammunition and other materiel levels and could lead to the inclusion of unit and depot stocks as topics for subsequent (CFE II) negotiations.

The U.S. Army's proposal for force structure reductions seeks a much more sweeping, immediate, and monitorable restructuring outcome. That is, the Army has proposed that logistical infrastructure (vice materiel) be dealt with in this round of CFE. This could be done through an exchange of information on forces of all types that each side intended to retain following the TLI reductions. The residual force structure depicted in this exchange could be subject to negotiation prior to the conclusion of a CFE agreement, and the outcome could constitute a treaty commitment to "build down" to the agreed-upon residual force structure levels. While each side would be free to change its respective force structure once the agreed-upon reductions had all been taken (thus avoiding any requirement to "freeze" force structure, which neither side would agree to), any changes would have to be preannounced and subject to monitoring by the other side.

From the Army's perspective, the key to defensive restructuring is an ability to ensure that neither side intended to retain, and could not build without immediate detection, service support units and other infrastructure necessary for a rapid mobilization or reinforcement from outside the ATTU. Obviously, without an in-place support base and sufficient service support force structure, neither side would be able to prepare itself logistically to attack except through very time-consuming and unambiguous activities. And because force structure is much more readily monitorable than materiel levels, the Army proposals appear to deserve more attention from governments and restructuring advocates alike.

(5) *Summary.*

While both sides acknowledge that the large, asymmetrical TLI reductions called for in CFE will greatly reduce Pact capabilities for a limited warning, large-scale offensive against NATO, neither side is eager to propose substantially deeper TLI reductions. Nor is either side ready to embrace proposals for a massive restructuring of its forces, or for the quantum alterations to operational practices, doctrine, and strategy that such a restructuring would require. On the other hand, both sides are proposing a geographic redistribution of TLI and limits on the quantities of TLI stationed and single country holdings; if accepted, these would constitute a form of geographic restructuring (but would not require major changes to the internal composition of military units). NATO has also called for storing a substantial quantity of the TLI, which would permit both NATO and the WTO to reduce dramatically the number of personnel each currently requires in its active, fully manned units.

The proposals of many defensive restructuring advocates are focused on substituting manpower-intensive infantry units for existing tank and artillery units—a possibility that most military leaders on both sides have examined and found wanting. To be sure, the WTO has proposed thin-out zones along the IGB, which would imply at least some Pact readiness to defend its side of the border area with only infantry and obstacles. For a variety of military, geographic, and political reasons, however, NATO is unlikely to accept the Pact thin-out zone proposal, and neither side has indicated any willingness to broaden the concept to include a larger area (as the more radical defensive restructuring proposals would suggest is necessary). Nor has either side been willing to substitute massive barrier plans for armored forces.

Finally, some members of the North Atlantic Alliance are at least looking at the possibility that logistical depots and logistical force structure may hold the key to a restructuring proposal that would be militarily significant and acceptable to both sides. As Napoleon once noted, armies do indeed "travel on their stomachs." Given the logistical consumption levels of modern armies, this truth appears to be even more valid today than in Napoleon's time. On the other hand, constraints on logistical elements appear to present special problems for arms control solutions, and these would have to be overcome before either NATO or the WTO would be willing to address such proposals seriously in CFE.

NOTES

1. The current NATO strategy cannot be executed, regardless of the threat, without a certain minimum force density. For estimates of the size of the necessary minimum, see Stephen J. Flanagan and Andrew Hamilton, "Arms Control and Stability in Europe," *Survival*, pp. 455–56, who determine that 30 front line divisions and 10 divisions for operational reserves are required, and Captain Daniel M. Gerstein, "In Search of NATO's Minimum Force Density Requirement," in Chapter 2 of this book.

2. Recent public opinion polling shows that most Europeans do not perceive a military threat from the Warsaw Pact. See, as an example, "West European Publics Counsel Caution in Responding to the Gorbachev United Nations Speech, Yet Confidence in the Soviet Union Continues to Rise," Research Memorandum, U.S. Information Agency, December 20, 1988, p. 1.

3. Jim Stewart, "Alliance Confronts New Adversary: Public Opinion," *The Atlanta Journal and the Atlanta Constitution*, April 2, 1989, p. 1.

4. Demographic constraints to NATO's force structure are briefly discussed in Hans Gunter Brauch, "West German Alternatives for Reducing Reliance on Nuclear Weapons," in *Rethinking the Nuclear Weapons Dilemma in Europe*, ed. by P. Terrence Hopmann and Frank Barnaby, New York: St Martin's Press, 1988, pp. 146–82. For more intensive analyses of constraints on NATO's strategy, see Hans Gunter Brauch and Robert

Kennedy, eds., *Alternative Conventional Defense Postures for the European Theater,* Vol. 1, *The Military Balance and Domestic Constraints*, New York: Taylor and Francis, forthcoming.

5. David Gates, "Area Defense Concepts: The West German Debate," *Survival*, July-August 1987, pp. 302–3.

6. For good surveys of these proposals published in English, see ibid., pp. 301–17; Jonathan Dean, "Alternative Defense: Answer to NATO's Central Front Problem?" *International Affairs*, Winter 1987/88, pp. 61–82; Egbert Boeker and Lutz Unterseher, "Emphasizing Defense," in *Emerging Technologies and Military Doctrine: A Political Assessment*, ed. by Frank Barnaby and Marlies ter Borg, New York: St Martin's Press, 1986, pp. 89–109; Brauch, "West German Alternatives," pp. 146–82; and Brauch and Kennedy, eds., *Alternative Conventional Defense Postures for the European Theater*, Vol 2, *NATO Strategy and Force Posture Alternatives*, New York: Taylor and Francis, forthcoming, especially Part 3.

7. Frank Barnaby and Egbert Bocker, "Non-Nuclear, Non-Provocative Defense for Europe," in *Rethinking the Nuclear Weapons Dilemma in Europe*, pp. 135–45.

8. Jonathan Dean, "The Exclusionary Zone" An American Approach," in *The New Force Reduction Negotiations in Europe: Problems and Prospects*, Proceedings from an AAAS Annual Meeting Symposium, 1989, pp. 5–8.

9. Boeker and Unterseher, "Emphasizing Defense," pp. 97–100.

10. Alvin M. Saperstein, "Non-Provocative Defense and Disengagement Zones," in *Defending Europe: Options for Security*, Philadelphia: Taylor and Francis, 1985, pp. 210–24.

11. Gene Sharp, *Making Europe Unconquerable*, Cambridge, Mass.: Ballinger, 1986.

12. Hans Gunter Brauch and Lutz Unterseher, "A Survey of the Debate on Alternative Conventional Force Structure for the Defense of Central Europe in the Federal Republic of Germany," a draft chapter for a forthcoming book edited by Brauch and Robert Kennedy, p. 35.

13. Ibid., pp. 25–26.

14. Ibid., pp. 26–28.

15. Ibid., pp. 28–30.

16. Boeker and Unterseher, p. 5.

17. Ibid.

18. Ibid., pp. 1–6.

19. Gates, "Area Defense Concepts," pp. 309–15.

20. Stephen J. Flanagan, "Nonoffensive Defense is Overrated," *Bulletin of the Atomic Scientists*, September 1988, pp. 46–48.

21. Flanagan and Hamilton, "Arms Control and Stability," pp. 460–62.

22. See, as examples, Flanagan, "Nonoffensive Defense," p. 48; David W. Tarr, "NATO Strategy: Can Conventional Forces Deter a Conventional Attack?" in *Rethinking the Nuclear Weapons Dilemma in Europe*, pp. 231–33; and Fen Osler Hampson, "The Role of New Technologies and Follow-on Forces Attack in NATO Strategy," in *Defending Europe: Options for Security*, p. 16.

23. Virtually all alternative defense strategists writing before the negotiation of a CAC agreement accepted the prevention of a Soviet fait accompli as the proper military objective. The position is made forcefully in H. Afheldt, "Tactical Nuclear Weapons in European Security," in *Tactical Nuclear Weapons*, by Stockholm International Peace Research Institute, New York: Crane, Russak & Co., 1978, p. 271.

24. See especially the comments of Alvin M. Saperstein in *Defending Europe: Options for Security*, p. 63.

25. Richard Smoke, "Force NATO Defensive Deterrent," in *Rethinking the Nuclear Weapons Dilemma in Europe*, pp. 214–15.

26. Gates, "Area Defense Concepts," p. 310, states this position cogently.

27. Ibid., p. 313. Some alternative defense strategists recognize the dangers of high dependence on a technological monoculture. See Boeker and Unterseher, p. 6.

11

Risks, Results, and Reflections

In the event NATO and the WTO conclude an agreement in the Negotiations on Conventional Armed Forces in Europe (CFE), the WTO will be required to reduce its conventional forces substantially, roughly to parity with NATO at force levels lower than current Alliance levels. If this occurs, the threat that the Soviet Union and its allies have heretofore posed to NATO, and to U.S. interests in Europe, could cease to be an overriding security policy concern for either European or U.S. publics. Recent demands from Eastern European nations for Soviet troop withdrawals have created uncertainties, however, that call for a cautious approach.

Even considering new uncertainties, progress in the CFE negotiations has been so spectacular that some Western leaders predict an agreement in 1990 and implementation within two to three years thereafter. The United States and its NATO allies are also committed to new negotiations to reduce U.S. and Soviet Short-Range Nuclear Force (SNF) weapons. Other arms negotiations are also in train, and together with CFE, they are perceived by European and U.S. publics alike to portend dramatic improvements in both U.S./European security and the larger fabric of East–West political and economic relations.

In fact, prospects for deep arms reductions and a politico-economic restructuring throughout Eastern Europe have seemingly given European and U.S. publics an abiding sense of optimism. This optimism has not been dampened either by the increasing Eastern political instability, which is accompanying the thaws in both East–East and East–West relations, or by the reality that many difficult problems remain to be resolved. Furthermore, most Europeans have yet to appreciate that a really dramatic improvement in East–West relations could result in a sea change in U.S. global strategy, and potentially in the force mix, priorities, and peacetime deployments of U.S. forces committed to NATO. From a U.S. perspective, however, a substantial reduction in both CONUS-based and forward-deployed

U.S. ground and air forces could be an entirely logical consequence of the positive changes occurring in Europe.

The impetus for a reduction in U.S. forward-deployed forces is not tied exclusively to CFE. Public criticism in the United States and Europe of current U.S. force levels in Europe has grown considerably in recent years and has become intertwined with the never-ending U.S./European burdensharing debates. In the very immediate future, deep budget cuts on both sides of the Atlantic seem certain to further aggravate Alliance burdensharing problems. Budget-driven force reductions on the order of 20,000 or more men from CONUS-based and forward-deployed U.S. forces may, for example, be required even before the CFE negotiations have been concluded, and without substantial prior Alliance consultation.[1] Similarly, smaller unilateral (and "pre–CFE") European reductions also appear imminent (e.g., the proposed withdrawal of Belgian forces from the FRG).

Moreover, should a CFE agreement be achieved, the U.S. defense budget will probably average $25-30 billion per year less than current projections, and U.S. force levels in Europe could decline precipitously. For example, budget-driven reductions between now and 1995 might be as large as 150-200 thousand men from all military services in addition to those who may come from U.S. forces in Europe.[2]

Furthermore, U.S. future commitments to European security may turn on allied willingness to forego proportionate shares of the allied CFE force reductions, thereby allowing the United States to take the lion's share (and then some). If NATO's European members nevertheless insist on also substantially reducing their own force levels—which, in fact, they are very eager to do for their own political, economic, and demographic reasons—U.S. force levels could decline even more precipitously.

As will be discussed, this projection may not occur, and should not be permitted to occur, if at all possible. On the other hand, some combination of CFE and "extra–CFE" U.S. and European force cuts does seem certain, leaving NATO at force levels well below those envisioned in the arms negotiations, and potentially well below the levels heretofore assumed essential for the "forward defense" of Central Europe. If so, the conceptual fabric of NATO's current strategy of forward defense and Flexible Response could begin to unravel.

To be sure, the relatively high ceilings specified in NATO's CFE arms control proposals will leave NATO free in the future to rebuild Alliance forces (up to those ceilings), should events ever make this necessary. Furthermore, the warning time available to NATO for force mobilization should increase with reduction of WTO force levels and imposition of regional limits. Also, if political and military situations in the East take a threatening turn, a timely rebuilding might be possible. Thus, the prospect of greatly reduced, post–CFE Alliance force levels should, however, require what could be a very politically divisive strategy revision.

Apart from any purely military adjustments, such a revision would require a new apportionment of Alliance defense burdens. This cannot help but be an arduous process. Clearly, the larger political environment will also have a major influence on the strategy, force posture, and derivative burdensharing choices that will have to be made. NATO's future security decisions could, for example, be influenced by the European economic integration planned for 1992, by Alliance differences over trade and foreign policies toward Eastern Europe and the USSR, by perturbations in the "German question" and the stability/instability of Eastern Europe, and by evolutions in U.S. nuclear posture and strategy (especially as the result of the promised SNF negotiation). And yet, if NATO is to remain viable, the post–CFE U.S. and allied programmatic priorities and force postures, and the strategies that justify them, must be politically as well as militarily supportable in both Europe and North America, and in a larger context of rapidly evolving East–West and trans-atlantic relationships.

The purposes of this chapter are to discuss these challenges and prospects, and their implications for future U.S. and allied nuclear and conventional force requirements. The focus of the chapter is on NATO Europe, and in particular, on the future of U.S. commitments to the Alliance. U.S. (and allied) forces and strategies oriented on regions of potential conflict outside of Europe are, of course, also potentially very important, but they are not discussed in this chapter. Suffice it to say that non-European threat scenarios will continue to be qualitatively different from European scenarios, but as the Panamanian operations demonstrated, less demanding in terms of the force levels that might be required.

CFE AND THE ASSUMPTIONS UNDERLYING NATO'S CURRENT STRATEGY FOR DETERRENCE AND DEFENSE

Given the offensive potential of existing Soviet and other Warsaw Pact ground and air forces opposite Western Europe, the seminal, pre–CFE strategy assumptions have been that credible deterrence and effective defense were beyond the means of the European members of NATO alone. However, it was also assumed that credible deterrence and effective defense could nevertheless be achieved, provided that:

- There was a continuous, visible, and substantial presence of U.S. Army, Navy, and Air Force units forward deployed and postured to participate immediately in the collective defense of NATO Europe;
- The United States could and would rapidly reinforce NATO's defenses should deterrence fail or appear to falter; and
- The United States would maintain effective and survivable nuclear weapons in Europe sufficient to deny the WTO a decisive battlefield advantage and capable of credibly coupling NATO's conventional and nuclear defenses to the destructive and (therefore) deterrent potential extant in the U.S. strategic nuclear arsenal.

Consistent with these assumptions, Alliance strategy has been based on the precepts of forward defense and Flexible Response, which together define NATO's concept for meeting force with countervailing levels of deterrent force. It has always been accepted that NATO would probably not be able to sustain a forward defense for more than a few weeks in the face of the WTO's overwhelming quantitative advantages. On the other hand, NATO's members generally accepted the economic and other burdens associated with maintaining conventional force levels sufficient to contain an attack at or near the IGB, at least until a deliberate escalatory decision could be made. Which is to say that Alliance strategy has also been predicated on the threat of deliberate nuclear escalation, both as a credible deterrent and as a means to terminate the conflict rapidly. In this regard, the stationing of U.S. conventional and nuclear forces in Europe has generally been accepted by most Europeans as a means to couple the U.S. strategic escalatory potential to Europe's strategy both for deterrence and—should deterrence fail—for avoiding the certain devastation of a prolonged conventional war.

From a U.S. perspective, nuclear escalation against the USSR could only be considered under circumstances where NATO's defenses were in immediate danger of collapse: after NATO had tried but failed to defend conventionally, and after NATO had at least attempted to end the Soviet/WTO aggression with an initial employment of shorter-range, theater nuclear weapons. U.S. leaders have not been prepared to justify to U.S. publics a strategy of precipitous strategic nuclear escalation, especially against Soviet targets. On the other hand, European leaders have not been prepared to explain to their publics a strategy in which Europe would have to be destroyed by conventional or theater nuclear war before the United States would act. Whereas Americans have generally emphasized the necessity for effective forward defenses, Europeans have placed emphasis on maintaining the credibility of Flexible Response as extended nuclear deterrence.

Fortunately, MC 14/3, NATO's agreed-upon strategy document, succeeded in papering over these public policy differences. Admittedly, the differences have had less to do with conventional or nuclear "warfighting," per se, than with articulating in peacetime a politically acceptable concept for deterrence and defense. The differences are nonetheless likely to be revisited in a post–CFE environment. That is, in the event CFE offers NATO the prospect of WTO tank, artillery, armored troop carrier, combat helicopter, and combat aircraft holdings equal to those of the Alliance (as seems likely), the necessity for a U.S. commitment to a strategy requiring either rapid strategic nuclear escalation, or very substantial forward-deployed conventional force levels in peacetime, seems virtually certain to be questioned in the United States. In the absence of clear U.S. conventional and strategic nuclear commitments, the presence of large numbers of U.S. theater nuclear weapons on European territories would probably just as certainly be questioned in Europe.

Conventional parity at the force levels being considered in CFE will not require NATO to absorb any substantial force reductions. The WTO, on the other hand, will be required to undertake massive reductions. For precisely that reason, NATO's European members will be perceived by many Americans as more than capable of providing for their own defense. This is not to say that the United States will seek to withdraw all of its forces from Europe. Rather, it only says that most Americans will probably feel that only two or three of the four and two-thirds forward-deployed Army divisions, and a comparable number of Air Force wings, will be required in order to sustain NATO's post-CFE strategy. Furthermore, compensating for a one or two division/wing U.S. reduction will probably be perceived in the United States as something well within the means of NATO's European members.

From European perspectives, however, a reduction of even one U.S. division would leave NATO short of the force minimum required to execute a forward defense. And because the U.S. presence has been perceived to add credibility to U.S. nuclear commitments, any significant troop reduction could also diminish the credibility of Flexible Response. If a CFE agreement were followed rapidly be agreements to reduce U.S. and Soviet strategic and short-range nuclear weapons, the entire conceptual fabric of NATO's current strategy could be perceived in Europe to have lost credibility as a deterrent, and military efficacy as a basis either for planning or executing Europe's defense in the event deterrence failed.

Even the announced U.S. force reductions (i.e., the 80,000 Army and Air Force personnel that would have to be demobilized under NATO's current CFE proposal) are seen in some European circles to create a requirement for a strategy reappraisal. From the perspective of European leaders, a much larger U.S. force reduction (e.g., an entire 60,000-man Army corps, and a comparable slice of the U.S. Air Forces in Europe) would be decisive, making a potentially "avoidable" strategy revision totally unavoidable. (*NOTE*: At least in European minds, U.S. troop reductions, per se, do not have to translate into U.S. force structure reductions. However, the Bush administration has made it clear that the United States intends to reduce both the forward-deployed manpower and its associated force structure.)

As questionable as these European perspectives may seem to Americans, they are nevertheless likely to be an important part of the political landscape on which the post-CFE transatlantic relationship and strategy will be reconstructed. At issue will be the nature and extent of future U.S. commitments to NATO, the credibility of those commitments as a deterrent, and the utility of those commitments should deterrence fail. On one hand, some Europeans are likely to view CFE as a welcome reduction in European dependence on U.S. forces. On the other, more sophisticated Europeans are certain to appreciate the extent to which the increasing political instabilities in Eastern Europe could still pose a threat to their security. European defense intellectuals will probably remain wary of the changes occurring in the East—and supportive of both relatively high Alliance force levels and of a substantial continued U.S. military presence. Working against these objectives, however, will be public perceptions in the United States and Europe of the benign nature and limited extent of the WTO military threat following anything like a good-faith implementation of a CFE agreement.

POST–CFE: WITHER THE THREAT?

Soviet/WTO agreement with NATO's CFE proposals could result in the elimination of roughly 80,000 WTO tanks, artillery pieces, armored troop carriers, combat helicopters, and combat aircraft. This could mean as much as a 50 percent reduction in the WTO's offensive military potential, notwithstanding NATO's own CFE force reductions. More to the point, were the WTO to reduce the quantities of these five principal weapon systems to parity with NATO, and also distribute them according to NATO's regional reductions proposals, there could be little if any question that the WTO would thereby render itself politically as well as militarily incapable of rapidly overrunning Europe.

Furthermore, even from a purely technical-military perspective, it is highly improbable that the Soviet Union and other WTO members would either agree to the reductions under negotiation in CFE or embark on the unilateral reductions and internal military reorganizations that are already in train, while also harboring an intent to attack. The wholesale political dissolution of the WTO, which also appears possible in the not too distant future, would make it even less likely that the Soviets would or could attempt successfully to overrun Europe. Moreover, should a conflict nevertheless occur in such a post–CFE environment, the WTO would almost certainly fare very poorly.

All that aside, the political instabilities sweeping Eastern Europe must be seen as a clear and present threat to peace. While the WTO may be willing in CFE to render itself much less capable of a deliberate surprise attack, the almost daily upheavals in Eastern Europe make flash conflicts in Eastern Europe, and even between East and West, more rather than less likely. To be sure, any conflict that did occur, post–CFE, might initially be concerned with only a very limited objective and with the commitment of relatively modest means. On the other hand, it is impossible to take for granted the containment of even a limited military engagement potentially involving the USSR.

Even without the support of its WTO allies, the Soviet Union will be entitled by a CFE agreement to maintain as many as 12-14 thousand tanks and comparable quantities of other major weapon systems in Eastern Europe and in the Western half of the USSR.[3] Soviet force levels east of the Ural Mountains will remain totally unconstrained. In short, the Soviet Union will continue to possess the wherewithal to initiate and sustain a very major conflict. And although it seems highly improbable that Soviet military and political leaders will deliberately seek such a conflict after reducing their forces (and the cohesiveness of the military alliance) so substantially, this does not, and cannot, be interpreted to mean that future events in Eastern Europe could not impose on Soviet (or other WTO) leaders a perceived requirement to consider the use of force as an option preferable to other alternatives.

For example, while some may very correctly consider the unfolding events in East Germany to be highly fortuitous, this does not, should not, and cannot also mean that those events do not pose a potential threat to peace. Possibilities for miscalculations and/or misbegotten resorts to force (and to countervailing force) are clearly present. Whether or not historic events, such as the dismantlement of the Berlin Wall, will, for example, lead to armed oppression cannot be predicted, but the possibilities that accompany these and other events argue for added Western caution and solidarity.[4] Similarly, changes occurring inside the Soviet Union and to valued Soviet interests in Eastern Europe may produce sudden shifts in Soviet leadership and in the policy directions of that leadership. It is not at all farfetched to suggest that those shifts could once again plunge Europe into a period of political and military confrontation.

Despite the potential for instability and confrontation—and, in some cases, even because of this potential—some in the West have begun extolling the necessity for still deeper force reductions, either in the current round of CFE or in what has come to be termed "CFE II."[5] Arms control approaches to the problems of instability are at best naive, and at worst dangerous. It is not naive to believe that both NATO and the WTO may elect unilaterally to reduce their respective force levels for budgetary reasons, especially if the political climate improves and as the other side also reduces. It is dangerous, however, to pin any hope for greater stability on arms reductions per se; and it is naive to expect that all 23 of the CFE participants will marshal the political wherewithal to conclude a negotiated agreement to impose lower ceilings on their forces as long as the potential for sudden shifts in leadership and policy could produce renewed confrontation.

In the context of a successful CFE agreement leading to improved relations and less turbulence in Eastern Europe, reductions to levels lower than those envisioned in CFE are entirely possible; ceilings lower than those agreed to in CFE are not, however, either negotiable with many of the 23 at this time, or militarily desirable in the absence of greater political stability. Furthermore, the promised SNF negotiations, which are expected to commence immediately upon conclusion of a CFE agreement, seem certain to tax the political cohesion of the Alliance in ways that will make a serious CFE II negotiation virtually impossible. Until NATO's members have successfully digested both the conventional reductions following from CFE I and any nuclear reductions required by a subsequent SNF agreement, the attention of their political and military leaders will be consumed with the formulation of Alliance strategy, doctrine, and derivative burdensharing formulas (to include, specifically, an apportionment within the Alliance of adjusted nuclear and conventional roles and missions). Thus, until NATO has formulated a new strategy and a mutually acceptable burdensharing formula, and CFE II negotiation will remain a low priority, to be kept at arms length until the dust from the current round of CFE negotiations has settled.

These conclusions are not offered in order to dismiss the positive aspects of arms controls. CFE, for example, has always been understood in the West as an opportunity, not just for redressing the current military imbalance, but also for creating less threatening politico-military conditions throughout Europe and globally. Indeed, even the WTO's objectives in CFE have seemingly been concerned at least as much with creating favorable East–West political and economic relations as with requiring deep Alliance force reductions. In fact, it is not at all farfetched to suggest that a primary WTO objective has been, and still is, to achieve politico-military and economic conditions sufficiently promising to win Western military forbearance in the face of the Eastern political instabilities.

Any precipitous reduction in Alliance force levels could, however, entail a substantial reduction in Alliance cohesion and solidarity, and it could diminish the potential of the West to deal constructively with the political and economic problems and aspirations of the East. Such an outcome would not be in the interest of peace, crisis stability, or the military security of either East or West. The threat to peace will go up, not down, for example, if the United States and its NATO allies permit precipitous armament and budget reductions to render the Alliance ineffective as a political entity and, therefore, incapable of exercising collective approaches to Europe's rapidly evolving problems and prospects.

While it is beyond the scope of this chapter, the requirement for U.S./European cooperation, forbearance, and perseverance with regard to the economic integration of Europe in 1992 is also relevant, and related to the requirement for politico-military solidarity within NATO. The political and economic cohesion of Europe is, like the military solidarity of the Alliance, threatened by the potential for precipitous, unilateral responses to events unfolding in the East. Suffice it to say that the maintenance of U.S. and allied force levels, post–CFE, and restraint with respect to achieving rapid reductions in defense budgets, will have an impact on the ability of Alliance members to also agree on economic and trade policy, technology transfer and foreign policy, and policy responses to any Eastern oppression of political and/or human rights.[6] Not to belabor the point further, but the future security and stability in Europe will depend much more on maintaining a strong transatlantic Alliance than it will on diminishing the military threat that the WTO would still pose, post–CFE, to NATO.

In conclusion, NATO's members have been willing to offer modest arms reductions in CFE as a symbol of NATO's intent to avoid any direct intervention in Eastern affairs. NATO has, however, heretofore eschewed reductions to armament ceilings lower than those required for credible deterrence and effective defense. This does not mean that lower ceilings could never be considered. Rather, it only says that Alliance reductions to ceilings lower than those called for in CFE should only be considered when the political conditions (i.e., the conditions that made the current force levels necessary in the first place) have improved. Until there has been a big improvement, further reductions, and especially lower ceilings, would be ill advised. Wars are fought with weapons, but sufficient—or even excessive—weapons levels are not, and never have been, the direct causes of war.

ADJUSTING TO THE POLITICO-MILITARY AND ECONOMIC REALITIES: NATO'S REQUIRED POST-CFE FORCE POSTURE

Although implementation of a CFE agreement would impose on the WTO a requirement for substantial reductions and change, NATO could comply with all treaty provisions without undertaking any quantum modification of existing Alliance force structure, defensive doctrine, or strategy.[7] As noted previously, however, economic considerations (qua budget reductions) and the politics of Alliance burdensharing nevertheless seem likely to impose on NATO a requirement for force structure and strategy modifications similar in scope to those required of the WTO.

The real issues, therefore, are probably not concerned with whether NATO will need to make compensating strategic changes along with reductions; rather, they are concerned with when, how, and how much change will be required, and with how politically divisive the changes will be permitted to become when they occur. A strong case can be made for deferring any really dramatic changes until the WTO has at least implemented the arms reductions called for in a CFE agreement. An equally valid argument can be made that further reductions (and change) by the West should await a period of greater political stability and certainty in the East. And finally, a very sound argument can also be made that the determination of future Alliance force reductions (and residual force postures) should await the formulation of new doctrine and strategy.

On the other hand, the desire among NATO publics for immediate relief from the expense of maintaining current Alliance force levels is real and pervasive. As an alliance, NATO has always accepted a large amount of military risk. Budget-reduction proponents will argue that NATO can and should cut its military forces now, and that a net decrease in the level of risk (risk that NATO accepted prior to CFE) will still obtain. Despite the threat to Alliance cohesion (and, as argued previously, to European security), the proponents of immediate budget reductions may prevail over their more cautious political opponents.

The longer NATO can defer such reductions, and the more that appetites for trading upon risk in order to achieve greater savings can be dampened, the better. That said, it is also true that Alliance members must get on with the task of formulating their future force requirements, doctrine, and strategy. This task will be politically and militarily divisive, but it should not be all that conceptually difficult. For example, analysis suggests that Alliance reductions in Central Europe of as little as 15 percent will necessitate the abandonment of forward defense as it has heretofore been understood. This is not to suggest that NATO will ever cede German territory without a fight, or that forward defense will not remain a byword of any future strategy. Rather, it simply says that at force-to-space densities 15 percent lower than NATO's current densities, military prudence will require commanders to orient their forces on the opposing force rather than on the terrain they will nevertheless be expected to defend.

The reasons for this are not all that hard to describe. First and foremost, the terrain along the IGB will remain a constant. Urban areas may spread, and highways may be made more or less useful as high speed axes of advance. However, the fundamental defensive requirement to prevent deep penetrations across the 750-900 kilometer international border will probably not change. Large reductions, even to parity, will leave both sides woefully lacking in readily available forces sufficient to establish a robust defensive line, and if NATO (or the WTO) were to attempt a linear defense at low force levels, the result would almost certainly be a catastrophic defeat. Strategically significant objectives could be seized by fast-moving attacks, and the coherence of static defensive positions could be decisively undermined before the defender could even begin to regroup and respond.

Inasmuch as a 15 percent reduction in NATO's forces seems probable, military prudence obviously argues for a new approach to achieving NATO's defensive objectives. NATO could, for example, adopt a force-on-force concept of defense, based primarily on capabilities for highly mobile warfare. Under such a concept, a small fraction of the defending force would still be used to conduct covering force operations in the immediate border area. The rest would remain in reserve, ready to respond when and where attacks occur. Such an approach, while viable, will require changes fundamental to NATO's existing force structure, doctrine, and strategy. For example:

- Following really deep reductions, NATO will need to optimize its C^3I (Command, Control, Communications, and Intelligence) capabilities in order to better locate and attack the other side's forces before they penetrate to strategic depths and/or unhinge Alliance defenses.

- A mobile defense will require the political will (and military flexibility) to risk trading space for both time and maneuver room (a requirement that has heretofore been anathema to West German and other NATO allies).

- Most important, a mobile defense will depend on retaining a competitive edge in terms of the agility, mobility, target acquisition, command and control, and firepower/lethality of the residual force(s).

- And finally, a mobile defense will entail retaining in the reduced force structures a high level of peacetime manning and training readiness (i.e., force-on-force operations are substantially more difficult to execute than the relatively static forms of defense currently employed by NATO, and therefore, they rely on a nucleus of ready—vice mobilizable—forces).

While a mobile defense does pose an alternative on NATO's current commitment to more static forms of defense, it is problematic whether a force designed for mobile warfare could be differentiated from a force optimized for offensive operations. Moreover, despite the potential for manpower and force structure savings, the dollar costs of maintaining the requisite levels of force modernization and readiness could be prohibitive. It is precisely with these challenges in mind that budget and force reduction advocates have continued to search for other alternatives such as those discussed in Chapter 10. These have frequently included proposals to restructure all or most of NATO's armor-heavy formations into a much larger number of infantry and anti-tank units, to emplace elaborate, technologically sophisticated barriers, and to denude the existing forces (on both sides) of armored vehicles, longer-range artillery, air power, and other weapons that could potentially give either side a combination of speed, range, mobility, and lethality.[8]

Such proposals should be viewed with extreme skepticism. Given the potential of the USSR to reinforce with forces located behind the Urals, NATO's force composition and posture should not be based on the composition or posture of only those WTO forces directly opposite the IGB. Rather, Alliance forces must remain capable of meeting aggression by optimally equipped and trained Soviet armored forces, fully supported by equally capable air forces.

NATO really has only three cardinal choices. First, the Alliance can elect to retain its current concept for defense (a largely static linear defense predicated on achieving force-to-space densities sufficient to occupy and defend terrain all along the IGB). Given sufficient warning and an effective utilization of the available time for mobilization, reinforcement, and defensive preparation, this option could remain viable. It would entail the acceptance of considerable risk, but such an approach would at least require little in the way of new investment.

The viability of this option will, however, decline in almost direct proportion to reductions in U.S. force levels (which could not be rapidly reconstituted). It will also hinge on European readiness levels (which, if reduced, would need to remain rapidly reversible). Finally, it would require that the United States and its NATO allies take action to correct the current shortfall in a strategic sea lift. An investment in barriers, while tactically desirable, would—despite the claims of restructuring advocates—do little to reduce the strategic risk.

Second, NATO could adopt a doctrine and force posture designed for a mobile defense. Peacetime European force levels could be reduced substantially, and the difference shifted into mobilizable reserves. On the other hand, the materiel and training readiness of the remaining active forces would need to be kept very high. Their capability to cover the mobilization of the reserves would be critical, as would the agility, lethality, and maneuver potential of the nucleus of active, ready forces when employed as NATO's counterattack force. In this regard, a sustained level of Alliance investment in additional C^3I, longer-range artillery, and better air- and ground-delivered munitions would be necessary. As the most modern forces in the Alliance, retention of U.S. and German Army and Air Force units could also be critical to the near-term viability of a "mobile defense" doctrine.

Finally, NATO could elect to "lower the nuclear threshold" as the de facto consequence of conventional forces wholly inadequate for either a static or mobile defense. As long as European security were perceived in Europe, in the United States, and by the Soviet Union to be an interest vital to U.S. security, such a high risk option would not be without historical precedent and could, therefore, be adopted. If the United States were to retain a substantial ground and Air Force presence in Europe (as seems likely even after CFE and "extra-CFE" force reductions), this might be sufficient to assuage near-term European paranoias about extended nuclear deterrence. The prospect imminent U.S. (and Soviet) strategic and SNF nuclear arms-reduction agreements could be a problem, however, if not in combination with drastic Soviet reductions and NATO conventional modernization programs.

On balance, NATO will probably attempt to cobble together elements of each of these approaches. A true "mobile defense" is almost certainly beyond the means of most Alliance members, and its execution would be difficult if not impossible to coordinate among so many disparate national entities in any case. On the other hand, given a strategic concept predicated on achieving a capacity for linear defense through European mobilization and U.S. reinforcement, the creation of a mobile covering force will probably be critical. Once NATO has been fully mobilized and reinforced, the defense could once again take a linear form. On the other hand, unless the risks of inadequate mobilization and reinforcement were diminished by high states of readiness and abundant lift, the credibility of a nuclear "trip wire" might once again be the sine qua non of NATO's declaratory deterrence and war-termination strategy.

SQUARING THE CIRCLE: NUCLEAR REQUIREMENTS POST-CFE

The INF treaty, which banned the only ground-based U.S. missiles that could reach Soviet territory from NATO Europe, also raised serious European concerns about the credibility of U.S. commitments to NATO's strategy of Flexible Response. Although the INF missiles were hardly necessary for the United States to threaten Soviet targets, the fielding of the longer-range missiles was perceived by many European defense intellectuals, and especially the Germans, as a unique symbol of the intent of the United States to hold Soviet targets at immediate nuclear risk. The subsequent U.S.–Soviet agreement to eliminate all such missiles did, however, underscore in European minds the possible reticence of the United States to undertake a credible, politically acceptable (in terms of European concerns) escalatory commitment.

U.S.–German discord over the "Follow-on to Lance" (FOTL) missile has accelerated this intellectual ferment. The United States has been (and still is) seeking from the West German and other allied governments a commitment to field modernized, short-range surface-to-surface missiles, ostensibly to replace the obsolete Lance. Despite U.S. assurances that the FOTL missiles are required primarily to deter nuclear and conventional attacks against NATO, and only secondarily as a means to enable NATO to respond forcefully to an attack (i.e., by offsetting any gain anticipated by the WTO, and without resorting immediately to weapons in the U.S. strategic arsenal), the doubts remain; but then, so do the ambiguities in European thinking about the means to achieve deterrence and defense.

France and Great Britain are, for example, seeking to compensate for the declining credibility of U.S. nuclear deterrence (as they perceive it) by enhancing their own longer-range nuclear forces. What makes this prospect particularly troublesome to the United States is that increasing the number of such European missiles is unlikely to have the effect of enhancing either deterrence or defense. Rather, despite the capability of some European weapons to initiate escalation against Soviet targets, a larger number of such weapons might only serve to decouple the U.S. deterrent from NATO. Furthermore, because French and British nuclear enhancements are certain to be gained at the expense of French and British conventional modernization programs (thereby once again linking the credibility of nuclear escalation to the vulnerability of NATO's conventional defenses), the United States could be confronted with the politically difficult prospect of a lower nuclear threshold. Given the derivative loss of U.S. control over Alliance escalatory decisions, and the prospect of a low nuclear threshold, the United States could be driven to distance itself politically form NATO's nuclear strategy and, by implication, from NATO.

Finally, there is the question of Alliance participation in any future SNF negotiation. The outcome of the SNF negotiations could establish common NATO and WTO ceilings on theater nuclear holdings, which might then be instrumental in justifying to Alliance publics the levels and kinds of theater nuclear weapons that could and should be retained by NATO following the conventional and SNF reductions. In this sense at least, the SNF negotiations might work to NATO's advantage.

Justifying (which is to say, rationalizing) the level and mix of U.S. and allied nuclear weapons to European and U.S. publics will, however, be politically difficult in a post–CFE environment. For example, were the Soviets to offer the total elimination of Soviet SNF weapons in exchange for the elimination of all comparable U.S. and allied weapons, this could make the retention of such weapons (and rejection of the Soviet offer) inordinately difficult to justify publicly. Especially in a post–CFE environment, such justification would require a considerable degree of sophistication with respect to the technical-military prerequisites of Alliance deterrence strategy. Because meeting this public diplomacy requirement seems so difficult, many Western governments have been opposed to the SNF negotiations.

The intra-Alliance debate over the follow-on to Lance missiles, like intra-Alliance disharmony over the prospect of an SNF negotiation, is very much about the public acceptability (especially in the United States, FRG, Britain, and France) of the surface-to-surface component of NATO's nuclear force posture. SNF negotiations and FOTL are inextricably linked, especially in the sense that the SNF negotiations are strongly supported by the West Germans as a means to avoid the fielding of FOTL on German territory. From the perspective of the U.S., French, and British governments, however, the Germans must be made to accept FOTL for several salient reasons. German intransigence could, they believe, deprive NATO of a weapons system important to the flexibility of the nuclear deterrent (a U.S. concern), set in motion efforts by other European publics and governments to also shed theater nuclear burdens (a concern of the U.S. and many European governments) and worse still, undermine public support in Britain, France, and even the United States for the nuclear programs and strategies that they deem essential to deterrence (a key concern especially in Britain and France).[9]

For precisely these reasons, German opposition to FOTL and insistence on the SNF negotiation have already brought to a head the issue of nuclear burdensharing among Alliance members. The immediate burdensharing issue is concerned primarily with West Germany's inability to sustain politically the presence of so many nuclear weapons on German territory in peacetime, and to justify to German publics the probability that FOTL missiles would land predominantly on German territory (be it East or West Germany), should deterrence fail. Over the longer term, however, the debate over FOTL and the SNF negotiations is about the maintenance of public support in all NATO countries for shouldering their share of the costs and risks of NATO's nuclear strategy. In this regard, the nuclear members of the Alliance—the United States, France, and Great Britain—are insistent that the other members—the FRG, Netherlands, Belgium, and Italy, but especially the FRG—continue to accept the stationing of weapons on their territories, and continue also to provide delivery capabilities important to projecting the collective nature of Alliance escalatory commitments.

German opposition to FOTL threatens to upset the cohesiveness of the Alliance, and with it public support for stationing nuclear weapons essential to nuclear burdensharing. On the other hand, opposition to stationing FOTL on German territory is nearly unanimous among cognizant German publics and political leaders of all political persuasions. Not only does FOTL provide a visible symbol of Germany's uniquely vulnerable position in Europe's military geography, but some Germans also perceive FOTL to be an attempt by allies, and especially the United States, to make Germany's security interests subservient to their own. The United States, France, and Great Britain may view FOTL and the SNF negotiations as a Rubicon of German support for Alliance nuclear strategy and burdensharing, but the Germans are equally (if not more) adamant that with or without an SNF agreement, maintaining the credibility of Alliance strategy will not be permitted to impose a disproportionately large nuclear burden on their country.

All of the FOTL/SNF debate might be perceived as idle ramblings were it not for the probability that the Germans will remain steadfast in refusing to accept any new surface-to-surface missiles. If so, either the United States will be forced to use the SNF negotiations as a means to defuse the confrontation with the FRG, or U.S. leaders will have to find some other way to defer or forgo the fielding of FOTL in the mid-1990s. At the same time, however, the United States will also need to find ways to mollify the British and French governments, both of which are likely to take exception to any U.S. effort to compromise with the Germans.

Such a conclusion may not be well received by those who remain convinced that NATO's nuclear requirements can be defined precisely, and justified publicly, with or without a CFE agreement. As suggested previously, however, this would be a politically futile undertaking. NATO's nuclear requirements, which have never been pegged to a nuclear warfighting strategy, are a function of political acceptability and sufficiency for deterrence. Especially in a post–CFE environment, even a large reduction in the quantities of nuclear weapons stationed in and dedicated to the defense of Europe will be possible if Alliance members deem the residual levels adequate. Whether FOTL is eventually deployed either in the FRG or elsewhere in Europe is of little consequence compared to the requirement to settle within the Alliance the issues of nuclear burdensharing as they relate to credible deterrence and to a mutually acceptable concept for Flexible Response.

CONCLUSION

What all of this suggests is that the threat assumptions underlying NATO's current strategy are changing dramatically, and that CFE will make change within the Alliance necessary and explicit. To the extent that Europeans are concerned politically about the rapidity with which the United States will risk a strategic nuclear exchange, their best course of action would be to minimize their strategic dependence on the timeliness of such a U.S. decision. This should almost certainly include encouraging the United States to maintain at least a forward-deployed Army Corps and Air Force in Europe.

Suffice it to say that parity in NATO and WTO conventional forces will enable NATO to eventually consider reductions in European as well as U.S. conventional force levels. If the WTO is prepared to also reduce, the risks to both sides may remain within acceptable limits. At 15 percent below current NATO levels, however, Alliance members will need to seriously consider whether the current doctrinal approach to forward defense is still militarily viable. With sufficient warning, there should be little question that Alliance force levels sufficient for even a linear forward defense could be reconstituted. On the other hand, given the instabilities that clearly exist in Eastern Europe, NATO should probably not count heavily on the availability of time. For this reason, a force posture doctrinally designed for an initial mobile defense would seem more flexible and less risky, especially in the current environment.

There is no magic number of ground force divisions or Air Force wings that must be maintained for a mobile defense. Rather, the quantities must only be sufficient to deny an attacker a decisive quantitative advantage. Within this broad parameter, the requirement is to retain qualitative advantages primarily in terms of agility, lethality, and precision. C^3I capabilities seem likely to be at a premium, but advantages in long-range target acquisition, modern munitions and delivery systems, and highly maneuverable armored reserves will also be important.

The nuclear requirements in a post–CFE environment are even less possible to define precisely. What is not difficult to define, however, is the potential for political rifts within NATO that, if left unattended, could threaten the security of Europe. It is somewhat incongruous that really dramatic reductions in the military threat posed by the Soviet Union could potentially lead to dangerous reductions in the cohesion of the transatlantic community at a time when the solidarity of that community would appear to be absolutely essential. Thus, if there is a bottom line to this chapter, it can only be that all Alliance governments need to come to their senses. Their proclivities for dramatic near-term savings; precipitous, "extra-CFE" arms reductions; and divisive burdensharing arguments present the primary threat to their own security and to the security of all of Europe. Even the instabilities rampant in Eastern Europe will only be a threat to peace if NATO renders itself incapable of credibly standing by or responding coherently if required.

NOTES

1. Patrick E. Tyler, "Pentagon Says Troop Strength Might Decline by 10 Percent," *The Washington Post*, November 9, 1989, p. 1.

2. Ibid.

3. *CFE: Negotiation on Conventional Armed Forces in Europe*, Pamphlet distributed by the United States Arms Control and Disarmament Agency, Office of Public Affairs, October 1989, passim.

4. John M. Goshko and Ann Devroy, "Moscow Warned on Use of Force," *The Washington Post*, November 11, 1989, p. A23.

5. Jonathan Dean, "Defining Long-Term Western Objectives in the CFE Negotiations," *Washington Quarterly*, Winter 1990, Vol. 13, No. 1, pp. 169–84.

6. Jim Hoagland, "Leaders Worry How German Events Might Affect EC Integration Plans, *The Washington Post*, November 11, 1989, p. A23.

7. See Chapter 6.

8. Andreas von Bulow, "Restructuring the Ground Forces," in *Non-Provocative Defense as a Principle of Arms Reduction*, ed. by Marlies ter Borg and Wim A. Smit, Amsterdam: Free University Press, 1989, pp. 161–74.

9. Arnold Kanter, "Nuclear Weapons and Conventional Arms Control," in *Conventional Arms Control and East–West Security*, ed. by Robert D. Blackwell and Stephen Larrabee, Durham, N.C.: Duke University Press, 1989, pp. 422–60.

Appendix A: Mandate for Negotiation on Conventional Armed Forces in Europe

a. Preamble.

The representatives of Belgium, Bulgaria, Canada, Czechoslovakia, Denmark, France, the German Democratic Republic, the Federal Republic of Germany, Greece, Hungary, Iceland, Italy, Luxembourg, the Netherlands, Norway, Poland, Portugal, Romania, Spain, Turkey, the Union of Soviet Socialist Republics, the United Kingdom and the United States of America, held consultations in Vienna from the 17th February 1987 to [. . .] the 9th of January 1989.

—These states:

—Conscious of [the] their common responsibility [which they have] for seeking to achieve greater stability and security in Europe;

—Acknowledging that it is their armed forces which bear most immediately on the essential security relationship in Europe, in particular, as they are signatories of the Treaties of Brussels (1948), Washington (1949) or Warsaw (1955), and accordingly are members of the North Atlantic Treaty or parties to the Warsaw Treaty;

—Recalling that they are all participants in the CSCE process;

—Recalling that, as reaffirmed in the Helsinki Final Act, they have the right to belong or not to belong to international organizations, to be or not to be a party to bilateral or multilateral treaties including the right to be or not to be a party to treaties of alliance;

—Determined that a negotiation on conventional armed forces in Europe should take place in the framework of the CSCE process;

—Reaffirming also that they participate in negotiations as sovereign and independent states and on the basis of full equality;

—Have agreed on the following provisions.

b. Participants. The participants in this negotiation shall be the 23 above-listed states hereinafter referred to as "the Participants."

c. Objectives and Methods.

—The objectives of the negotiation shall be to strengthen stability and security in Europe through the establishment of a stable and secure balance of conventional armed forces, which include conventional armaments and equipment, at lower levels; the elimination of disparities prejudicial to stability and security; and the elimination, as a matter of priority, of the capability for launching surprise attack and for initiating large-scale offensive action. Each and every Participant undertakes to contribute to the attainment of these objectives.

—These objectives shall be achieved by the application of militarily significant measures such as reductions, limitations, redeployment provisions, equal ceilings, and related measures, among others.

—In order to achieve the above objectives, measures should be pursued for the whole area of application with provisions, if and where appropritate, for regional differentiation to redress disparities within the area of application and in a way which precludes circumvention.

—The process of strengthening stability and security should proceed step-by-step in a manner which will ensure that the security of each Participant is not affected adversely at any stage.

d. Scope and Area of Application.

—The subject of the negotiation shall be the conventional armed forces, which include conventional armaments and equipment, of the Participants based on land within the territory of the Participants in Europe from the Atlantic to the Urals.

—The existence of multiple capabilities will not be a criterion for modifying the scope of the negotiation.

—No conventional armaments or equipment will be excluded from the subject of the negotiation because they may have other capabilities in addition to conventional ones. Such armaments or equipment will not be singled out in a separate category.

—Nuclear weapons will not be a subject of this negotiation.

—Particular emphasis will initially be placed on those forces directly related to the achievement of the objectives of the negotiation set out above.

—Naval forces and chemical weapons will not be addressed.

—The area of application [*] shall be the entire land territory of the Participants in Europe from the Atlantic to the Urals which includes all European island territories of the Participants. In the case of the Soviet Union the area of application includes all the territory lying west of the Ural River and the Caspian Sea. In the case of Turkey, the area [is understood to] includes the [land] territory of [Asian] Turkey north and west of a line running [from Gurbulak, through Dogu Beyazit, Agri, Eleskirt, Tekman, Pulumur, Ovacik, Kemaliye, Kultepe, then southwest to Derinkuyu, Meke Mountain and then to the south to Mut, and Ovaick*] along the 39th degree parallel west to Muradiye, then to Patnos, Karayazi, Tekman, Kemadite, Feke, Ceyhan, Gosne, and Erdemli.

e. Exchange of Information and Verification.

—Compliance with the provisions of any agreement shall be verified through an effective and strict verification regime which, among other things, will include on-site inspections as a matter of right and exchanges of information.

—Information shall be exchanged in sufficient detail so as to allow a meaningful comparison of the capabilities of the forces involved. Information shall also be exchanged in sufficient detail so as to provide a basis for the verification of compliance.

—The specific modalities for verification and the exchange of information, including the degree of detail of the information and the order of its exchange, shall be agreed at the negotiation proper.

f. Procedures and Other Arrangements.

—The procedures for the negotiation, including the agenda, work programme and timetable, working methods, financial issues and other organizational modalities, as agreed by the Participants themselves, are set out in Annex 1 of this mandate. They can be changed only by consensus of the Participants.

—The Participants decided to take part in meetings of the states signatories of the Helsinki Final Act to be held at least twice during each [session/]round of the negotiations on conventional [. . .] armed forces in Europe in order to exchange views and substantive information concerning the course of the negotiation on conventional [. . .] armed forces in Europe. Detained modalities for these meetings are contained in Annex 2 to this mandate.

—The Participants will take into consideration the views expressed in such meetings by other CSCE participating states concerning their own security.

—Participants will also provide information bilaterally.

—The Participants undertake to inform the next CSCE follow-up meeting of their work and possible results and to exchange views, at that meeting, with the other CSCE participating states on progress achieved in the negotiation.

*The Participants recall here the relevance of the language on noncircumvention in the section on objective and methods.

—The Participants foresee that, in the light of circumstances at the time, they will provide in their timetable for a temporary suspension to permit this exchange of views. The appropriate time and duration of this suspension is their sole responsibility.

—Any modification of this mandate is the sole responsibility of the Participants, whether they modify it themselves or concur in its modification at a future CSCE follow-up meeting.

—The results of the negotiation will be determined only by the Participants.

g. Character of Agreements.

—Agreements reached shall be internationally binding. Modalities for their entry into force will be decided at the negotiation.

h. Venue.

—The negotiation shall commence in Vienna [on . . .] no later than in the 7th week following the closure of the Vienna CSCE follow-up meeting.

—The representatives of the 23 Participants, whose initials appear below, have concluded the foregoing mandate, which is equally authentic in the English, French, German, Italian, Russian and Spanish languages.

—The representatives, recalling the commitment of their states to the achievement of a balanced outcome at the Vienna CSCE meeting, have decided to transmit it to that meeting with the recommendation that it be attached to its concluding document.

—Palais Liechtenstein (formula reproduced in all six languages in correct order) Vienna, Austria, the [. . .] 9th day of [. . .] January 1988.

—Meetings will not be extended beyond the day on which they convene, unless otherwise agreed.

—The chair at the first meeting will be taken by the delegation chosen for this purpose by lot. The chair will then rotate among the 35 states represented in alphabetical order according to the French alphabet.

—Further practical arrangements may, if necessary, be agreed by consensus, taking due regard of relevant precedents.

Annex 1. Procedures for the Negotiation on Conventional Armed Forces in Europe

The representative of the 23 states listed in the mandate [to which these procedural arrangements are annexed], hereinafter referred to as "the Participants," held consultations in Vienna from 17 February 1987 to [. . .] 9 January 1989, and agreed on the following procedural arrangements for the conduct of the negotiation on conventional armed forces in Europe.

These procedural arrangements have been adopted by the consensus of the Participants. They can be changed only by consensus of the Participants.

I. Agenda.

   1. Formal opening.

   2. Negotiations, including presentation of proposals by the Participants, elaboration of mesures and procedures for their implementation, in accordance with the provisions of the mandate of the negotiation on conventional armed forces in Europe.

II. Work Programme.

The first plenary of the negotiation on conventional armed forces in Europe will open [on . . .] at 3 p.m. on the Thursday of the week specified in the section of the mandate on venue [in building] in (Vienna) beginning at 11 a.m. A work programme for the meetings of the plenary during the first two weeks of the [session/]round is attached. Thereafter, the plenary will agree further work programmes for the remainder of the first [session/]round, and for subsequent [sessions/]rounds. [The first session/round will conclude on . . . .] A decision on the date for conclusion of the round will be taken at the first plenary.

In 1989, there will in principle be four [sessions/]rounds.

The Participants will, in setting their timetable, take due account of the practical needs of all delegations, including those participating in other negotiations within the framework of the CSCE process.

III. Working Methods.

With the exception of the formal opening, all business under the agenda will—unless otherwise agreed—be dealt with in closed plenary and in such subsidiary working bodies as are established by the plenary. The work of such subsidiary bodies will be guided by the plenary.

Decisions shall be taken by consensus of the Participants. Consensus shall be understood to mean the absence of any objection by any Participant to the taking of the decision in question.

The proceedings of the negotiation shall be confidential unless otherwise agreed at the negotiation.

Unless otherwise agreed, only accredited representatives of the Participants shall have access to meetings.

During the plenary meetings all Participants shall be seated in the French alphabetical order.

IV. Languages.

The official languages of the negotiation shall be: English, French, German, Italian, Russian and Spanish. Statements made in any of these languages shall be interpreted into the other official languages.

V. Role of the Chairman.

The chairman of the first plenary will be the representative of (country chosen by lot in Vienna). The chair thereafter will rotate weekly according to the French alphabetical order.

The chairman of any meeting shall keep a list of speakers and may declare it closed with the consent of the meeting. The chairman shall, however, accord the right of replay to any representative if a speech made following closure of the list makes this desirable.

If any representative raises a point of order during a discussion, the chairman shall give that representative the floor immediately. A representative raising a point of order may not speak on the substance of the matter under discussion.

The chairman shall keep a journal which shall record the date of the plenary, and the names of the chairman of the plenary and of speakers in the plenary. The journal shall be handed from chairman to chairman. It shall be made available only to Participants.
VI. Decisions, Interpretative Statements, and Proposals and Related Documents on Matters of Substance.

Decisions on matters of substance shall be attached to the journal. Interpretative statements, if any, shall be attached to the journal at the request of the originator.

Formal proposals and related documents on matters of substance and amendments thereto shall be submitted in writing to the chairman and shall be registered at the request of the originator. They shall be circulated in writing to the Participants.
VIII. Financial Issues.

The following scale of distribution has been agreed for the common expenses of the negotiation subject to the reservation that the distribution in question concerns only this negotiation and shall not be considered a precedent which could be relied on in other circumstances:

[10.0] 9.95 percent for	France, Federal Republic of Germany, Italy, Union of Soviet Socialist Republics, United Kingdom, United States of America
[6.3] 6.35 percent for	Canada
5.0 percent for	Spain
[3.9] 3.85 percent for	Belgium, Democratic Republic of Germany, Netherlands, Poland, [Spain]
[2.3] 2.25 percent for	Czechoslovakia, Denmark, Hungary, Norway
[0.9] 0.85 percent for	Greece, Romania, Turkey
[0.7] 0.65 percent for	Bulgaria, Luxembourg, Portugal
[0.2] 0.15 percent for	Iceland

Payment of contributions by the Participants shall be made into a special account of the negotiation. Accounts shall be rendered by the host country in respect of each [session/]round or at intervals of 3 months, as appropriate. Accounts shall be expressed in the currency of the host country and shall be rendered as soon as technically possible after the termination of a billing period. Accounts shall be payable within 60 days of presentation in the currency of the host country.
VIII. Host Country Support.

The government of Austria shall provide security and other necessary support services for the negotiation.

The host country shall be asked to appoint an administrator, agreed by the Participants, to make and manage arrangements for the negotiation. The administrator shall be a national of the host country [and employed by the government of the host country]. The task of the administrator shall include, in liaison with the appropriate host country authorities:

—A. To arrange accreditation for the Participants,

—B. To manage the facilities of the negotiation,

—C. To ensure the security of, and control access to, the facilities and meetings,

—D. To employ and manage interpretation staff.

—E. To make available appropriate technical equipment,

—F. To ensure the availability of translation services in all official languages; the practical arrangements for their use being agreed at the negotiation,

—G. To deal with financial matters,

—H. To make available to Participants as necessary facilities for press briefings and to arrange appropriate media accreditation.

The administrator shall act at all times in conformity with these rules of procedure. Liaison between the administrator and the plenary will be effected by the chairman.

Annex 2. On Modalities of Meetings to Exchange Views and Information Concerning the Course of the Negotiation on Conventional Armed Forces in Europe (Exchange Meetings)

The Participants have, for their part, agreed the following modalities for the meetings which are to be held between Participants in the negotiation on conventional armed forces in Europe and other CSCE participating states.

Unless otherwise agreed, meetings will take place at least twice in the course of each [session/]round of the negotiation. [And specifically:]

[– on the second (day X of the week) of each session/round of the negotiation on conventional armed forces in Europe, and on every fourth (day X of the week) thereafter during the [session] round.]

Accordingly the first meeting will take place at 10:30 a.m. on the second (day X of the week) of the first session/round.

Representatives of:

Der Bundesrepublik Deutschland:	Der Deutschen Demokratischen Republik:
The Federal Republic of Germany:	The German Democratic Republic:
La Republica Federal de Alemana:	La Republica Democratica Alemana:
La Republique Federale d'Allemagne:	La Republique Democratique Allemande:
La Republica Federals di Germania:	La Republica Democratica Tedesca:
(Russian)	(Russian)

Appendix B: NATO Chapter One

Negotiations on Conventional Armed Forces in Europe

Postition Paper Provided by the Delegations of Belgium, Canada, Denmark, Federal Republic of Germany, France, Greece, Iceland, Italy, Luxembourg, Netherlands, Norway, Portugal, Spain, Turkey, United Kingdom and United States

Objectives

    1. The objectives of these negotiations are agreed in the mandate, are:

      —the establishment of a secure and stable balance of conventional forces at lower levels;

      —the elimination of disparities prejudicial to stability and security;

      —the elimination, as a matter of high priority, of the capability for launching surprise attack and for initiating large-scale offensive action.

    2. Through the approach outline below the Western Delegations will seek to establish a situation in which surprise attack and large-scale offensive action are no longer credible options. We pursue this aim on the basis of equal respect for the security interests of all. Our approach offers a coherent whole and is intended to be applied simultaneously and in its totality in the area of application.

Rationale

    3. The rationale for our approach is as follows:

      —the present concentration of forces in the area from the Atlantic to the Urals is the highest ever known in peacetime and represents the greatest destructive potential ever assembled. Overall levels of forces, particularly those relevant to surprise attack and offensive action such as tanks, artillery and armored troop carriers, must therefore be radically reduced. It is the substantial disparity in the numbers of these systems, all capable of rapid mobility and high firepower, which most threatens stability in Europe. These systems are also central to the seizing and holding of territory, the prime aim of any aggressor;

      —no one country should be permitted to dominate Europe by force of arms: no participant should therefore possess more than a fixed proportion of the total holdings of all participants in each category of armaments, commensurate with its needs for self defence;

—addressing the overall number and nationality of forces will not by itself affect the stationing of armaments outside national borders: additional limits will also be needed on forces stationed on other countries' territory;

—we need to focus on both the levels of armaments and state of readiness of forces in those areas where the concentration of such forces is greatest, as well as to prevent redeployment of forces withdrawn from one part of the area of application to another. It will therefore be necessary to apply a series of interlocking sublimits covering forces throughout the area, together with further limits on armaments in active units.

4. The following specific measures within the area of application would fulfill these objectives:

Rule 1: Overall Limit
The overall total of weapons in each of the three categories identified above will at no time exceed:

—main battle tanks	40,000
—artillery pieces	33,000
—armored troop carriers	56,000

Rule 2: Sufficiency
No one country may retain more than 30 percent of the overall limits in these three categories, i.e.

—main battle tanks	12,000
—artillery pieces	10,000
—armored troop carriers	16,800

Rule 3: Stationed Forces
Among countries beloging to a treaty of Alliance neither side will station armaments outside national territory in active units exceeding the following levels:

—main battle tanks	3,200
—artillery pieces	1,700
—armored troop carriers	6,000

Rule 4: Sub-limits
In the areas indicated below, each group of countries belonging to the same treaty of Alliance shall not exceed the following levels:

(1) In the area consisting of Belgium, Denmark, the Federal Republic of Germany, France, Greece, Iceland, Italy, Luxembourg, the Netherlands, Norway, Portugal, Spain, Turkey, the United Kingdom, Bulgaria, Czechoslovakia, the German Democratic Republic, Hungary, Poland, Romania and the Territory of the Soviet Union west of the Urals comprising the Baltic, Byelorussian, Carpathian, Moscow, Volga, Urals, Leningrad, Odessa, Kiev, Trans-Caucasus, North Caucasus military districts:

—main battle tanks	20,000
—artillery	16,500
—armored troop carriers	28,000 (of which no more than 12,000 AIFVs)

(2) In the area consisting of Belgium, Denmark, the Federal Republic of Germany, France, Italy, Luxembourg, the Netherlands, Portugal, Spain, the United Kingdom, Czechoslovakia, the German Democratic Republic, Hungary, Poland and the territory of the Soviet Union west of the Urals comprising the Baltic, Byelorussian, Carpathian, Moscow, Volga, Urals military districts in active units:

—main battle tanks	11,300
—artillery	9,000
—armored troop carriers	20,000

(3) In the area consisting of Belgium, Denmark, the Federal Republic of Germany, France, Italy, Luxembourg, the Netherlands, the United Kingdom, Czechoslovakia, the German Democratic Republic, Hungary, Poland and the territory of the Soviet Union comprising the Baltic, Byelorussian, Carpathian military districts in active units:

—main battle tanks	10,300
—artillery	7,600
—armored troop carriers	18,000

(4) In the area consisting of Belgium, the Federal Republic of Germany, Luxembourg, the Netherlands, Czechoslovakia, the German Democratic Republic and Poland in active units:

—main battle tanks	8,000
—artillery	4,500
—armored troop carriers	11,000

(5) Rule 4 is to be seen as an integrated whole which will only be applied simultaneously and across the entire area from the Atlantic to the Urals. It will be for the members of each Alliance to decide how they exercise their entitlement under all of these measures.

Rule 5: Information Exchange

Each year holdings of main battle tanks, armored troop carriers and artillery pieces will be notified, disaggregated down to battalion level. This measure will also apply to personnel in both combat and combat support units. Any change of notified unit structures above battalion level, or any measure resulting in an increase of personnel strength in such units, will be subject to notification, on a basis to be determined in the course of the negotiations.

Measures for Stability, Verification and Non-Circumvention

6. As an integral part of the agreement, there would be a need for:

—stabilizing measures: to buttress the resulting reductions in force levels in the ATTU area. These should include measures of transparency, notification and constraint applied to the deployment, movement, storage, and levels of readiness of conventional armed forces which include conventional armaments and equipment;

—verification arrangements: to include the exchange of detailed data about forces and deployments, with the right to conduct on-site inspection, as well as other measures designed to provide assurance of compliance with the agreed provisions;

—non-circumvention provisions: inter alia, the ensure that the manpower and equipment withdrawn from any one area do not have adverse security implications for any participating state;

—provision for temporarily exceeding the limits set down in Rule 4 for pre-notified exercises.

The Longer Term

7. In the longer term, and in the light of the implementation of the above measures, we would be willing to contemplate further steps to enhance stability and security in Europe, such as:

—further reductions or limitations of conventional armaments and equipment;

—the restructuring of armed forces to enhance defensive capabilities and further to reduce offensive capabilities.

Appendix C: NATO Chapter Two

Negotiations on Conventional Armed Forces in Europe

Proposal Submitted by the Delegations of Belgium, Canada, Denmark, France, Federal Republic of Germany, Greece, Iceland, Italy, Luxembourg, Netherlands, Norway, Portugal, Spain, Turkey, United Kingdom and United States
Objectives

1. The agreed objectives of this negotiation are:
—the establishment of a secure and stable balance of conventional forces at lower levels;
—the elimination of disparities prejudicial to stability and security;
—the elimination, as a matter of high priority, or the capability for launching surprise attack and for initiating large-scale offensive action.

2. Through the proposals set out below the Delegations of Belgium, Canada, Denmark, France, the Federal Republic of Germany, Greece, Iceland, Italy, Luxembourg, the Netherlands, Norway, Portugal, Spain, Turkey, the United Kingdom and the United States seek to establish a situation in which surprise attack and large-scale offensive actions are no longer credible options. We pursue this aim on the basis of equal respect for the security interests of all. Our proposals make up a coherent whole and are intended to be applied simultaneously and in their totality in the area of application, as defined in the mandate.

Rationale
3. The rationale for our proposals is as follows:
—the present concentration of forces in the area from the Atlantic to the Urals is the highest ever known in peacetime and represents the greatest destructive potential ever assembled. Overall levels of forces, particularly those relevant to surprise attack and offensive action such as tanks, artillery and armored troop carriers, must therefore be radically reduced. It is the substantial disparity in the numbers of these systems, all capable of rapid mobility and high firepower, which most threatens stability in Europe. These systems are also central to the seizing and holding of territory, the prime aim of any aggressor;
—no one country should be permitted to dominate Europe by force of arms: no participant should therefore possess more than a fixed proportion of the total holdings

of all participants in each category of armaments, commensurate with its needs for self-defence;

—addressing the overall number and nationality of forces will not by itself affect the stationing of armaments outside national borders: additional limits will also be needed on certain forces stationed on other countries' territory;

—we need to focus on both the levels of armaments and state of readiness of forces in those areas where the concentration of such forces is greatest, as well as to prevent redeployment of ground forces withdrawn from one part of the area of application to another. It will therefore be necessary to apply a series of interlocking sublimits covering certain forces throughout the area, together with further limits on armaments in active units.

—it was decided at the meeting of Alliance Heads of State and Government in Brussels on 29th/30th May 1989 that aircraft and helicopters should also be reduced because of their relevance to the conventional balance. We envisage appropriate measures of verification and non-circumvention taking account of the particular characteristics of these weapons systems;

—the Summit meeting in Brussels on 29the/30th May 1989 also decided to supplement these provisions with an equal ceiling on U.S. and Soviet ground and air force personnel stationed in Europe outside their national territory. Such a measure reflects the particular responsibilities of the two major powers in the reduction of military confrontation and the building of mutual confidence in Europe on a basis of mutual equality, as well as the fact that these two countries maintain substantial forces outside the zone of application.

Proposals
Chapter 1: Limitation on Major Weapons Systems

a. Ground Forces

Our proposals on ground forces have been made public on 6th March in Vienna. Those main battle tanks, artillery pieces and ATCs withdrawn from service in order to achieve compliance with the rules proposed in March shall be destroyed, in accordance with procedures to be agreed.

b. Air Assets
Rule A: Overall Limits
The overall total of combat aircraft and compat helicopters will at no time exceed:

Combat Aircraft	11,400*
Combat Helicopters:	3,800*

*Attached are definitions and lists of types on which these ceilings are based.
Rule B: Sufficiency
No one country may retain more than 30% of the ovrall limits in these two categories, i.e.

Combat Aircraft:	3,420
Combat Helicopters:	1,140

Rule C: Sub-Limits
Within the area of application delineated under Rule 4(1), each group of countries belonging to the same treaty of alliance shall not exceed the following levels:

Combat Aircraft:	5,700
Combat Helicopters:	1,900

Rule D: Disposition of Reduced Weapons Systems

Those aircraft and helicopters withdrawn from service in order to achieve compliance with Rules A to C above shall be destroyed in accordance with procedures to be agreed.

Chapter II: Limits on U.S. and Soviet Ground and Air Force Personnel Stationed in Europe Outside National Territory

The United States and the Soviet Union shall not station outside their national territory within Europe from the Atlantic to the Urals more than, in each case, 275,000 ground and air force personnel. United States and Soviet Union personnel withdrawn from service in order to achieve compliance with this limit shall be demobilized.

Chapter III: Measures of Information Exchange, Stabilization, Verification and Non-Circumvention

In addition, there will, as an integral part of the agreement, be a need for further measures of information exchange, stabilization, verification and non-circumvention.

a. Information Exchange

Each year holdings of main battle tanks, armored troop carriers, artillery pieces, combat aircraft and helicopters will be notified, disaggregated down to battalion/squadron level. This measure will also apply to personnel in both combat and supporting units. Any change of notified unit structures above battalion/squadron level, or any measures resulting in an increase of personnel strength in such units or in aggregate personnel levels, will be subject to notification on a basis to be determined in the course of the negotiations.

b. Stabilizing Measures

We shall shortly present proposals designed to buttress the resulting reductions in force levels in the ATTU area. These will include measures of openness and constraint applied to the deployment, movement, storage and levels of readiness of conventional armed forces, including their armaments and equipment. There will also need to be provision for temporarily exceeding the limits set out in Chapters I and II, inter alia, for pre-notified exercises.

c. Measures of Verification

We shall also propose verification arrangements designed to provide assurance of compliance with the agreed provisions.

d. Non-Circumvention Provisions

We will propose provisions which will ensure that actions of the parties do not circumvent the agreement and do not have adverse security implications for any participant.

Chapter IV: The Longer Term

In the longer term, and in the light of the implementation of the above measures, we would be willing to contemplate further steps to enhance stability and security in Europe, such as:

—further reductions or limitations of conventional armaments and equipment;

—the restructuring of armed forces to enhance defensive capabilities and further to reduce offensive capabilities.

Definitions and Lists to Support Proposed Ceilings

1. Definition of Combat Aircraft

For the purpose of the CFE negotiation, a combat aircraft is a fixed-wing or swing-wing aircraft permanently land-based of a type initially constructed or later converted to drop bombs, deliver air-to-air or air-to-surface missiles, fire guns/cannons, or employ any other weapons of destruction. Any permanently land-based version or variant of these aircraft is also included. An aircraft type should not, however, be included unless a combat variant of the type concerned exists within the ATTU area in the armed forces of a member state of the same treaty of alliance to which the participating state owning the aircraft belongs.

2. Aircraft Type List

F-4	MB-339
F-5	Hunter
F-15	G-91
F-16	Mirage IV
F-18	Mirage F-1
F-84	Mirage III
F-104	Mirage 5
F-111	Mirage 2000
PD-808	F-35 Draken
Buccaneer	Hawk
Canberra	T-2
P-3	T-38
A-7	T-33
A-10	Nimrod
Alpha Jet	S-2
Fouga	HU-16 Albatross
Harrier	T-37
Tornado	AM-X
Lightning	Atlantic
Jaguar	Casa-101
MB-326	

3. Definition of Combat Helicopters

For the purposes of the CFE negotiation, combat helicopters are permanently land-based, rotary wing aircraft constructed or later converted to employ air-to-air or air-to-surface ordnance such as guns, cannons, rockets, bombs, missiles or any other weapons of destruction. Any permanently land-based version or variant of these helicopters which has been modified to perform another military function is also included. A helicopter type should not, however, be included unless a combat variant of the type concerned exists within the ATTU area in the armed forces of a member state of the same treaty of alliance to which the participating state owning the aircraft belongs.

Appendix D: NATO Chapter Three

21 September 1989

Negotiations on Conventional Armed Forces in Europe

Position Paper Presented by the Delegations of Belgium, Canada, Denmark, Federal Republic of Germany, France, Greece, Iceland, Italy, Luxembourg, Netherlands, Norway, Portugal, Spain, Turkey, United Kingdom, and United States

CHAPTER III. Measures of Information Exchange, Stabilization, Verification and Non-Circumvention

I. Introduction

1. The proposals table by the member states of the Atlantic Alliance on 9th March and 13th July are designed to eliminate disparities in key categories of combat equipment relevant to surprise attack and offensive action and thereby to contribute towards the achievement of a more stable and secure balance of forces at lower levels. Full implementation of these proposals will dramatically reduce the capacity to conduct offensive operations. But a numerical parity in conventional forces in Europe, even at lower levels, will not by itself guarantee stability and security. Further measures are necessary to ensure that, insofar as is possible, the arms reductions we propose will in fact result in the lasting stability and security that we seek.

2. The additional measures necessary are:

—Exchange of Information

—Stabilizing Measures

—Verification Provisions

—Measures to Prevent Circumvention.

II. Exchange of Information

3. There will be an exchange of data on forces, sites and weapon systems as outlined

below. Each state will be responsible for its own data; receipt of this data and subsequent notifications will not imply validation or acceptance of the data.

4. Information to be Exchanged

(A) Each participant shall provide the following information about the structure of its land, air and air defence forces in the area of application:

(i) Its land forces command organization, showing the designation and subordination of all combat, combat support and combat service support formations and units at each level of command down to the level of battalion or equivalent,* indicating whether the unit is active duty or not.

(ii) Its air and air defences command organization,** showing the designation and subordination of formations and units at each level of command down to squadron or equivalent.

(B) For each of the above formations and units holding treaty-limited items, each participant shall provide the following information:

(i) The normal peacetime location of its headquarters component and of formations and units at which treaty-limited items are stationed or held, with exact geographical terms or coordinates and peacetime planned/authorized personnel strength.

(ii) The holdings at such locations of the following categories of treaty-limited equipment, specifying numbers and types:

—main battle tanks

—artillery pieces

—armored troop carriers

—combat aircraft

—combat helicopters

(iii) The locations and holdings of Armored Vehicle Launched Assault Bridges (AVLB), in active units.

*This is to include "low strength units"—See Stabilizing Measure 3 (D) (1).

**This is to include naval aviation permanently based on land.

(C) Each participant shall also provide information on the following within the area of application:

(i) The location, including exact geographical terms or coordinates, of storage depots monitored under the stabilizing and verification arrangements of this agreement, and the numbers and type of treaty-limited equipment held at such depots.

(ii) The numbers, types and permanent locations of treaty-limited items not belonging to the formations and units declared under (B)(i) above, and not in monitored storage.

(iii) The location, including exact geographical terms or coordinates, and the number of personnel assigned to low strength units* designated under Stabilizing Measure 3(D).

(iv) The location, including exact geographical terms or coordinates, of other sites where treaty-limited equipment may be present on a regular or periodic basis, such as repair and maintenance depots, training establishments, storage depots other than those subject to monitoring under verification measures of this agreement, and alternative operating airfields, and the numbers of any treaty-limited equipment permanently located at such sites.

(v) The numbers and location, including geographical terms or coordinates of AVLB in monitored storage and in any other sites not covered by 4(B)(iii).

(D) The U.S. and Soviet Union shall provide information on the number and location of their ground and air force personnel stationed on the territory of other participants in the area of application.

(E) Each participant shall also indicate the location of any sites which held equipment of the types subject to limitation under Chapter I after 1st January 1989, and from which such equipment has been withdrawn; each of these sites will have to be declared for (x) years following such withdrawal.
*As declared in Stabilizing Measure 3(D).

(F) In addition, each participant shall also provide information on the numbers, type and location of any main battle tanks, artillery pieces, armored troop carriers, combat aircraft and combat helicopters present on the territory of participants in the area of application, not subject to treaty limitation but with a potential for circumvention, e.g., equipment held by paramilitary forces and equipment which has been produced within the area of application but which is not in service with the armed forces of any participant.

5. Information required by paragraph 4 above shall be communicated in writing through diplomatic channels in accordance with an agreed format.

6. Each participant shall provide the stipulated information on its military structure, forces and equipment in the area of application:
—on signature of the Agreement, with information effective as of that date;
—on coming into force of the Agreement, with information effective as of that date;
—on 15th December of that year and the 15th December of every year thereafter (with information effective as of the 1st day of January the following year); and
—immediately after completion of reductions.

7. Notification of Changes in Organizational Structures or Force Levels

(A) Each participant shall notify all other participants 42 days in advance of any permanent change in the organizational structure of its existing units in the area of application or the permanent addition of any new unit of at least battalion/squadron or equivalent size to its forces in the area of application.

(B) Each participant shall notify all other participants of changes of 10 percent or more in the peacetime planned/authorized strength of personnel and of treaty-limited equipment in any of its treaty-limited equipment-holding combat, combat support or combat service support units down to the battalion/squadron or equivalent level in the area of application since the last annual report. All such changes shall be reported in the preceding annual information exchange or as they occur.

III. Stabilizing Measures

Measure 1: Notification of Call-up of Reservists

Any participant intending to call up 40,000 or more reservists in the area of application shall notify all other participants at least 42 days in advance. Such notification shall be in writing in an agreed format and shall include the number of reservists involved, the designation and location of the units affected, and the purpose and intended duration of the call-up.

Measure 2: Notification of Movements

(A) Any participant intending to move ground treaty-limited equipment from one location to another within the area of application shall notify all other participants at least 42 days in advance if such movements will exceed within 14 days the following levels:

Main Battle Tanks	600
Artillery	400
Armored Troop Carriers	1,200

(B) Notification made in compliance with this Measure shall be in writing, in an agreed format, and shall specify the number of items of treaty-limited equipment to be moved, their normal peacetime locations, the route of their movement to and from the new locations, and the purpose and intended duration of their presence in the new locations.

Measure 3: Monitored Storage

(A) Monitored Storage Requirement

(1) For each group of states belonging to the same treaty of alliance, equipment in active units shall not exceed the following levels in the area of application:

Main Battle Tanks	16,000
Artillery	14,500
Armored Troop Carriers	25,500

(2) Treaty-limited equipment which is within the total authorized ceilings but in excess of the ceilings for active units stated in paragraph (A)(1) shall be placed either in monitored storage sites as specified in (B) below or in monitored low strength units as specified in (D) within the area 4.2. Equipment located in area 4.3 shall, however, be placed in monitored storage sites.

(B) Monitored Storage Sites

(1) Only equipment placed in declared, monitored storage as specified in this Section shall be regarded as equipment in storage for compliance with the requirements of paragraph (A)(2) above.

(2) The location of monitored storage sites for treaty-limited equipment shall be declared and communicated to all CFE participants, along with information specifying the quantities of treaty-limited equipment stored at them.

(3) Monitored storage sites declared in accordance with paragraph (B)(2) shall be configured to ensure:

—an effective separation of stored equipment from active equipment;

—ease of monitoring;

—clearly defined boundaries with limited entrance and exit points.

(4) Participants may maintain as much treaty-limited equipment in non-monitored storage sites as they desire, but equipment kept at such sites shall be counted, solely for the purpose of this agreement, as being in active units.

(C) Removal from Monitored Storage

(1) Except as permitted by (C)(4) below, equipment may be removed from monitored storage only when the state intending to remove that equipment has notified all CFE participants at least 42 days prior to removal. Such equipment shall not remain out of storage for more than a period of 42 days.

(2) Equipment removed from monitored storage under (C)(1) by states belonging to the same treaty of alliance shall at no time exceed the following levels:

Main Battle Tanks	600
Artillery	400
Armored Troop Carriers	1,200

(3) Notification of the intended removal of equipment from monitored storage in compliance with (C)(1) shall specify the locations(s) of the site(s) from which the equipment is to be removed and shall provide details on the intended use of the equipment during the period of its removal from storage.

(4) Small (up to 10 percent of the figures in (C)(2) above) amounts may be removed for maintenance or other purpose without being subject to the time limit in (C)(1) and without prior notification except to any observer at the storage site.

(5) Replacement of equipment in monitored storage shall be notified by the state making the replacement at the time it takes place and shall include the dispositon of any removed equipment.

(D) Equipment in Monitored Low Strength Units

(1) For the purpose of the agreement, a definition of low strength units shall be agreed among the participants.

(2) The location of such units shall be declared and communicated to all CFE participants, along with information specifying the quantities.

(3) The treaty-limited equipment in such units shall be subject to observation and monitoring to the same level of confidence as that for treaty-limited equipment stored pursuant to (B) above.

(4) Participants may hold as many additional non-monitored low strength units as they desire, but equipment kept at such units shall be counted, solely for the purpose of this Agreement, as being in active units.

Measure 4: Limitation and Monitored Storage of Bridging Equipment

(A) For each group of states belonging to the same treaty of alliance, there shall be in active units in the area of application no more than 700 armored vehicle launched assault bridges.

(B) All armored vehicle launched assault bridges above the levels specified in (A) above shall be placed in monitored storage, as defined in Measure 3. A maximum of 50 items of such equipment may only be removed from monitored storage in accord with the provisions of Measure 3(C) above.

Measure 5: Constraint on the Size of Military Activities

(A) No participant shall conduct in the area of application any military activity involving more than 40,000 troops or 800 main battle tanks, if organized into a divisional structure or into at least 2 brigades/regiments not necessarily subordinate to the same division, except as permitted in (B) below.

(B) A participant may conduct one military activity exceeding the limits stated in (A) above within a period of 2 years. Such an activity shall require prior notification to other participants at least 12 month before the activity is to be conducted. The notification shall include the information specified under paragraph 56 of the Stockholm Document, supplemented by:

(1) The planned area of the military activity, indicated by geographic coordinates, and geographic features if appropriate.

(2) The planned duration of the activity, indicated by projected start and end dates.

(3) The envisaged total number (rounded to the nearest hundred) of troops taking part in the military activity. For activities involving more than one participant, the host state will provide such information for each participant involved.

(4) The planned level and designation of direct operational command under which the activity will take place.

(5) For each participant, the number, type and designation of each ground formation unit down to division or equivalent level whose participation is envisaged.

Air Stabilization Measures

8. The possibility of additional stabilizing measures to deal specifically with combat aircraft and helicopters should be addressed in due course.

IV. Verification Measures

Conceptual Approach

9. The CFE treaty will need to include a verification regime designed to:

—provide confidence that all parties are in compliance with treaty provisions;

—deter violation of treaty provisions;

—enable violations to be detected in a timely fashion.

Such a verification regime must be simple, reliable and as inexpensive as possible, consistent with the needs of effective verification.

10. Implementation of CFE verification provisions and judgments about treaty compliance will be the responsibility of each sovereign state party to the treaty, but treaty provisions should not impede whatever cooperative arrangements allies may choose to make in the exercise of those responsibilities.

11. The three major tasks will be:

(A) validation of baseline data, relating to the forces to be reduced;

(B) monitoring of reductions;

(C) confirmation of compliance with agreed residual force limits and other provisions for the life of the treaty.

Measure 1: Declared Sites

(A) All sites declared under the terms of paragraphs 4(B), 4(C) and 4(E) above shall be subject to inspection at short notice, with no right or refusal, and in accordance with the provisions in paragraph 12.

(B) Each state shall be liable to receive on its territory an agreed quota of inspections. The quota will reflect relevant parameters. The quotas will be expressed in terms of the number of days' presence on the territory of the receiving state of inspection teams.

(C) The intensity of inspections shall be greater during the initial (x) month period after the entry into force of the treaty in order to facilitate the initial validation of the baseline data. The armed forces of participants will not be required to suspend out-of-garrison training (stand-down) for the entire period of the baseline inspection.

(D) Within the quota in (B) above, the participant sending the inspection teams will be free to decide for how long each team will stay on the territory of the inspected state and which declared sites it will visit during this period, but no team may stay more than (y) days at any one site. While it is understood that the full inspection quota must be capable of being fulfilled, there will be a limit to the number of inspection teams that a participant must receive at any one time, according to (B) above.

(E) Provisions will also be required for the application of the inspection regime to the information provided under paragraph 4(D) above.

Measure 2: Non-Declared Sites

Participants shall also have the right to request inspection of other sites on the territory of another participant in the area of application. While there would be a right of delay and ultimately refusal, these should be kept to a minimum. In any case an obligation to attempt in good faith to satisfy the concerns of the party requesting an inspection at an undeclared site will remain. Quotas for such inspections could be based on the same criteria as those for declared sites, but differently weighted. Participants will agree on detailed modalities to govern such inspections, taking into account the provisions of paragraph 12 below.

Measure 3: Monitored Storage Sites and Monitored Low Strength Units

In addition to the provisions outlined in Measure 1, these sites and units will be subject to appropriate monitoring measures to be agreed.

Measure 4: Monitoring of Reductions

(A) Destruction of treaty-limited equipment that is to be reduced shall be in accordance with procedures to be agreed by the participants. This destruction shall take place at designated sites and shall be completed according to an agreed timetable within a period of (x) years.

(B) All destruction of equipment above agreed ceilings shall be notified in advance and be subject to on-site monitorings without quotas or right of refusal. Treaty-limited equipment shall be considered destroyed when agreed prior notification procedures have been followed, the destruction has been carried out in accordance with agreed procedures, and notification has been received that such destruction has been completed. Participants will agree on notification, destruction and monitoring procedures to be followed.

(C) Reduction of U.S. and Soviet stationed personnel shall be completed according to an agreed timetable within a period of (x) months and the reductions shall be subject to monitoring by any of the participants.

Measure 5: Monitoring the Stabilizing Measures

Participants shall also have the right to monitor, under appropriate conditions, the call-up of reservists (Stabilizing Measure 1), movements from one location to another (as notified under the terms of Stabilizing Measure 2), and the size of military activities (Stabilizing Measure 5).

Measure 6: Aerial Inspection

A CFE regime will include provisions for aerial inspection. Modalities and quotas require further study. The parties shall consider cooperative measures to enhance aerial inspection.

Measure 7: Possible Special Measures for Verification of Aircraft and Helicopter Limits

The possibility of additional measures to deal specifically with the verification of combat aircraft and combat helicopters, such as identification by number or perhaps tagging of aircraft and helicopters permanently land based in the area of application, requires further study.

Measure 8: National or Multinational Technical Means

(A) No participant shall interfere with national or multinational technical means of verification, or use concealment measures which impede verification of compliance with the CFE treaty except cover and concealment practices associated with normal training, maintenance, and operations.

(B) The participants shall consider cooperative measures to enhance national or multinational technical means of verification.

Measure 9: Joint Consultative Group

Participants will establish a Joint Consultative Group in the framework of which they will resolve ambiguities, address questions of compliance as well as promote the treaty's viability.

12. General Considerations

(A) No state shall exercise inspection rights on the territory of other parties who belong to the same treaty of alliance. Each inspection or monitoring team shall be the responsibility of one state. That state may include representatives of other members of the treaty of alliance to which it belongs on its inspection or monitoring team if it chooses. In conducting on-site inspections, the inspecting party should be permitted access, entry and unobstructed survey within the site that is being inspected except at sensitive areas or points.

(B) Each participant shall be entitled to conduct an agreed number of inspections upon the territory of other participants in the area of application. These active quotas are to be determined among the members of the same alliance. Unused quotas may be transferred to other members of the same alliance, however, no participant will be obliged to accept more than 50 percent of its passive quota of inspections in each calendar year from the same participant. The number of inspections available for the participants in each alliance should be sufficient for effective verification.

(C) Other details of modalities for verification provisions and the specific rights and duties of inspecting and inspected states will be agreed and contained in an inspection protocol.

V. Non-Circumvention

13. Each shall, in exercising its national sovereignty, have the right to withdraw from the treaty if it decides that extraordinary events related to the subject matter of the treaty have jeopardized its supreme interests. A party intending to withdraw shall give notice of its decision to withdraw to all other parties three months in advance of its withdrawal. Such notice shall include a statement of the extraordinary events the party regards as having jeopardized its supreme interests.

14. Each party shall, in particular, in exercising its national sovereignty, have the right to withdraw from this treaty if a party were to increase its holdings in tanks, artillery pieces, armored troop carriers, land-based combat aircraft or land-based combat helicopters, as defined in Chapter I, which are outside the scope of the limitations of the treaty, in such proportions as to pose a direct and obvious threat to the balance of forces within the area of application.

VI. Other Issues

15. Measures will also be required for the notification and monitoring, under appropriate circumstances to be worked out, of arrivals of main battle tanks, artillery pieces, armored troop carriers, land-based combat aircraft and land-based combat helicopters in the area of application, exits being duly taken into account so as to provide necessary assurance that the agreed ceilings under Chapter I will not be exceeded or circumvented.

16. Measures will be required to provide necessary assurance that the agreed ceilings under Chapter I are not exceeded or circumvented through the disposition in the zone of newly produced main battle tanks, artillery, armored troop carriers, land-based combat aircraft and land-based combat helicopters.

Appendix E: Western CSBM Proposal

Negotiations on Confidence- and Security-Building Measures in Europe

CSCE/WV.1/Amplified
Vienna, June 9, 1989
Original: English

Proposal Submitted by the Delegations of Belgium, Canada, Denmark, France, The Federal Republic of Germany, Greece, Iceland, Italy, Luxembourg, The Netherlands, Norway, Portugal, Spain, Turkey, The United Kingdom and The United States of America

The delegations of Belgium, Canada, Denmark, France, the Federal Republic of Germany, Greece, Iceland, Italy, Luxembourg, the Netherlands, Norway, Portugal, Spain, Turkey, the United Kingdom and the United States of America

—Recalling that the adoption of the Stockholm Document in September 1986 was a politically significant achievement and that its measures are an important step in efforts aimed at reducing the risk of military confrontation in Europe,

—Encouraged by the satisfactory implementation of these measures thus far,

—Determined to build upon and expand the results achieved at the Stockholm Conference and to carry forward the dynamic process of confidence-building,

—Stressing the complementary nature within the framework of the CSCE process of negotiations on further confidence- and security-building measures and negotiations on conventional armed forces in Europe,

—Determined

—to create greater transparency about military organization;

—to create greater transparency and predictability about military activities;

—to improve contacts and communications between the participating States;

—And determined, in the forthcoming negotiations, to promote an exchange of views on military policy,

—In conformity with the Madrid Mandate of 1983 as confirmed by the CSCE Review Meeting in Vienna in 1989, propose confidence- and security-building measures, including the following:

I. Transparency About Military Organization

These measures are designed to create more openness and confidence about the military force disposition of each participating State. This will be achieved by regular exchange of information on forces on land in the zone and on major weapons deployment programs. The information exchanged will be subject to evaluation.

Measure 1: Exchange of Military Information.

1. Each participating State will exchange information annually concerning its military organization, manpower and equipment in the zone. Such information will be provided to all other participating States, will be exchanged no later than the 15th day of December of each calendar year, and will be effective as of the first day of January the following year.

2. Each participating State will provide in writing, in an agreed format, the following information on its land forces:

(a) Its land forces command organization in the zone, including the designation and subordination of formations* and main combat units** at each level of command down to the level immediately below but not necessarily subordinate to division (brigade/regiment, or equivalent). The information given for each formation and main combat unit will include the normal peacetime locations of its HQ components with exact geographic terms or coordinates, and indicate whether the unit is active duty or not.***

*Formations are "army, corps, division."

**Combat units are defined as infantry, artillery, armoured, mechanized, motorized rifle, combat engineer or army aviation units.

***Active duty would be defined as any unit manned with at least 5 percent of war authorized strength (WAS).

(b) For each information and main combat unit identified in (a), the following details will be given:

(1) the authorized/planned peacetime troop strength;

(2) the weapon system and equipment holdings organic to the formation or main combat unit, specifying numbers and types, in the following categories:

—battle tanks

—antitank guided missile launchers permanently/integrally mounted on armoured vehicles.

—artillery pieces, mortars and multiple rocket launchers (100 mm calibre and above).

—helicopters.

—armoured troop carriers, i.e., Armoured Infantry Fighting Vehicles (AIFVs) and Armoured Personnel Carriers (APCs).

—mobile assault bridging.*

*Mobile assault bridging includes complete bridges, or bridge sections, carried on self-propelled or towed transporters or launchers. The unit of account is the number of specialized bridging vehicles in which the bridge/bridge section and its transporter are an integrated system.

3. Each participating State will also provide in writing, in an agreed format, the following information on its air forces:

(a) Its air forces command organization in the zone, stating the designation and subordination of land-based air formations** and main combat units at each level of command down to wing, air regiment or equivalent unit, including the location of the headquarters, with exact geographic terms or coordinates.

**Land-based air formations include air defense aviation units and those naval aviation units that operate permanently from land.

(b) For each formation and main combat unit identified in (a), the following details will be given:

(1) the authorized/planned peacetime troop strength.

(2) the number and types of fixed-wing aircraft and helicopters organic to the unit.

4. If a participating State transfers a formation or main combat unit identified in paragraph 2(a) above, together with its organic equipment, from one normal peacetime location to another inside the zone and the formation or main combat unit in question will remain in the new location for more than 30 days, the participating State involved will duly inform other participating States in Writing, in an agreed format, no later than the commencement of the transfer of the formation or main combat unit in question, of the change in the information provided under paragraph 2(a) above, giving the designation of the formation or main combat unit transferred, its new location and its old one.

5. If a participating State calls at least 40,000 reservists in the zone to active duty in addition to the troop strength already declared in paragraph 2(b)(1) above, and this recall is planned to last longer than seven days, the participating State involved will inform other participating States, in writing in an agreed format, not later than the planned time of call-out, of the change in the information provided under paragraph 2 above, including the number of troops and the designation and location of the units involved.

6. Clarification of any information provided under this measure may be requested through normal diplomatic channels.

Measure 2: Information Exchange on Major Conventional Weapon Deployment Programs.

1. Every year each participating State will exchange with all other participating States its program of planned weapon deployment in the zone for the subsequent year. This will indicate major weapon and equipment systems, in the categories specified in paragraphs 2(b)(2) and 3(b)(2) of Measure 1 above, planned to be introduced into service with formations and main combat units in its land and air forces in the zone.

2. This information will be communicated in writing through diplomatic channels by no later than the 15th December of each calendar year with effect from the first day of January of the following year and will be in accordance with the following format:

(a) the type and name of weapon /equipment system(s) (e.g. main battle tank Leopard II);

(b) the total number of weapon/equipment system(s) to be deployed;

(c) the numbers to be deployed in each formation and, to the degree possible, each main combat unit;

(d) whether the deployment will add to or replace existing weapon/equipment system(s).

Measure 3: Establishment of a Random Evaluation System Related to the Exchange of Information.

1. To evaluate the information provided under Measures 1 and 2 above, a random evaluation system will be set up. The system will provide for access to the active duty formations and main combat units reported under paragraphs 2(b) and 3(b) of Measure 1 in their normal peacetime locations in order to check the validity of the information provided.

2. Each participating State will accept a number of evaluation visits each year equal to 10 percent of the total number of its main combat units (brigades/regiments, or equivalent) declared under paragraphs 2(a) and 3(a) of Measure 1, or a minimum of three visits per year, whichever is higher. Any individual formation or main combat unit can only be visited twice a year and only once by a particular State. No State will have to accept more than 1/5 of the total or eight (whichever is the lower) visits by the same State in any one year.

3. Requests will be submitted through diplomatic channels giving seven days' notice to the host State. The host State will respond to the request within 72 hours of the request being received, indicating whether the specified formation or main combat unit will be available at its normal peacetime location for evaluation at the time the visit is to be made. If the formation or main combat unit is absent from its normal peacetime location, and therefore unavailable for evaluation, the reasons for its absence (e.g., its participation in exercise activity away from its normal peacetime location) should be stated and the duration of its absence indicated. However, a formation or main combat unit's absence from its normal peacetime location for training or other activity need not prevent the host State from accepting an evaluation visit to its normal peacetime location if the requesting State so desires. If the formation or main combat unit is at its normal peacetime location but unavailable for evaluation, reasons should also be stated and the duration of unavailability indicated. In those cases where units are unavailable for evaluation whilst in their normal peacetime location, each State is entitled to refuse a request for evaluation up to five times per year for an aggregate of no more than 30 days per year. If, for any reason, visits are not carried out as a result of nonavailability of the unit in question, a request for evaluation will not count against the quota of either State.

4. Evaluation visits to specified normal peacetime locations, lasting for a working day of up to 12 hours' duration, will be carried out by teams of up to two military or civilian personnel either already accredited to the Government of the host State or designated by the visiting State for the purpose of the visit. In the latter case, visiting personnel will be accredited to the Government of the host State and will be granted, during their mission, the privileges and immunities accorded to diplomatic agents in the Vienna Convention or Diplomatic Relations.

5. The evaluation visit will begin with a meeting with the officer commanding the active duty formation and/or main combat units with headquarters at the location in question (or his representative). With a view to facilitating the evaluation, the officer commanding will be required to account for the personnel, vehicles and weapon systems declared under paragraph 2(b) or 3(b) of Measure 1 and provide the opportunity to observe them in their normal locations. Immediate access to equipment is at the discretion of the unit being visited. Access will not be granted into sensitive facilities, such as command posts, communications facilities, equipment and ammunition storage. The use of photographic equipment will not be permitted. The evaluation teams will be accompanied at all times by representatives of the host State. The visit will not interfere with the activities of the units involved. Further, no scheduled training or other activity requiring a unit's absence from garrison will be cancelled for a random evaluation visit.

6. The host State may delegate some of its responsibilities as host to another participating State with troops stationed in locations declared under Measure 1 on the territory of the host State. In such cases the host State will specify the division of responsibilities between it and the other State in its response to a request in accordance with paragraph 3 above.

7. Costs for the transportation and accommodation of personnel carrying out a random evaluation will be borne by the sending State.

8. A report of the evaluation visit will be prepared by the visiting State and communicated to all CSCE participating States without delay.

II. Transparency and Predictability of Military Activities.

These measures will build upon those agreed in Stockholm by refining them in order to enhance openness and produce greater predictability of military activities.

Measure 4: Enhanced Information in the Annual Calendar.

1. Military activities subject to prior notification will be included in the annual calendars of both the participating State conducting the activity and the State on whose territory the activity takes place.

2. In addition to the information included under Measure 56 of the Stockholm Document, annual calendars will include:

(a) Planned area of the military activity, indicated by geographic coordinates, and geographic features if appropriate.

(b) Planned duration of the activity indicated, by projected start and end dates.

(c) The envisaged total number (rounded to the nearest hundred) of troops taking part in the military activity. For activities involving more than one State, the host State will provide such information for each State involved.

(d) The planned level and designation of direct operational command under which the activity will take place.

(e) For each participating State, the number, type and designation of each land force formation down to divisional level whose participation is envisaged.

Measure 5: Enhanced Information in Notification.

In addition to the information included under Measure 35 of the Stockholm Document, participating States will indicate:

(a) The number of reservists (i.e., military personnel to be called up) taking part in the military activity (i.e., ground troops, amphibious troops, airmobile, airborne troops) and the number of reservists participating for each State involved, if applicable.

(b) The designation, subordination, number and type of land force formations participating for each State down to brigade/regiment level.

(c) Numbers of fixed-wing aircraft sorties by functional missions (e.g., air defense, attack, electronic warfare, reconnaissance or transport).

(d) The designation, subordination, number and type of land force formations and main combat units down to bridge/regiment level, which are to be transferred into the zone.

Measure 6: Improvements to Observation Modalities

1. At the commencement of the observation program, the host State will give a briefing covering:

(a) the purpose, the basic situation and the phases of the activity;

(b) the dispositions of the brigades/regiments involved, with their unit designations;

(c) possible changes as compared with the notification.

2. The host State will normally provide the observers with:

(a) a map with a scale of 1 to no more than 250,000 depicting the area of the military activity and the tactical situation (smaller-scale maps may be used to depict the entire exercise area);

(b) an observation program with a daily schedule.

3. As part of the commencement briefing, participating States are encouraged, whenever possible and with due consideration for the security of the observers, to provide a helicopter survey of the area of the activity so that at least one observer from each participating State gets an impression of the scope and scale of the activity. Helicopters may be provided either by the host State, or by another participating State in accord with the host State. If such surveys are provided, the observers will be given the opportunity to observe the disposition of combat and support units of the participating brigades/regiments.

4. Observers will be provided with appropriate observation equipment; in addition, the observers will be permitted to use their own binoculars, maps, photo cameras, dictaphones

and hand-held passive night vision devices. The above-mentioned equipment will be subject to examination and approval by the host State.

5. In the course of the observation program, the observers will be given daily briefings, aided by maps with an overlay or overprint depicting the disposition of participating brigades/regiments with their unit designations. In addition, the briefing will provide information on the various phases of activity. In the case of a land force activity conducted in combination with air or naval components, briefings will be given by representatives of these forces.

6. The host State will provide opportunities to observe directly forces of the State/States engaged in the military activity so that the observers get an impression of the flow of the entire activity. To this end, the observers will be given the opportunity to observe combat units of the participating brigades/regiments and, whenever possible, to visit elements of these units and to communicate with commanders and troops. Commanders or other senior personnel of participating formations as well as of the visited units will inform the observers of the mission and disposition of their troops. When the nature of the activity makes it appropriate, the host State will provide the observers with the opportunity to divide into two sub-groups to carry out their functions.

7. At the close of each observation, the host State will provide an opportunity for the observers to meet together and with host State officials to discuss the course of the observed activity.

8. The host State will determine a duration of observation which permits the observers to observe a notifiable military activity from the time that agreed thresholds for observation are met or exceeded until 24 hours after the number of troops participating in the activity falls below the observation threshold.

Measure 7: Changes to Thresholds.

Notifiable activities will be subject to observation whenever the number of troops engaged meets or exceeds 13,000 or if more than 300 tanks participate in them, except in the case of either an amphibious landing or a parachute assault by airborne forces, which will be subject to observation whenever the number of troops engaged meets or exceeds 3,000 troops.

Measure 8: Improvements to Inspection Provisions.

1. No participating State will be obliged to accept on its territory within the zone of application for CSBMs more than five inspections per calendar year.

2. A receiving State's reply to an inspection request will be given within 16 hours. Inspection teams will be permitted to enter the territory of the receiving State not earlier than 24 hours after the issuance of the request.

3. Preliminary aerial survey.

(a) At the request of the inspecting State, a preliminary aerial survey of the specified area may be conducted after the arrival of the inspecting team. The time used for such a preliminary aerial survey will precede and not count towards the 48-hour period allotted for inspection as stipulated in the Stockholm Document. An inspecting State requesting a preliminary aerial survey will have the right to conduct such a survey for up to four hours. All rights, immunities and privileges applicable to the conduct of an inspection will be extended to the team for the conduct of the preliminary aerial survey.

(b) Should an inspecting State request a preliminary aerial survey, it may include its preferred flight plan in its inspection request. If such a flight plan has been included, the receiving State will either indicate its approval or specify changes, indicating the reasons (to avoid sensitive points or for safety considerations) in its reply to the inspecting State.

(c) Such a survey will begin from a point as close as possible to the point of entry. The survey will end at, or as close as possible to, the point designated in the request for the beginning of the inspection.

(d) A fixed-wing aircraft or helicopter will be provided by the receiving State, or by another State participating in the activity, in concert with the receiving State.

(e) The receiving State will have the right to accompany the inspection team aboard the aircraft during a preliminary aerial survey.

4. Improvements to Inspection Modalities.

(a) There will be no more than six members in an inspection team. While conducting the inspection, the inspection team may divide into no more than two sub-teams.

(b) The inspection team will have the use of its own maps, photo cameras, binoculars, dictaphones and any hand-held passive night vision devices as well as aeronautical charts.

(c) The inspection team will have access to appropriate telecommunications equipment of the receiving State for the purpose of communicating with its embassy or other official missions and consular points located on the territory of the receiving State and for continuous communication between the sub-teams.

(d) At their request, inspectors will be given briefings at agreed times by commanders of units/formations conducting military activities within the specified area.

Measure 9: Lowering the Threshold for Longer Notice of Larger-Scale Activities.

Participating States will not carry out military activities subject to prior notification involving more than 50,000 troops unless they have been the subject of communication defined in Measure 59 of the Stockholm Document.

III. Contacts and Communication.

These measures are designed to increase the knowledge about the military capabilities of the participating States by developing communications and military contacts.

Measure 10: Improved Access for Accredited Personnel Dealing with Military Matters.

1. In order to implement the principle of greater openness in military organization and activities and to enhance mutual confidence, restrictions on the activities in the CDE zone of personnel dealing with military matters and accredited to the host Government will be reduced substantially.

2. Therefore the participating States will:

(a) Reduce any existing requirements for advance notification to host State authorities of travel in connection with their duties by accredited personnel in the CDE zone. The notice required for such advance written notification will not exceed 48 hours (not including Saturdays, Sundays or holidays) before the anticipated departure. The host State will indicate in writing whether the requested dates and time of departure and return, itinerary, mode of travel and contacts with specified officials are approved. Accredited personnel will not be required to delay travel if host State response is not given before the time of departure.

(b) Reduce restrictions on those travel arrangements which must be made through host State authorities; specifically, accredited personnel may select the routes they wish to take and the commercial overnight accommodation they wish to use. Nonavailability of accommodation should not be used as an excuse of frustrate travel.

3. The number and size of areas not open to accredited personnel should be as small as possible and be restricted to military sites and restricted areas relevant to State security. Areas ordinarily restricted to the citizens of the host State may also be closed to accredited personnel.

4. Subject to the national regulations of the host country and international commitments, accredited personnel should have the opportunity to use any communication means available to them to maintain continuous contact with their embassies or other official missions and consular posts, including the carrying and use of their own communications equipment, including two-way radios.

5. Nothing in this Measure may be construed to diminish or otherwise affect the privileges extended to accredited personnel dealing with military matters under any applicable existing or future bilateral arrangements, understandings, or international agreements.

Measure 11: Development of Means of Communication.

Diplomatic channels will be used for communications concerning measures agreed upon in this document. Each participating State will designate a point of contact of receiving such information, preferably on a 24-hour basis. Participating States may consider additional arrangements, such as public telex lines, for transmitting diplomatic communications related to agreed measures.

Measure 12: Equal Treatment of Media Representatives.

Participating States are encouraged to permit media representatives from all participating States to attend observed military activities. In such instances, media representatives from all participating States will be treated without discrimination and given equal access to those facets of the activity open to any members of the media.

Exchanges of Views on Military Policy.

Confidence-building is a dynamic process which is enhanced by the free and frank interchange of ideas designed to reduce misunderstanding and misrepresentation of military capabilities. To this end, participating States will, in the forthcoming negotiations, avail themselves of the following opportunities:

—to discuss issues concerning the implementation of the provisions of the Stockholm Document;

—to discuss, in a seminar setting, military doctrine in relation to the posture and structure of conventional forces in the zone, including, inter alia:

—exchanging information on their annual military spending;

—exchanging information on the training of their armed forces, including references to military manuals;

—seeking clarification on developments giving rise to uncertainty, such as changes in the number and pattern of notified military activities.

Glossary

ABM	Anti-Ballistic Missile Treaty
ACDA	U.S. Arms Control and Disarmament Agency
ACV	Armored Combat Vehicle
AFAP	Artillery-Fired Atomic Projectile
AFCENT	(NATO) Allied Forces, Central Region
AFNORTH	(NATO) Allied Forces, Northern Region
AFSOUTH	(NATO) Allied Forces, Southern Region
AFV	Armored Fighting Vehicle
AIFV	Armored Infantry Fighting Vehicle (vehicle with a turret)
APC	Armored Personnel Carrier
ARSTAF	Army Staff
ARTY	Artillery
ATACMS	Army Tactical Missile System
ATC	Armored Troop Carrier
ATTU	Atlantic-to-the-Urals
AVLB	Armored-Vehicle-Launched Bridge
CAA	U.S. Army Concepts Analysis Agency
CAS	Close Air Support
CBT	Combat
CDE	Conference on Confidence- and Security-Building Measures and Disarmament in Europe
CFE	Negotiations on Conventional Armed Forces in Europe
CONUS	Continental United States

CS	Combat Support
CSBM(s)	Confidence- and Security-Building Measure(s)
CSBM Talks	Negotiations on Confidence- and Security-Building Measures
CSCE	Conference on Security and Cooperation in Europe
CSS	Combat Service Support
C^3I	Command, Control, Communications, and Intelligence
DC	Deputies Committee, National Security Council
DCA	Dual-Capable Aircraft
DCS	Dual-Capable Systems
DOD	U.S. Department of Defense
EEC	European Economic Community
EEP	Exit–Entry Point
F_{DEP}	Forward Deployed Units in West Germany
F_{MIN}	Minimum Force Density Requirement
FOFA	Follow-on Forces Attack
FOTL	Follow-on to Lance
FRG	Federal Republic of Germany
GDP	Gross Domestic Product
GDR	German Democratic Republic
HLTF	High Level Task Force
IC	(Allied) Intelligence Communities
IFV	Infantry Fighting Vehicle
IGB	East/West/Inter/German Border
INF	Intermediate-Range Nuclear Forces
IPB	Intelligence Preparation of the Battlefield
I&W	(NATO's) Indications and Warning (Systems)
JCS	Joint Chiefs of Staff
LBNA	Land-Based Naval Air
LOSAT	Line of Sight Anti-Tank
LRINF	Long-Range Intermediate Nuclear Forces
MBFR	Mutual and Balanced Force Reduction
MBT	Main Battle Tank
MC 14/3	NATO Military Committee Document Number Fourteen Slant Three
MDs	Military Districts
MLRS	Multiple Launch Rocket Systems
NAC	North Atlantic Council
NDU	National Defense University

NGA	NATO Guidelines Area
NNA	Neutral and Nonaligned Nations
NORTHAG	Northern Army Group
NSC	National Security Council
NSD-1	National Security Directive 1
NSWP	Non-Soviet Warsaw Pact
NTM	National Technical Means
OJCS	Office of the Joint Chiefs of Staff (staffers, not principals)
OSI	On-Site Inspection
PC	Principals Committee, National Security Council
PCC	Policy Coordination Committees, National Security Council
PGM	Precision Guided Missile
POMCUS	Pre-positioning of Materiel Configured to Unit Sets
R_{ATTU}	Reinforcing Units from within Western Europe
R_{CONUS}	Reinforcing Units from the Continental United States
REFORGER	Return of Forces to Germany
SACEUR	Supreme Allied Commander Europe
SALT	Strategic Arms Limitation Treaty
SAM	Surface-to-Air Missile
SAS	European Study Group on Alternative Security Policy
SC	Subcommittees
SHAPE	Supreme Headquarters, Allied Powers Europe
SLCM	Sea-Launched Cruise Missile
SNF	Short-Range Nuclear Forces
SSI	Strategic Studies Institute
SSM	Surface-to-Surface Missile
START	Strategic Arms Rductions Talks
STC	SHAPE Technical Center
SYDP	Six-Year Defense Program
TBD	To Be Determined
TLE	Treaty Limited Equipment
TLI	Treaty Limited Items
TOE	Table of Organization and Equipment
TRS	Theater Reserve Stocks
USG	United States Government
WEU	Western European Union

WP	Warsaw Pact
WRM	War Reserve Materiel
WRS	War Reserve Stock
WTO	Warsaw Treaty Organization

Bibliography

Adams, Peter. "Complex Issues Confront Conventional Arms Talks." *Defense News*, February 13, 1989, p. A3.

Allison, Graham. "Success is Within Reach." *The New York Times*, February 19, 1989, p. E19.

Arendt, Hannah. "What is Authority?" In *Between Past and Future*. New York: Viking Press, 1968, p. 93.

Baker, Caleb. "Marine Corps' Mission Debate Rekindles as Threat Changes." *Defense News*, September 12, 1988, p. 4.

Baker, James A. III. Secretary of State. From a speech at the Berlin Press Club; excerpts reprinted in *The Washington Post*, December 13, 1989, p. A18.

Barnaby, Frank, and Boeker, Egbert, eds. *Rethinking the Nuclear Weapons Dilemma*. New York: St Martins Press, 1988. Pp. 134–45: "Non-Nuclear, Non-Provocative Defense for Europe."

Barnaby, Frank, and ter Borg, Marlies, eds. *Emerging Technologies and Military Doctrine: A Political Assessment*. New York: St Martins Press, 1986. Pp. 89–109: "Emphasizing Defense," by Egbert Bocker and Lutz Unterseher.

Blackwell, Robert D., and Larrabee, Stephen, eds. *Conventional Arms Control and East-West Security*. Durham, N.C.: Duke University Press, 1989. Pp. 422–46; "Nuclear Weapons and Conventional Arms Control," by Arnold Kanter.

Borawski, John; Weeks, Stan; and Thompson, Charlotte E. "The Stockholm Agreement of September 1986." *Orbis*, Winter 1987, pp. 643–62.

Brooke, James. "Cuba Pulls 450 Soldiers Out of Angola." *The New York Times*, January 11, 1989, p. A10.

Calleo, David. *Beyond American Hegemony: The Future of the Western Alliance*. New York: Basic Books, 1987.

Carlucci, Frank C. *Report of the Secretary of Defense Frank C. Carlucci to the Congress on the FY1990/FY1991 Bienniel Budget and FY1990–94 Defense Programs*. Washington, D.C.: U.S. Government Printing Office, 1989.

Chira, Susan. "Japan Ready to Share Burden, But Also the Power, with U.S." *The New York Times*, March 7, 1989, p. A1.

Cockburn, Patrick. "Third World: Stronger, Bolder." *The New York Times*, June 20, 1988, p. A19.

Cohen, Stephen F. Centrists Lack the Guts to Respond to Gorbachev." *The New York Times*, September 19, 1988, p. A23.

"Conceptual Approach to the Reduction of Conventional Armed Forces in Europe." Translation by USIS, presented as the March 9, 1989 Proposal by the Delegation of the Warsaw Pact to the CFE Negotiations, Vienna, Austria, March 9, 1989, pp. 2–6.

"Conventional Forces in Europe: The Facts." NATO Press Information Service, Brussels, Belgium, November 25, 1989.

Cox, Arthur Macy. "Mr. Gorbachev's Peaceful Coexistence Ploy." *The New York Times*, June 25, 1988, p. 27.

"CSSR Delegate Outlines Pact CFE Proposal." Translated from *Rude Pravo*, FBIS-EEU-89-128, July 6, 1989 (in Czech), June 30, 1989, p. 7.

Darilek, Richard. "The Future of Conventional Arms Control in Europe, A Tale of Two Cities: Stockholm, Vienna." *Survival*, January-February 1987, pp. 5–20.

Davis, Lynn E. "Arms Control and the Alliance." In *The Alliance at Forty: Strategic Perspective for the 1990s and Beyond*. Washington, D.C.: National Defense University, April 24–25, 1989, p. 3.

Dean, Jonathan. "Alternative Defense: Answer to NATO's Central Front Problem?" *International Affairs*, Winter 1987–88, pp. 61–82.

——— . "The Exclusionary Zone: An American Approach." In The New Force Reduction Negotiations in Europe: Problems and Prospects. Paper presented at an AAAS Annual Meeting Symposium, 1989, pp. 5–8.

——— . "Defining Long-Term Western Objectives in the CFE Negotiations." *Washington Quarterly*, Winter 1990, Vol. 13, No. 1, pp. 169–84.

"Declaration of the Heads of State and Government Participating in the Meeting of the North Atlantic Council in Brussels." Press Communique M-1 (89) 29, NATO Press Service, May 30, 1989, p. 4.

Deibel, Terry L., and Gaddis, John Lewis, eds. *Containment: Concept and Policy*, Vol. 1. Washington, D.C.: National Defense University Press, 1986. P. 219: "Military Instruments of Containment," by Paul A. Gorman (General, USA Retired).

"Documentation: Conference on Disarmament in Europe." *Survival*, January-February 1987, pp. 79–84.

Einvardsson, Johann. "Draft Interim Report of the Subcommittee on Confidence- and Security-Building Measures," Internal Secretariat, North Atlantic Assembly, May 1989, pp. 8–9.

Farah, Douglas. "Salvadoran Guerrillas Step up Armed Attacks." *The Washington Post*, October 20, 1988, p. A34.

Ferguson, Yale H., and Mansbach, Richard W. *The State, Conceptual Chaos, and the Future of International Relations Theory, 1989*. Lynne Rienner Publishers, Fall 1988–Winter 1989.

Flanagan, Stephen J. "Nonoffensive Defense Is Overrated." *Bulletin of the Atomic Scientists*, September 1988, pp. 46–48.

Gaillard, Regina. "The Trilateral Commission; Its Goals and World Policy: Is There a Latin American Connection?" Unpublished dissertation, University of Miami, 1984, p. 70.

Gates, David. "Area Defense Concepts: The West German Debate." *Survival*, July-August 1987, pp. 302-3.

Gilpin, Robert G. *The Political Economy of International Relations*. Princeton: Princeton University Press, 1987, pp. 224-27.

Gordon, Michael. "Warsaw Pact Offers Details of Its European Arms Proposal." *The New York Times*, May 31, 1989, p. 15.

Goshko, John M., and Devroy, Ann. "Moscow Warned on Use of Force." *The Washington Post*, November 11, 1989, p. A23.

Greenberger, Robert S., and Carrington, Tim. "Peace is Proliferating in Many Trouble Spots from Mideast to Asia." *Wall Street Journal*, July 29, 1988, p. 1.

Guertner, Gary L. "Conventional Deterrence after Arms Control," *Parameters*, U.S. Army War College Quarterly, Carlisle Barracks, PA: Vol. 19, No. 4, December 1989, pp. 67-79.

Halloran, Richard. "Navy's Top Officer Says Military Cannot Halt Influx of Latin Drugs." *The New York Times*, July 23, 1988, p. 10.

Helprin, Mark. "Hypnotist Gorbachev Conjures an Arms Reduction." *The Washington Post*, December 13, 1988, p. A20.

Hoagland, Jim. "Leaders Worry How German Events Might Affect EC Integration Plans." *The Washington Post*, November 11, 1989, p. A23.

Hopman, Terrence, and Barnaby, Frank, eds. *Rethinking the Nuclear Weapons Dilemma in Europe*. New York: St Martins Press, 1988. Pp. 146-82: "West German Alternatives for Reducing Reliance on Nuclear Weapons," by Hans Gunter Brauch.

Ignatius, David, and Getler, Michael. "The Great Non-Debate on American Foreign Policy." *The Washington Post*, October 23, 1988, p. C1.

The International Institute for Strategic Studies. *Strategic Survey*. London: IISS, 1976, pp. 57-58.

——— . *Strategic Survey 1980-1981*. London: IISS, 1981, pp. 83-84.

——— . *Strategic Survey 1986-1987*. London: IISS, 1987, p. 70.

Karber, Phillip A. *NATO-Warsaw Pact Force Levels in a Conventional Arms Control Context*. Vol. 2, *Atlantic-to-the-Urals Summary*. Washington, D.C.: BDM Corporation, August 11, 1989.

——— . "Strategic Significance of the Western Conventional Arms Control Proposal: In the Context of the Gorbachev Unilateral Reductions and the CFE Negotiations in Vienna." Testimony before the Senate Armed Services Committee, April 6, 1989, pp. 1-6.

Karber, Phillip A., and Milan, John H. "Conventional Force Reductions in Europe: A Comparison of NATO and WTO CFE Proposals." A presentation before the New Alternatives Workshop: Arms Control and Technology, May 25, 1989, pp. 1-8.

Karkoszka, Andrzej. "A Modified Approach to Conventional Arms Control." Summarized in "An East-West Negotiating Proposal," *Bulletin of Atomic Scientists*, September 1988, pp. 41ff.

Kempe, Frederick, "Perez de Cuellar Wins U.N. New Respect." *Wall Street Journal*, September 26, 1988, p. 22.

Kenman, George F. "The Gorbachev Prospect." *New York Review of Books*, January 21, 1988, p. 3.

Kennedy, Paul. *The Rise and Fall of the Great Powers: Economic Change and Military Conflict from 1500 to 2000*. New York: Random House, 1987.

Keohane, Robert O., ed. *Neorealism and Its Critics*. New York: Columbia University Press, 1986. P. 293: "The Poverty of Neorealism," by Richard K. Ashley; Ibid., p. 137: "Continuity and Transformation in the World Polity: Toward a Neorealist Synthesis."

Lewis, Flora. "Salvador at a Crossroads." *The New York Times*, February 19, 1989, p. E19.

Lewis, Paul. "Third World Must Stem Arms Flow, Shultz Warns." *The York Times*, June 14, 1988, p. A15.

Lykke, Arthur F., ed. *Military Strategy: Theory and Application*. Carlisle Barracks, Pa: U.S. Army War College, 1989. Pp. 383-91: "Why Arms Control Has Failed," by Edward N. Luttwak.

McCartney, Robert J. "NATO Sets Goals for Arms Cuts." *The Washington Post*, March 3, 1988, pp. A27 and A30.

Markham, James J. "The Idea That Democracy Pays Helps Reshape East-West Ties." *The New York Times*, September 22, 1988, p. 1E.

Moore, Molly, and Wilson, George C. "Pentagon Drafts Major Cuts in Forces, Weapons." *The Washington Post*, November 28, 1989, p. A1.

Morganthau, Hans J. *Politics among Nations*. New York: Alfred A. Knopf, 1963, p. 5.

Morrocco, John D. "Defense Department Grapples with Massive Spending Cuts." *Aviation Week and Space Technology*, November 27, 1989, p. 16.

NATO Information Service. "Halifax Communique." Brussels, Belgium: NATO, 1986.

———— . *NATO Handbook*. Brussels, Belgium: NATO, 1983, p. 27.

Nunn, Sam. U.S. Senator. "NATO Challenges and Opportunities: A Three-Track Approach." *Congressional Record*, Vol. 133, No. 66, April 28, 1987, pp. 4-5.

———— . "The American/Soviet Disarmament Negotiations and Their Consequences for NATO." Speech to the Wehrkunde Conference. Munich, West Germany, February 8, 1988, pp. 5-6.

Oberdorfer, Don. "Bush Proposes Cutback in U.S. Troops in Europe." *The Washington Post*, May 30, 1989, p. A1.

Ottaway, David B. "Foreign Aid Largely a Failure, U.S. Report Says." *The Washington Post*, October 20, 1988, p. A34.

Preston, Julia. "Soviets Raise Profile, But Not Aid, in Managua." *The Washington Post*, November 6, 1988, p. A37.

Reagan, Ronald W. *National Security Strategy of the United States*. Washington, D.C.: The White House, 1988, pp. 3-4.

Robb, Charles S. "Support the Peace Plan and the Contras." *The Washington Post*, January 24, 1988, p. C7.

Rosenberger, Leif. "Toward a U.S.-Soviet Agreement in the Philippines." *SAIS Review*, Vol. 9, No. 1, Winter-Spring 1989, pp. 213-26.

Saperstein, Alvin M. "Non Provocative Defense and Disengagement Zones." In *Defending Europe: Options for Security*. Philadelphia: Taylor and Francis, 1985, pp. 210-24.

Scanlon, Michael E. "Conventional Armed Forces in Europe (CFE) Negotiations: Facts and Figures." In *CRS Report to Congress*. Washington, D.C.: Congressional Research Service, Library of Congress, October 30, 1989, p. 14.

Sharp, Gene. *Making Europe Unconquerable*. Cambridge, Mass.: Ballinger, 1986.

Shaver, David E. *Force Structures: The United States and Europe in the Coming Decade*. Carlisle Barracks, Pa.: Strategic Studies Institute, June 12, 1989, pp. 7-11.

Sloss, Leon, and Davis, M. Scott, eds. *A Game for High Stakes: Lessons Learned in Negotiating with the Soviet Union.* Cambridge, Mass.: Ballinger, 1986. Pp. 79–106: "East–West Arms Negotiations: The Multilateral Dimension," by Jonathan Dean.

Smith, R. Jeffrey. "NATO Arms Cut Proposal Faulted as Too Cautious." *The Washington Post,* April 17, 1989, p. A27.

Stewart Jim. "Alliance Confronts New Adversary: Public Opinion." *The Atlanta Journal and the Atlanta Constitution,* April 2, 1989, p. 1.

Stockholm International Peace Research Institute, ed. *Tactical Nuclear Weapons: European Perspectives.* New York: Crane, Russak & Co., 1978. Pp. 262–95: "Tactical Nuclear Weapons in European Security," by H. Afheldt.

Strategic Studies Institute, U.S. Army War College. *Conventional Arms Control in Europe: Army Perspectives.* Carlisle Barracks, Pa.: October 1987, p. 5.

——— . *How to Think about Conventional Arms Control: A Framework.* Carlisle Barracks, Pa.: June 24, 1988, pp. 13, 17, 23, 80.

Talbott, Strobe. "Of Deficits and Diplomacy." *Time,* March 6, 1989, p. 26.

ter Borg, Marlies, and Smit, Wim A., eds. *Non-Provocative Defense as a Principle of Arms Reduction.* Amsterdam: Free University Press, 1989. Pp. 161–74: "Restructuring the Ground Forces," by Andreas von Bulow.

Toufexis, Anastasia. "Too Many Mouths." *Time,* January 2, 1989, p. 48.

"Transcript of Bush's Remarks on Transforming Soviet–American Relations." *The New York Times,* May 13, 1989, p. 6.

Tyler, Patrick E. "Pentagon Says Troop Strength Might Decline by 10 Percent." *The Washington Post,* November 9, 1989, p. 1.

Tyson, Ann Scott. "Moscow to Help Speed Vietnam Pullout." *Christian Science Monitor,* September 6, 1988, p. 11.

U.S. Arms Control and Disarmament Agency (ACDA). "Negotiations on Conventional Armed Forces in Europe: NATO Objectives." In *ACDA Update,* No. 12, March 1989, pp. 4–5.

——— . *CFE: Negotiations on Conventional Armed Forces in Europe.* Washington, D.C.: Office of Public Affairs, October 1989.

U.S. Department of Defense. *Soviet Military Power: An Assessment of the Threat.* Washington, D.C.: U.S. Government Printing Office, 1988, p. 19.

U.S. Department of State. "Conference on Disarmament in Europe." *GIST,* January 1986, p. 1.

——— . "The Conference on Security and Cooperation in Europe." *Historical Issues Series,* October 1986, various pages.

——— . "Declaration on Conventional Arms Control December 12, 1986." *Department of State Bulletin,* March 1987, p. 43.

U.S. Government Memorandum U-427/DI-5. "NATO CFE–Related Aircraft Defense Aid." Washington, D.C.: U.S. Government Printing Office, July 17, 1989.

U.S. Information Service. "Conceptual Approach to the Reduction of Conventional Armed Forces in Europe (Proposal by Warsaw Pact)." Washington, D.C.: U.S. Government Printing Office, March 9, 1989, pp. 2–6.

U.S. National Security Council. "Description of the National Security Council Organization." Washington, D.C.: U.S. Government Printing Office, April 18, 1989, pp. 1–3.

van Loon, Henry, "An Exclusive AFJ Interview with: General John R. Galvin, USA." *Armed Forces Journal,* March 1988, p. 50.

Waltz, Kenneth N. *Theory of International Politics*. Reading, Mass.: Addison-Wesley, 1979.

Wayne, E. A. "Momentum Sought for Talks on Cutting Conventional Weapons." *Christian Science Monitor*, February 17, 1988, p. 5.

Williams, Phil. "American Troops in Europe: A New Great Debate?" *The World Today*, December 1987, p. 217F.

Index

About the Editors and Contributors

COLONEL RALPH A. HALLENBECK is Chief of the Army's Conventional Arms Negotiation Division, Office of the Deputy Chief of Staff for Operations and Plans, Headquarters, Department of the Army. His previous assignments have included command of two infantry companies in Vietnam, a mechanized infantry battalion in Europe, and a variety of staff positions in infantry brigades and divisions. He has served as Chief of Current Operations, U.S. European Command, as Assistant Professor of Political Science at the United States Military Academy, as Military Adviser to the U.S. Delegation to the Strategic Arms Limitation Talks (SALT II) in Geneva, and as Acting Deputy Assistant Secretary of State for Defense and Arms Control. Colonel Hallenbeck is a graduate of the United States Military Academy, the U.S. Army Command and General Staff and Senior Service Colleges, and he served an Army Fellowship at Harvard University. He holds a Ph.D. in Political Science from Pennsylvania State University and has written extensively on conventional arms control issues.

COLONEL DAVID E. SHAVER is a Strategic Research Analyst with the Strategic Studies Institute, U.S. Army War College. His previous assignments have included command of combat engineer battalions in the 1st and 8th Infantry Divisions; Chief, Military Engineering and Topography Division, U.S. Army Europe; and S-3, 937th Engineer Group. In Vietnam he served as a unit commander and staff officer in the 62nd Engineer Battalion (Land Clearing). He received a Bachelor's Degree from the University of Nebraska-Omaha and an M.S. from Florida Institute of Technology. Colonel Shaver is a graduate of the U.S. Army Command and General Staff College and the U.S. Army War College. He is a co-author of *Conventional Arms Control in Europe: Army Perspectives; How to Think about Conventional Arms Control: A Framework;* and *Burdensharing and Mission Specialization in NATO;* and he is author of *Force Structures: The United*

States and Europe in the Coming Decade and *Flex-Lease: An Acquisition Strategy for the 1990s*. He currently holds the General Douglas MacArthur Chair of Research at the U.S. Army War College.

COLONEL ARTHUR W. BAILEY is Chief Political-Military Analyst for Confidence- and Security-Building Measures at the U.S. Arms Control and Disarmament Agency, and a member of the U.S. Delegation to the Negotiations on Confidence- and Security-Building Measures in Vienna, Austria. His previous assignments have included infantry and armor combat service in Vietnam, company command and staff service in the 3rd Infantry Division, and in the Strategic Plans and Policy Directorate of the Army Staff. Prior to his current assignment he was Chief, Combat Maneuver Division and member of the Armor Anti-Armor Net Assessment Team in the Office of the Deputy Chief of Staff for Operations and Plans, Headquarters, Department of the Army. Colonel Bailey is a graduate of the Armed Forces Staff College, the U.S. Foreign Service Institute, and a member of Corresponding Studies Class of 1990 of the U.S. Army War College. He holds an M.A. in Political Science from the University of Arizona.

REGINA GAILLARD is a National Security Affairs Analyst at the Strategic Studies Institute, U.S. Army War College. She previously worked in government relations in Washington, D.C., and has written on international and economic policy issues. She is the author of *Military Civic Action and Low Intensity Conflict in Latin America: A Cases of Deja Vu?* and a co-author of *Conventional Arms Control in Europe: A Framework*. Her book, *After Containment: International Changes through a Non-Authoritarian Looking Glass*, is forthcoming from Praeger Publishers. Dr. Gaillard is a graduate in International Affairs from Hunter College and earned her Ph.D. in Inter-American Studies from the Center for Advanced International Studies of the University of Miami.

CAPTAIN(P) DANIEL M. GERSTEIN is an Arms Control Analyst with the Conventional Arms Negotiation Division, Office of the Deputy Chief of Staff for Operations and Plans, Headquarters, Department of the Army. His previous assignments have included command and staff positions in the 17th Signal Battalion and service with the U.S. Army Concepts Analysis Agency, where, as the lead analyst for conventional arms control and strategic mobility issues, he was selected as Outstanding Analyst of the Year. Captain Gerstein is a graduate of the United States Military Academy, holds an M.S. in Operations Research from Georgia Institute of Technology, and has been selected to attend the U.S. Army Command and General Staff College.

LIEUTENANT COLONEL DAVID R. TANKS is a Political-Military Analyst with the U.S. Arms Control and Disarmament Agency (ACDA), where he works on Conventional Forces in Europe negotiation issues. He was a primary staff officer for coordinating the expansion of POMCUS (pre-positioned sets of unit equipment) to six division sets and has worked extensively on NATO mobilization and reinforcement plans at both the Army Staff and on the staff of the U.S. European Command at Stuttgart, Germany. Lieutenant Colonel Tanks subsequently served three and one-half years in the 1st Armored Division at Nurenberg, Germany, in operational assignments, and then came to ACDA in 1987. He has a graduate degree in International Relations from the University of Southern California and is currently working on a Ph.D. in International Affairs with a primary focus on Sino–Soviet–European affairs and superpower relations. He is author of numerous studies including *The Coming Soviet Crisis: A Western Policy Dilemma.*

THOMAS L. WILBORN is a National Security Affairs Analyst with the Strategic Studies Institute, U.S. Army War College, and specializes in East Asian security problems. He earned a B.A. in Journalism and an M.A. and Ph.D. in Political Science from the University of Kentucky. Before joining the Strategic Studies Institute in 1975 he taught political science and international relations at James Madison University and Central Missouri State University, and served with the University of Kentucky educational assistance program in Bandung, Indonesia. Dr. Wilborn is the author of several studies dealing with Northeast Asia and other articles and chapters of books on nuclear strategy and Southeast Asia.